assimilation, american style

assimilation, american style

Peter D. Salins

A New Republic Book
BasicBooks
A Division of HarperCollins*Publishers*

Designed by Nancy Singer

FIRST EDITION

Library of Congress Cataloging-in-Publication Data
Salins, Peter D.
       Assimilation, American style / by Peter D. Salins. — 1st ed.
            p. cm.
       Includes index.
       ISBN 0-465-09817-7
       1. Americanization. 2. United States—Emigration and immigration—
History. 3. Immigrants—United States—History. I. Title.
E169.1.S198 1996
304.8'73—dc20   96-25595

97 98 99 00 01 ❖/RRD 10 9 8 7 6 5 4 3 2

To my wife Rochelle and the memory of Esther, Hyman, Ilse, and Irwin, our immigrant parents

Contents

Preface   ix

part I   **A Nation of Immigrants**

1   We're All Americans   3

2   The More Things Change   19

part II   **How Assimilation Actually Works**

3   Assimilation, American Style   43

4   Crucibles of Assimilation   61

5   Assimilation's Anglo Base   85

6   Americans United by Myths   101

7   Americans United by the Protestant Ethic   123

8   Americans United but Living Apart   143

9   Black Americans and Assimilation   167

part III   **Getting It Right**

10   Battlegrounds of Assimilation   185

11   An Assimilationist Immigration Policy   199

12   Living Together in Peace and Unity   219

Notes   227

Index   247

Preface

A number of things impelled me to write this book. My work on New York's economic problems and prospects led me inexorably to the issue of the growing role of immigrants in the city's economic and social life. Looking at New York's immigrants led me to think about immigration more generally. As the son of immigrants, I had a firsthand appreciation of America's unique status as a nation of immigrants. Seeing my parents come to grips with life in the United States, I also had a firsthand understanding of the promise and perils of assimilation. My parents were profoundly grateful for the sanctuary and economic opportunity America offered but continued to speak their native language and held on to many habits and attitudes forged in the land of their childhoods. Even my sister and I, as assimilated as we were, were occasionally embarrassed by our parents' somewhat alien ways and were shaped by aspects of our ancestral culture.

However, what really made this book an imperative for me was my fear that Americans no longer appreciate the value of assimilation as an indispensable means of integrating America's immigrants and unifying its ethnically diverse population. As a product and a student of immigration, I have long marveled at the way America effectively assimilated its immigrants. I marveled at both my parents' successful adjustment to American life. I marveled at the vitality of the new immigrant communities of New York, generally populated by non-Europeans. But my sunny perspective on this country's immigrant saga and generally harmonious ethnic relations has been increasingly beclouded by two sinister developments: on the Left, the rising tide of divisive ethnocentricity that has been engulfing my city and many other places in the United States and on the Right, the sudden reemergence, after a full half century of remission, of nativism. I was especially distressed to see these divisive tendencies emerge in my own backyard as it were: ethnocentricity dividing the faculty and students of my university and nativism clouding the judgment of my friends in the community of market-oriented conservatives.

As I reflected on these unfortunate developments, I realized that neither the ethnocentrists nor the nativists really understand how America's assimilation paradigm has actually worked—how uniquely effective it has been in reconciling national unity with ethnic diversity. The ethnocentrists do not understand that because of the magic of assimilation, American national unity has not been a threat to ethnic and cultural diversity, and the nativists do not understand that because of it, ethnic and cultural diversity have not been a threat to American national unity.

In writing *Assimilation, American Style* I hoped to harness my personal and professional insights as best I could to explain America's distinctive assimilation formula and to promote its revival. I may not persuade the ethnocentrists or the nativists of the error of their theories, but I hope that I can persuade many of my fellow Americans not to throw away thoughtlessly the secret of our country's success, chasing poisonous ideologies of ethnic discord in the one nation on earth whose unity has, until now, transcended ethnic distinctions.

This book could not have been completed without the support and assistance of a great many people. I want to thank Ron Unz, who encouraged me to embark on this project in the first place. I also want to thank my friends, Phil Kasinitz and Lou Winnick, whose work related to the book's concerns I especially respect, for hearing me out and critiquing many of my ideas and concepts. And I want to thank Nathan Glazer, the intellectual colossus in the field of immigration and ethnic scholarship, for immeasurably enriching my understanding of the subject and for giving me the opportunity to discuss some of the book's themes face-to-face.

I owe an especially geat debt to my editor, Paul Golob, whose persistent motivation (including just the right dose of nudging) saw the manuscript through to completion, whose keen editorial eye kept the book's argument on target, and whose deft and precise editorial hand enhanced the book's style without compromising its content.

Finally, I wish to express my deep appreciation and gratitude to the Manhattan Institute, particularly its president, Larry Mone, and former president, Bill Hammett, for providing the logistical and financial support without which the book could not have been written.

A Nation of Immigrants

1

We're All Americans

If ever a nation was laid out on a truly cosmopolitan basis and gifted with an irresistible power of attraction, it is the American. Here where our globe ends its circuit seems to terminate the migration of the human race. To our shores they come in an unbroken stream from every direction . . . They meet here on the common ground of freedom and equality, to renew their youth and to commingle at last into one grand brotherhood, speaking one language, pervaded by one spirit, obeying the same laws, laboring for one aim, and filling in these ends of the earth the last and richest chapter in the history of the world.

Philip Schaff, 1856[1]

My parents immigrated to the United States from Germany as young adults in 1938. We spoke German at home and ate German foods. My parents socialized with other German immigrants and joined German organizations. But not for one second during my German-speaking childhood did any of us—my parents, my sister, or I—doubt our Americanness. We took our Americanness for granted and were proud to be Americans. My national ancestors were not Otto von Bismarck or Frederick the Great, but George Washington and Thomas Jefferson. I thought *Father Knows Best* was about my family.

The town in central New Jersey where I grew up could have

served as the model for a series of Norman Rockwell paintings. But actually, most of my classmates' parents were foreign born, having come mainly from Italy and Poland. Did any of the kids I went to school with feel any the less American? Did they have conflicted ethnic loyalties? Absolutely not.

I also have friends who grew up in much more intensively ethnic enclaves—Italian, Russian, Middle Eastern, Cuban, and Chinese—in New York and other large cities. Their neighborhoods were replete with ethnic stores, restaurants, and social clubs, and few adults spoke English. They were invariably called "little" this or "little" that—fill in the ethnic blank. Like me, my friends spoke a foreign language at home, for their parents clung to most of their original folkways, and, culturally, lived in a world suspended somewhere between their birthplaces and the United States. But these young people grew up feeling every bit as American as I did. They accepted, perhaps even cherished, their Italian, Jewish, or other ethnic heritage, but they were proud to be Americans.

The story of my childhood may well strike the average reader as banal because we Americans take for granted that the immigrants of yesterday produced the Americans of today. And yet, assimilation, American style is more than just a historical artifact; it is nothing less than a miracle. For over two hundred years the United States has managed to pull off an almost impossible feat: It has forged a culturally unified nation, hundreds of millions strong, spanning a continent, at peace with itself, out of people drawn, literally, from every corner of the earth.

To maintain and deepen a sense of national cultural unity amid ethnic diversity has not been a simple task or one that other nations have easily accomplished. Canada, for example, has never been able to resolve the terms of coexistence between its two principal ethnic groups, both of which are northern European. One hundred and thirty years after its independence, Canada is, in most respects, an agreeable, prosperous, freedom-loving country, but it teeters on the edge of dissolution.[2]

In the Eastern Hemisphere things are much worse. Eastern Europe is a cauldron of ethnic hatreds from the Adriatic to the Urals. Long-united and almost ethnically indistinguishable Czechs and Slovaks recently split apart peacefully, but long-united and almost ethnically indistinguishable Yugoslavs are still splitting apart not so peacefully. Russians have been engaged in a devastating war with secessionist Chechens. Elsewhere in the former Soviet Union, one finds ethnic blood feuds among Georgians, permanent warfare between Armenians and Azerbaijanis, and long-resident Russians expelled from the Baltic states.

Even Western Europe harbors festering ethnic discord—in some cases among ancient ethnic antagonists, but in others, between natives and immigrants. The bitter conflict between Protestants and Catholics in Northern Ireland may be the most bloody, but there are countless examples of ongoing low-level ethnic discord. Greeks and Turks in Cyprus will never be reconciled. Flemish- and French-speaking Belgians maintain an uneasy ethnic truce that is dependent on formulas of power sharing and zones of influence. Italy is burdened with a north–south split that is at bottom ethnic, unhappy German-speaking South Tyrolians in Alto Adige, and discontented Slovenians and Croats in recently annexed Trieste. In Germany, working-class youths torch the homes of eastern European immigrants, and the country's naturalization policy denies citizenship to German-born descendants of Turkish guest workers who settled there more than thirty years ago. In France, the presence of large colonies of Islamic North Africans periodically triggers social unrest and prompts xenophobic political campaigns. Nor should one forget that only fifty years ago, a European power went on a genocidal ethnic rampage in which millions lost their lives. And this is the "good news" part of the world. In India, Sri Lanka, and many nations of Africa, ethnic conflict gives rise to unspeakable atrocities, unimaginable human suffering, year after year. The brutal images of Rwanda and Somalia are more often the rule than the exception.

Ethnic harmony is a fragile thing, and nations must work hard to maintain it. Thus, America's success as a multiethnic society is not simply a happy accident. As a country built on perpetual immigration, the United States has been struggling with the mission of maintaining national cultural and civic unity alongside ethnic diversity since colonial times. Throughout the nineteenth and early twentieth centuries, both the elites and the rank and file of "native" Americans aggressively and self-consciously promoted the idea of *assimilation*, or as they called it in the early years of this century, "Americanization."[3] Just as the Constitution of the United States was designed to create a unified, functional national society while preserving a maximum degree of individual liberty, so did its paradigm of assimilation aspire to the idea of *E Pluribus Unum*. (This Latin motto, "from many, one" is as old as the nation; it was chosen by a committee of the Continental Congress for the Great Seal of the United States and was adopted on June 20, 1782.)[4]

Assimilation, American style set out a simple contract between the existing settlers and all newcomers. Immigrants would be welcome as full members of the American family if they agreed to abide by three simple precepts: First, they had to accept English as the national language. Second, they were expected to take pride in their American identity and believe in America's liberal democratic and egalitarian principles. Third, they were expected to live by what is commonly referred to as the Protestant ethic (to be self-reliant, hardworking, and morally upright).[5] This basic framework, though minimal, proved highly effective. Since culture is transmitted by language, a single common language worked as a powerful force for cultural unity. Faith in the American Idea,[6] a unique, idealistic, and politically advanced set of liberal principles and institutions, promoted civic unity and national pride. The Protestant ethic, a belief system that judges individuals by their achievements, rather than by the circumstances of their birth, made ethnicity less relevant and united all Americans in a framework of shared values.

To seal the assimilation contract, immigrants were not only permitted, but encouraged to become citizens. The offer of citizenship was an advanced and radical idea in the eighteenth century,[7] and even today most countries, if they accept immigrants at all, merely allow them to be residents, or second-class citizens at best. According to Craig Whitney of the *New York Times*: "In Germany, it can be easier for a child whose family lived in Russia for 200 years to become a German citizen than it is for . . . the German-born child of a Turkish 'guest worker' [because] Germany defines citizenship by bloodline."[8] The United States, in contrast, always made immigrants eligible for a citizenship that conferred on them full membership in the American state and society, with all attendant rights and privileges (save one— the right to run for and be elected president).

To help implement the assimilation contract, most immigrant children were enrolled in free state-supported systems of public schools. The United States was one of the first nations to provide universal, compulsory, and free public education. As early as 1785, the federal government gave states land for public schools, and Massachusetts established the first free statewide public school system in the 1850s.[9] The public school movement was driven by the egalitarian desire to instill knowledge and civic virtue in all Americans, regardless of wealth or class. But, as the educational reformer Horace Mann persuasively argued, public schools were necessary, above all, to ensure the assimilation of immigrants.[10] Public school curricula were designed as much to acculturate immigrants and rural natives to the common values and demands of American society as they were to impart traditional learning. Schools fostered universal literacy and fluency in the English language. They explained and extolled the American Idea. They established norms of conduct, expectations, and attitudes. They fostered interethnic, interclass, and immigrant-native socialization.[11]

And it worked. This pervasive paradigm of assimilation served to unify the expanding population of the United States. Notwithstanding periodic bursts of nativism, faith in the paradigm made ordinary Americans willing to tolerate large-scale immigration. And as immigrants abided by the rules, Americans' faith in the paradigm was vindicated. At the same time, there was nothing especially coercive about the assimilation contract. All immigrants were free to be as ethnic as they pleased, especially at home or in their local communities. As the sociologist Richard Alba observed, "Assimilation need not imply the obliteration of all traces of ethnic origins, nor require that every member of a group be assimilated to the same degree."[12] From colonial times to the present, millions of these assimilated Americans from other lands have lived in their own ethnic enclaves, eaten ethnic foods, and even spoken their original languages. There is really no inconsistency between America's aggressive promotion of assimilation and its tolerance of ever-changing ethnic diversity. The assimilation contract, with its three ground rules, was the unofficial law of the land well into the 1950s, and it was clearly in play during my formative years.

*   *   *

But a funny thing happened in the middle of the twentieth centu-ry. America's opinion elites were persuaded or forced to reject assimilation, and to set aside all three of the assimilation contract's provisions. Bilingualism eroded English's monopoly as the only language of school instruction and government. Historical revi-sionism discredited the American Idea as a hypocritical myth. The welfare state superseded the Protestant ethic. Assimilation, both as a social process and a societal goal, came to be seen as anachronis-tic, irrelevant, and largely inapplicable to contemporary American social realities. In a 1993 essay aptly entitled "Is Assimilation Dead?" one of the most eminent observers of American ethnic relations, sociologist Nathan Glazer, noted:

> Assimilation is not today a popular term. Recently I asked a group of Harvard students taking a class on race and ethnicity in the United States what their attitude to the term "assimilation" was. The large majority had a negative reaction to it. Had I asked what they thought of the term "Americanization," the reaction, I am sure, would have been even more hostile. Indeed, in recent years it has been taken for granted that assimilation, as an expectation of how different ethnic and racial groups would respond to their common presence in one society or as an ideal regarding how the society should evolve . . . is to be rejected. Our ethnic and racial reality, we are told, does not exhibit the effects of assimilation; our social science should not expect it; and as an ideal, it is some-what disreputable, opposed to the reality of both individual and group difference and to the claims that such differences should be recognized and celebrated.[13]

How could a two-hundred-year-old idea be discredited in so short a time? One can only speculate, but it appears that in many respects assimilation was a casualty of the 1960s, the tumultuous decade between the assassination of John F. Kennedy in 1963 and the resignation of Richard M. Nixon in 1974. This era represent-ed, for better and for worse, a sea change in elite and popular atti-tudes on many aspects of America's traditions and social relations. On the positive side, Americans became less tolerant of race and gender discrimination, poverty, environmental degradation, and the mistreatment of handicapped persons. Less happily, intellectuals and the young adults they influenced challenged long-standing worthy social mores and the agents of authority who enforced them. Sexual restraint, strictures on drug use, standards of dress and decorum, competition, and achievement all came under concerted attack. And so did assimilation and ethnic harmony in general. The revolution may have been led by a generation of middle-class college students and their professors, but it was ratified by America's leadership as youthful rebellion was joined with establishment permissiveness. Officials in positions of authority capitulated to the revolution's demands, the mass media and organs of popular culture chronicled and rationalized each capitulation, and the institutional matrix of American society—laws, policies, and programs—codified and entrenched them.

To begin with, the rejection of assimilation as a concept was founded on a radical misconception of what assimilation entails. Assimilation was viewed by its antagonists as a means of imposing cultural conformity on America's minority groups. So defined it thus ran aground on two key staples of the 1960s revolution: heightened ethnic consciousness and the rejection of all manner of cultural conformity. But as this book emphasizes, assimilation, American style is not about cultural conformity; it is about national unity.

But national unity did not fare so well after the 1960s either. The 1960s was a period not only of social iconoclasm and self-righteous idealism but of aggressive disillusionment. Indeed, the disillusionment was seen as a necessary precursor to reform. Disillusionment prompted some of America's most influential intellectual leaders to scoff at the nation's past, even as their idealism led them to promote a new social contract and a new paradigm of ethnic relations, of whose perverse consequences they were blissfully unaware.

In the wake of this disillusionment, revisionist historians and political scientists were determined to discredit the official, rose-colored portrait of "America the virtuous" and to expose American idealism as hypocrisy. Whether in scholarly books of the "new historians"[14] or in ideological books like Howard Zinn's *The Politics of History*,[15] the revisionists tried to show that the United States was as unprincipled a nation as any other. They contended that American wars were fought for territorial and economic gain, rather than for lofty principles, and that American human rights invariably gave way to exploitation; racism; and, in the case of American Indians, even genocide. The unpopular and militarily unsuccessful Vietnam War did much to fuel the 1960s' social revolution, and it convinced educated Americans in the revolution's vanguard that the United States was not the world's idealistic beacon, but one of its most predatory states.

In the same revisionist spirit, scholars of social history debunked assimilation itself, as embodied in the cherished metaphor of the melting pot.[16] The phrase, first coined by writer Israel Zangwill in his 1908 play, *The Melting Pot*,[17] was enthusiastically embraced by turn-of-the-century Americans who were eager to find a unifying national concept at a time when the United States was becoming more ethnically diverse than ever before. The image of the melting pot represented a compelling way of reconciling ethnic diversity and national unity: The American was a sturdy alloy fashioned from innumerable ethnic base metals; each ingredient was represented in the alloy, but the alloy was different from each of its ingredients. The metaphor was hugely popular when it was introduced, and the play was a big success with the general public. President Theodore Roosevelt was so enamored of the play's message that he compared Zangwill favorably to George Bernard Shaw and Henrik Ibsen. Popular faith in the melting pot survived both the Great Depression and World War II. But it did not survive the 1960s.

Two books, in particular, effectively articulated the revisionist view. In *Beyond the Melting Pot*, which appeared in 1963, authors Nathan Glazer and Daniel Patrick Moynihan looked at ethnic enclaves in New York whose residents, even after several generations, seemed not to have "melted," culturally speaking.[18] A decade later, Michael Novak, in *The Rise of the Unmeltable Ethnics*, railed against the premises of the melting pot, this time from an insider's perspective, explaining why some ethnics couldn't or wouldn't "melt."[19] Both books perpetuated the notion that assimilation was to be equated with cultural conformity, and by documenting the survival of ethnic cultural disparities, they created an impression that assimilation couldn't and shouldn't happen. Notably, both books' titles played off the melting-pot metaphor, and both did so in a spirit of irony and disparagement.

But melting-pot revisionism only kindled a growing antiassimilationist bonfire. Weakened in the 1960s by iconoclasm and revisionism, the assimilation contract was struck its fatal blow by an emerging view of American ethnic relations in the 1970s and 1980s that goes under the general heading *multiculturalism*.[20] A better term might be *ethnic federalism*. Antiassimilationist to the core, this new paradigm explicitly rejects the notion of a transcendent American identity. Richard Sennett, articulating this view, referred to the "evil of a shared national identity."[21] Gone was faith in *E Pluribus Unum*—the old idea that out of ethnic diversity, there would emerge a single, culturally unified people, or in Philip Schaff's words in the epigraph to this chapter, "one grand brotherhood."[22] It was to be replaced by what Arthur M. Schlesinger, Jr., called "the ethnicity cult"[23] and Sheldon Hackney, chairman of the National Endowment of the Humanities, labeled "the new tribalism."[24] Now, the United States was to be viewed as a vast multiethnic confederacy, Canada's Anglo-French arrangement, raised to the nth power. As members of a federation, rather than a union, each ethnic group had "rights." Ethnic Americans had the right to function in their "native" language (even if it was not their language of birth or they had never learned to speak it), not just at home, but in the public realm. Ethnic Americans had the right to proportional representation in matters of power and privilege. And ethnic Americans had the right to demand that their "native" culture and their putative ethnic ancestors be accorded recognition and respect.[25]

Ethnic federalism is, at all times and in all places, an ideology of ethnic grievances and invariably leads to (and justifies) ethnic conflict. All the nations that have ever embraced it, from Yugoslavia to Lebanon, from Belgium to Canada, have had to live with perpetual ethnic discord. The ascendancy of ethnic federalism in the United States after the 1960s, as Chapter 9 explains, grew out of the disappointed hopes of the civil rights revolution. As such, it marked a 180-degree departure from the civil rights movement's ideological roots, which were firmly anchored in the unifying civic precepts of the American creed. Only by appealing to Americans' better instincts and their allegiance to the nation's founding principles, using courts of law and public opinion, had black Americans made great strides in reclaiming their long-denied basic civil rights. The disappointment came when formal civil rights did not quickly produce an end to poverty, discrimination, and social isolation among blacks.

Glazer tried to explain how the unhappy circumstances of black Americans led blacks and white liberals to reject assimilation and embrace ethnic federalism.[26] Many Americans assumed that once formal discriminatory barriers were breached, blacks might quickly assimilate, just as immigrant ethnics had in the past, and join the American mainstream by achieving economic success and gaining social acceptance. When they didn't do so as completely or quickly as anticipated, many blacks and their white liberal allies rejected the ideal of assimilation altogether.

> For one group, assimilation, by some key measures, has certainly failed. . . . most black children do attend black-majority schools. Most live in black neighborhoods. Why should not multiculturalism . . . become compelling as one way of understanding one's situation, perhaps overcoming it? The large statements of an American national ideal of inclusion, of assimilation, understandably ring false.[27]

This loss of faith in assimilation has inexorably led blacks and many of their white advocates to demand that blacks' fair share of economic and social status should be granted on the basis of ethnic rights in a federalist or "multicultural" commonwealth. Multiculturalism reached full flower when the concept was embraced by Latinos and, to legitimate its application to blacks and Latinos, was extended to all other ethnic groups.

It is a great irony that the United States entered its postassimilationist era, beginning about 1965, precisely when it was also entering an era of renewed large-scale immigration, under rules that would result in a far more ethnically varied mix of immigrants than the country had seen before. Just when it might have been dusted off and put to effective use again, the old assimilation contract was turned on its head. Assimilation (often cast in terms of the melting-pot metaphor) was now only a myth. It was said to have robbed America's disparate ethnic groups of their cultural heritages. Some even called it "cultural genocide."[28] According to the new orthodoxy, all Americans (especially those of non-European origin)—everyone but WASPs (White Anglo-Saxon Protestants) and Jews—were to get in touch with their ethnic roots, nurture them, take pride in them, and defend them from attack or extinction by the mainstream American culture. More to the point, U.S. institutions—governmental, educational, philanthropic, and corporate—were to be forcibly harnessed to the new mission. In the service of the new American ideology of ethnic federalism, a new assimilation contract was drawn up, one that is a precise mirror image of the old. The terms of this new contract are as follows:

English is a linguistic option. Although proficiency in the English language may still be a desirable objective for all American residents to achieve, it cannot and should not be forced on the foreign born or their children. Immigrant children should be instructed in their (or, more accurately, their parents') "first" language as they are gradually acclimated to English. Government-issued documents and signs in places with many non-English speakers must be multi- or bilingual. Even the private sector should be encouraged to function multilingually. (On cash machines in banks in New York City, for example, the first choice users are confronted with is the language in which the transaction is to be conducted.)

Taking pride in being American is not possible because the American Idea is a hypocritical myth. Ethnic Americans should not be conned into trading their ethnicity for a specious "American" identity. Americans betrayed the American Idea a long time ago, if they ever really believed in it. American history is a story of oppression, racism, and genocide aimed at American Indians, blacks, and most immigrants other than northern Europeans. The new American Idea is that individuals can secure their guaranteed American rights and enjoy the fruits of the American way of life only by appealing to their ethnic identities. Governmental and other institutions must make sure that all ethnic groups get a fair share of power, privilege, and status.

The Protestant ethic is dead. Celebration of that ethic, as mythologized in the Horatio Alger stories, has merely served to ratify class inequality. In any case, the Protestant ethic is the cultural product of a particular class, a particular national and religious group, and a particular time, all of which are irrelevant to modern multicultural America. Worse yet, its premises are flawed. The poor cannot be expected to raise themselves by their bootstraps because they are trapped in poverty by adverse economic conditions and discrimination. To preach the Protestant ethic is to "blame the victim." Poor immigrants are victims, too, and are especially subject to exploitation. The poor, native and immigrant alike, need public assistance for a range of functional needs to overcome their inherent disadvantages.

It no longer matters whether immigrants become U.S. citizens. Citizenship is a personal choice, and if it weakens immigrants' identification with their ethnic roots, it may actually do more harm than good.

Public schools should be crucibles of ethnic consciousness-raising. Public schools must accommodate ethnic diversity, not assimilation. In multilingual communities the schools must be multilingual, too. Instead of propagating American mythology and the glorification of racist hypocrites like Washington and Jefferson or genocidal monsters like Christopher Columbus, schools should celebrate the authentic traditions and heroic ancestors of today's (ethnically diverse) schoolchildren. Schools should promote sensitivity to ethnic differences and respect for all ethnic backgrounds.[29]

The new antiassimilation contract is not just a matter of changes in attitude and sentiment. It is hardwired into a growing set of laws and rules. Bilingual education is mandated by the Bilingual Education Act of 1968 and a 1974 Supreme Court ruling.[30] The school curricula that mandate ethnic recognition while disparaging the American Idea and traditional American heroes are the products of state education initiatives like that developed by New York State's Social Studies Review and Development Committee.[31] Key tenets of the American Idea are also undermined by ethnic quotas and preferences built into a host of national, state, and local laws.[32] Those features of the social welfare system that disengage immigrants from the Protestant ethic reflect policies set at the highest levels of government.[33]

The most alarming thing about Americans' rejection of the old assimilation contract in favor of its new multicultural antithesis is its impact on the immigrants' children. The most thorough and lasting benefits of assimilation have always been those that have been accrued in the social and cultural integration of succeeding generations. It may not matter that much if the new immigrants from Latin America or Asia learn to speak English well or at all. (There are, after all, still Italian and Polish Americans who barely speak English.) But it matters a great deal if their children don't. It may not matter much if the new immigrants don't take pride in being American or believe in the American creed. It matters a great deal if their children don't. And though immigrants are more than willing to abide by the Protestant ethic, it certainly matters a great deal if their children aren't.

How could America's intellectual and political leaders be so short-sighted as to cast away thoughtlessly the paradigm of assimilation that had proved invaluable in unifying the nation for over a century and a half? There was never actually a moment of decision. What happened was that these leaders' faith in the validity, or even the necessity, of the paradigm eroded at the same time that some key social and political developments were at work. Policies of race-conscious preferences replaced those of color blindness ostensibly to speed up the economic progress of blacks. Bilingual education began as a poorly thought-out pedagogical response to the sudden influx of Spanish-speaking youngsters in the schools and then became a way of cutting Latinos into the game of ethnic federalism. Trashing American history and dismissing the American Idea may have provided the rationale for such "un-American" policies, but it was also the product of post–Vietnam War cynicism and a specious sophistication that viewed old-fashioned patriotism and American exceptionalism as dated and corny. The demise of the assimilation paradigm actually occurred, under cover of media darkness, in barely noticeable increments, as one assimilation-subverting policy was piled upon another.

The history of the past thirty years has shown that America's opinion and policy elites made a terrible mistake by turning away from assimilation and negating the assimilation contract. And it has, indeed, been the country's leaders—in the media, in education, in government, and in corporate America—who have been specifically responsible. The rank and file of ordinary Americans were never consulted, and if they had been, they would have rejected the abandonment of the assimilation paradigm. But regardless of where the fault lies, if ever there was a time to promote assimilation, it is today, when the volume of U.S. immigration is approaching levels the nation has not seen since the turn of the century and ethnic conflict is the most salient feature of "the new world order." It is disheartening to contemplate the long-term outlook for America's large new immigrant communities, whether Mexicans in California, Asians in the Pacific Northwest, Cubans in Florida, or people from the Caribbean in New York, if they remain unassimilated. Most of all, it would be tragic if black Americans traveled any farther down the road of antiassimilationism. The United States' two-hundred-year history of maintaining national unity while accommodating ethnic diversity may be robust enough to withstand a temporary defection from the ethos and practice of assimilation, but it cannot withstand it for long before a host of unhappy consequences is unleashed.

Among the most bitter fruits of antiassimilationism has been the resurgence of nativism among nonimmigrant Americans.[34] The past few years have witnessed a growing antagonism against immigrants across the United States. In 1994 Californians voted for Proposition 187, whose supporters tapped deep pools of general anti-immigrant sentiment. Under the provisions of Proposition 187, illegal immigrants would be denied publicly funded education, health care, and other benefits and, when possible, would be deported. Proposition 187 was aimed ostensibly only at illegal immigrants, but its adoption reflects Californians' mounting dislike of all immigrants, legal or not. An even more threatening development was Congress's consideration in 1996, with little opposition from the White House, of the most restrictive immigration legislation in decades. This bill would sharply reduce quotas for legal immigration and deal harshly with illegal immigrants entering or residing in the United States. Also in 1996, Congress passed, and the president signed, a bill that denies unnaturalized legal immigrants many social welfare benefits. Congress's action merely reflects the results of public opinion polls, which have showed that an increasing number of Americans are favoring a reduction in the number of new immigrants and the curtailment of the rights of those already here.

The swing in attitudes toward immigrants has a number of causes, including hard economic times in California between 1987 and 1992. But there is considerable evidence that one of the most potent concerns of those who are alarmed by the growing number of immigrants is that these new arrivals and their children cannot or will not assimilate. According to immigration scholar John Miller, "Nativists complain that the current wave of immigrants won't assimilate, . . . that the newcomers are too different, too non-Western for our society to absorb them."[35] John O'Sullivan and Laurence Auster, both writing in the *National Review*, based their vehement polemics against the current immigration levels on a conviction that the United States is unwilling to promote the assimilation of its newest immigrants.[36] Undoubtedly, many neonativists would oppose the admission of a large number of immigrants, no matter how effectively or quickly they assimilated, but a revival of the assimilationist ethos might get a majority of ordinary Americans to smile on immigration again.

In the end, though, the greatest danger looming for the United States is interethnic conflict, the scourge of almost all other nations with ethnically diverse populations. Assimilation has been our country's secret weapon in diffusing such conflict before it occurs, and without a strong assimilationist ethos, we leave ourselves open for much misfortune. Assimilation is not really about people of different racial, religious, linguistic, or cultural backgrounds becoming alike; it is about people of different racial, religious, linguistic, or cultural backgrounds believing they are irrevocably part of the same national family. It is this belief that allows them to transcend their narrow ethnic loyalties and that blunts, to the point of insignificance, the spurs of ethnic conflict and discord.

At a time when the United States is admitting a million legal immigrants a year (and perhaps a few hundred thousand illegal ones as well), it is critical that our paradigm of assimilation is up and running in top form. Even if immigration was to be curtailed in the near term, there remains the task of assimilating the 18 million immigrants who came to the U.S. during the past two decades.[37] Only if the American society reaffirms its faith in the value of assimilation and Americanization will its newest generation of immigrants be as effectively integrated as were earlier ones.

This book is devoted to explaining and interpreting the true meaning of assimilation, American style. Assimilation is an intrinsic aspect of America's tradition of tolerance. As such, assimilation does not require immigrants to surrender their ethnic heritage. It does not require their children to turn themselves into characters out of 1950s suburban sitcoms. In fact, assimilation is not about making people do much of anything they don't really want to do. Assimilation is about the expectations and attitudes of natives. It is about feeling unabashedly proud to be American. It is about having faith in the American creed. It is about achieving national civic unity. It is about keeping English as the national language. It is about letting the public schools promote assimilation and Americanization. It is about indulging our hopes for the future at least as much as documenting our failures of the past. It is about reviving American myths. It is about rediscovering the virtues of the Protestant ethic. It is about making sure that black Americans are fully included in the American Dream, but not letting our guilt over past injustice keep them from assimilating or believing in the American Idea. It is about allowing the largest possible number of new immigrants to come to the United States, but changing the criteria for admission a little and getting tougher on gate-crashers.

If the United States can revive its historic and unique assimilation paradigm, it will continue to serve as a proud and secure example to the world of a nation-state that is able to sustain ethnic harmony amid diversity and personal freedom amid national unity. If it can't, it will soon join the dismal ranks of the world's other multiethnic nations as a battleground of perpetual ethnic discord.

2

The More Things Change

It is an incontrovertible truth that the civil institutions of the United
States of America . . . now stand in imminent peril from the rapid and
enormous increase of the body of residents of foreign birth, imbued with
foreign feelings, and of an ignorant and immoral character, who receive,
under the lax and unreasonable laws of naturalization, the elective franchise and the right of political office. . . . [because of] the suicidal policy
of these United States . . . a large proportion of the foreign body of citizens and voters now constitutes a representation of the worst and most
degraded of the European population—victims of social oppression or
personal vices, utterly divested, by ignorance or crime, of the moral and
intellectual requisites for political self-government. The mass of foreign
voters . . . will leave the Native citizens a minority in their own land!

Platform, Native American (Know-Nothing) Party, 1845[1]

The epochal Immigration Act . . . triggered a renewed mass immigration,
so huge and so systematically different from anything that had gone
before as to transform—and, ultimately, perhaps, even to destroy—
. . . the American nation, as it had evolved by the middle of the twentieth
century. . . . The mass immigration so thoughtlessly triggered in 1965
risks making America an *alien nation* . . . not merely in the sense that
America will become a freak among the world's nations because of the
unprecedented demographic mutation it is inflicting on itself; not merely
in the sense that Americans themselves will become alien to each other.

Peter Brimelow, 1995[2]

19

From the moment the United States won its independence from Great Britain, Americans have been animated by two primordial impulses that have distinguished them from the people of other nations (including Canada and other British outposts): a millenarian faith in their country's historic destiny as the world's exemplar of liberal principles of governance and an unrelenting determination that the United States should expand on all fronts: in population, territory, and economic supremacy.[3] Immigration was intimately bound up with both these impulses. Without America's political principles, far fewer immigrants would have come, and those who did might not have been so easily integrated into a stable and prosperous society. Without America's expansionist drive, far fewer immigrants would have been welcome.

The writing and thinking of Americans throughout the nineteenth century were suffused with faith in the uniqueness of the American political experiment and a belief in the inherent superiority of its central tenets: government legitimated only by the consent of the governed, ironclad guarantees of certain fundamental individual rights and liberties, rigid adherence to due process in the enforcement of law, contempt for class distinctions, and glorification of individualism and individual achievement. Historian Henry Steele Commager noted: "The moral superiority of his country was . . . axiomatic to the American."[4]

There was also a belief in the universality of the American paradigm. Shortly after independence, Tom Paine wrote in 1792: "The world is my country. All mankind are my brethren."[5] Fifty years later, William Lloyd Garrison stated: "My country is my world, my countrymen are mankind."[6] Jefferson called America "the world's best hope."[7] And Americans were determined to share their universalist values with as much of the world as would heed them. According to Commager:

> Successive generations [of Americans] were . . . eager to spread the American idea over the globe and exasperated that foreign ideas should ever intrude themselves into America.[8]

Such self-confident and self-aggrandizing idealism made it easy for Americans in the early years of the republic to contemplate two fairly radical ideas. One was to admit, without limitation, immigrants from what then were seen as "all corners of the globe." By the early nineteenth century, a large number of people had come to the United States from a variety of northern European nations, most of whom differed markedly from the original British settlers in language, religion, and dress. Admitting such a diverse group of immigrants was considered to be—both at home and abroad—an unprecedented expression of universalism and idealistic magnanimity and made the United States one of the world's most cosmopolitan societies.

Equally radical was America's early determination to make the immigrants "citizens," vesting them, after only a few years of residence, with all the rights of natives.[9] Under the new constitutional order of the United States, this policy meant conferring on immigrants the civil liberties of the Bill of Rights, including the right to vote (a right denied, it must be noted, to most black Americans at the time). It also meant accepting immigrants as members of the national family, officially erasing the social barriers and distinctions usually faced by foreigners. Citizenship was no small gift in the late eighteenth and early nineteenth centuries, especially citizenship in a democracy dedicated to observing unprecedented new human rights. In most countries citizenship, and such rights as it conferred, was a status reserved for the indigenous population. If immigrants were welcome at all, they were received as temporary sojourners; at best they could undergo a long apprenticeship to become citizens. Even in European colonies, things were not much better. Most of the colonial European nations, including Britain, were willing to offer settlers a form of colonial citizenship that conferred few rights beyond the right to live in a colony, was usually not transferable to the home country, and often was not extended to immigrants after independence.[10]

Whatever idealistic motives postindependence America had for admitting immigrants were powerfully reinforced by its expansionist impulse: the United States as not only the freest, but the greatest nation. By the middle of the nineteenth century, that drive was characterized as America's "manifest destiny," a term first coined by journalist John L. O'Sullivan in 1845.[11] Since the entire American population at the turn of the nineteenth century was barely more than 5 million (including the 20 percent in slavery), the only way the United States could grow was through immigration.

As the United States expanded westward throughout the nineteenth century, an infusion of immigrant labor was necessary to fuel its economic growth. Immediately after independence, immigrants were welcomed to add demographic and economic heft to the newly created nation and to compensate for the departure of English loyalists who fled to Canada during the revolutionary war. As the United States increased its territorial expanse at a breathtaking rate in the first half of the nineteenth century (beginning with the Louisiana Purchase of 1803 and completing its contiguous continental design with the Gadsden Purchase of 1853), immigrants were eagerly recruited to settle the new territories. After the Civil War, as the United States rapidly industrialized and urbanized, immigrants were again needed—this time to work in the new factories, mines, and service businesses of the burgeoning cities.[12]

Thus was the United States' destiny as a nation of immigrants irrevocably woven into its history and the national psyche. The actual course of American immigration in the nineteenth century must be one of the most remarkable human sagas of all time, and all the more remarkable because of its largely happy ending. Between 1820 and 1860, the country admitted more than 5 million immigrants, and its population swelled from 9.6 million to over 31 million, with a third of the growth accounted for by immigration itself or the natural increase of the immigrant population. In 1860 about a quarter of the population was foreign born or had foreign-born parents, and more than half had foreign-born grandparents.

Immigration did not even abate during the decade of the Civil War. Between 1860 and 1870, the United States admitted more than 2 million additional immigrants, and by 1890, the national population had doubled to 63 million, this time with half the increase owing to immigrants and their offspring. In 1890 well over a third of all Americans were foreign born or children of the foreign born, and two-thirds had living foreign-born relatives.[13] (See Table 1.)

TABLE 1. U.S. IMMIGRATION 1820–1991

Period	Immigrants	Cumulative Immigrants	U.S. Population at the End of the Period
1820–40	751,000	751,000	17,069,000
1841–60	4,311,000	5,062,000	31,443,000
1861–80	5,127,000	10,189,000	50,189,000
1881–1900	8,935,000	19,124,000	76,212,000
1901–30	18,638,000	37,762,000	123,203,000
1931–60	4,079,000	41,841,000	179,323,000
1961–80	7,815,000	49,656,000	226,546,000
1981–91	9,165,000	58,821,000	252,500,000

Source: U.S. Immigration and Naturalization Service, *1991 Statistical Yearbook of the Immigration and Naturalization Service* (Washington, D.C.: U.S. Government Printing Office, 1992).

The surge in immigration continued well into the twentieth century, until it was abruptly curtailed by the country's first real immigration-restricting legislation in the 1920s. The decades preceding the cutoff, 1890 to 1920, saw the entrance of the largest cohort of immigrants in American history, 18 million strong. By 1920, thanks to a century of immigration, the American population had reached 106 million, a population larger than that of any European nation other than Russia. The cumulative demographic and economic impact of America's immigration had been staggering, making the United States at least twice as populous as it otherwise would have been and more than twice as rich.[14]

By the time the era of mass immigration ended in 1929, more Americans than ever had strong immigrant roots. Immigrants were not spread uniformly across the nation, however. Most immigrants were concentrated in the states of the Northeast and Midwest. Few were to be found in the South, and nobody much, immigrant or native, lived in the West until after World War II. In particular, more immigrants than ever dominated the demography and politics of American cities. Most immigrants and their children lived in cities; most residents of large cities were immigrants or their children. Immigrants clustered, naturally, near the immigration gateways, the busiest one being New York City. In New York and other large eastern cities, immigrants for a long time made up more than half the population, and their extended immigrant families accounted for three-fourths. Even the midwestern farm states were largely immigrant-dominated places. Throughout the late nineteenth and early twentieth centuries, first-, second-, and third-generation Germans and Scandinavians constituted the majority of the population in Wisconsin, Minnesota, and Illinois.[15] As their share of the urban population grew, first- and second-generation immigrant voters decisively tipped the political balance in New York, Boston, Philadelphia, Chicago, and even smaller cities like Milwaukee and St. Louis and formed the constituencies of increasingly powerful big-city political machines.[16]

Impressive as America's nineteenth- and early-twentieth-century immigration saga was, it proceeded in the face of vociferous opposition and noisy agitation. This nation of immigrants and celebrators of immigration continually struggled to contain the fresh outbursts of antagonism directed at each new cohort of immigrants. American history is littered with the landmarks of anti-immigrant legislation: the Alien and Sedition Acts of 1798, the Chinese Exclusion Act of 1882, and the Immigration Act of 1924. It is also pockmarked by the ugly nativist movements that agitated for such legislation: the Know-Nothings of the 1840s, the American Protective Association of the 1880s, the Immigration Restriction League of the 1890s, and the notorious Ku Klux Klan of the 1920s. Over the long and checkered history of the American immigration dialectic—loving immigration but hating immigrants—America's principles and interests ultimately triumphed over nativism and bigotry, but not without some serious lapses of reason and decency along the way. America's continuing ambivalence about immigration is well summarized by the nativist musings of Jesse Chickering in 1848, written at a time when all immigrants were northern Europeans:

But is the country truly benefited by this great foreign immigration? Have the people been made wiser or better or happier? It has been said that without these foreigners our railroads and canals could not have been constructed . . . [Yet] the progress of [these] internal improvements, a year or two in advance of what they would have been without this foreign labor, will be a very poor compensation, if offset by the corruption of manners, the forfeiture of freedom, and the transfer of power to those who know not how to use it wisely.[17]

One recurrent theme animating American nativism has been the unacceptable "alienness" of whoever happened to be the immigrants du jour. Peter Brimelow, in his 1995 book, *Alien Nation*, asserted that Americans will be unable to cope with the current wave of immigrants because of their alien characteristics.[18] In Brimelow's view, "alienness" is reflected by the fact that most new American immigrants are non-Europeans but, rather, Asians or Latin Americans. It will distort the fabric of American society, Brimelow argued, if the country must contend with the racial distinctiveness of Asians and the linguistic distinctiveness of Spanish-speaking Latin Americans.

Brimelow is in crowded historical company in his complaint because successive groups of immigrants, including those from northern Europe, have always been seen as too alien. Even someone as deeply identified with basic American universalist values as Benjamin Franklin could not abide the "alien" Germans who were overrunning Pennsylvania in his day and compromising its English-language dominance:

Why should the Palatine boors be suffered to swarm into our settlements and by herding together establish their language and manners to the exclusion of ours? Why should Pennsylvania, founded by the English, become a colony of aliens who will shortly be so numerous as to Germanize us instead of our Anglifying them?[19]

It doesn't take much, after all, for the people of any society to find others alien. And the narrower one's world and the less contact one has had with people of other nations or cultures, the more likely that even insignificant ethnic distinctions can loom large. But the ethnic distinctions among Europeans during America's century of mass immigration between 1820 and 1920, involving diverse religions, languages, and political traditions, were anything but insignificant. They are not insignificant in Europe even today.

One of the great myths of imagined American ethnic history is the hegemony of the British stock. In no decade since immigration statistics were first collected in 1820 did people coming from Great Britain (exclusive of Ireland) constitute the majority of immigrants. After 1850, in fact, Anglo-Americans were no longer even the largest national ethnic cohort. The high-water mark of British immigration actually occurred late in the nineteenth-century immigration cycle, the decade of the Civil War, when 26 percent of all immigrants came from Britain.[20] In rebutting a *New York Times* columnist's assertion that WASPs "invented America,"[21] journalist Robert Christopher pointed out:

> The reality is that America was invented and built not just by Anglo-Saxon Protestants but by people of diverse ethnic origins and religious beliefs . . . the culture and institutions we generally think of as WASP creations were from the very start very heavily influenced by people whose ancestors had never set foot in England, and that we owe many of our most cherished symbols of the American past to ethnic groups whose heritage was emphatically not Anglo-Saxon.[22]

The largest source of immigration, by far, in the first half of the nineteenth century was Ireland. Between 1820 and 1860, nearly 2 million Irish arrived, almost 40 percent of all immigrants during those decades. And the Irish were considered *very* alien in pre–Civil War America. The Native American Party (the Know-Nothings) of the 1840s was the first of many virulent organized nativist movements in American history, and its fire was directed, almost exclusively, at the Irish.[23] The epithets that today's most outspoken opponents of immigration might hurl against the poorest contemporary immigrant nationalities pale in comparison to the vilification of the Irish. The Irish were characterized as "destitute in our streets . . . they are found in our almshouses, and in our hospitals; they are found at the bar of our criminal tribunals, in our bridewell [jail] and our penitentiary and our State prison,"[24] as well as "ignorant and vicious" and "priest-ridden slaves of Ireland."[25] What stuck most in the nativist craw at the time was the fact that the Irish were Catholic. But the anti-Irish animus also extended to Irish people's impoverished status and purportedly loose morals. Anti-Irish prejudice was the strongest in the Northeast, and in places like New York and Massachusetts, it vastly exceeded the bigotry aimed at free blacks. Journalist Ellis Cose described the anti-Irish mood on the East Coast in the 1830s as follows:

> Around [this] time [the 1830s], the Massachusetts legislature urged enactment of a federal antipauperism statute [aimed at the impoverished Irish]. A group of New Yorkers, fretting over the newcomers' religious orientation, established the *Protestant*, a weekly newspaper . . . for the purpose of inculcating "Gospel doctrines against Romish corruptions." Similar anti-Catholic publications sprouted in Philadelphia, Baltimore, and elsewhere.[26]

Close on the heels of the Irish came the Germans, who began arriving in large numbers around 1840 and continued to come in an almost uninterrupted surge through the end of the century, eventually overtaking the Irish in number. Between 1840 and 1890, the United States admitted 4.5 million German immigrants, and to this day German descent is claimed by more Americans than any other national origin.[27] The Germans may not have been as detested as the Irish, but they also provoked strong nativist reactions and were widely considered almost as unassimilable. To begin with, the majority of Germans were Catholic, and their number further increased the Catholic influence in Protestant America. In many states, like New York, the German Catholic presence helped to make Catholicism the dominant religion. But the Germans brought another serious problem: They spoke German rather than English, and not just at home. Foreshadowing current disagreements about bilingualism, the Germans aggressively resisted English-language dominance and made strong claims for allowing German to be the language of instruction in public schools in German-speaking neighborhoods and towns. According to immigration scholar Thomas Muller, the Germans "assiduously sought to preserve their language. Their attitude was based on a deeply ingrained belief that German 'high' culture, as expressed in music, literature, and art, was superior to anything England or America had to offer."[28]

The period immediately following the Civil War, though marked by historically high levels of immigration, was nonetheless one of ethnic tranquillity and tolerance of immigrants. The Know-Nothing Party vanished into obscurity, and nativism was in disrepute. As historian Maldwyn Jones wrote:

> [A] preoccupation with material growth led Americans rather to emphasize the economic value of immigrants. Thus the 1860s and 1870s produced a flood of efforts to encourage immigration rather than to restrict it. Dislike and distrust of immigrants persisted, but remained in most places beneath the surface.[29]

A constant buzz of low-level bigotry may have marked many Americans' reactions to the various strains of alien immigrants during the nineteenth century, but surprisingly little of this animus actually found its way into legislation or policy, with one major exception: the anti-Chinese sentiment of the 1870s and 1880s. Even before the Civil War, the influx of Chinese who came as gold miners and farmers triggered a wave of anti-immigrant Sinophobia. Welcomed in 1852 by California governor John McDougal as "one of the most worthy classes of our newly adopted citizens," the Chinese were branded before the end of that decade by a San Francisco newspaper as "semi-human Asiatics" and "morally a far worse class to have among us than the negro."[30]

Right after the war, the east–west race to complete the transcontinental railway (1866 to 1869) led the California-based Central Pacific Railroad to recruit thousands of Chinese laborers to speed its lagging track-laying efforts. (Its eastern competitor, the Union Pacific, used Irish immigrants and Civil War veterans. Much hinged on the speed of track laying because federal land grants and loans were doled out to the competing railroads as they laid track.) The new wave of Chinese immigrants precipitated a virulent campaign of anti-Chinese bigotry that continued for decades until 1882, when federal legislation cut off all further Chinese immigration.

Because the Chinese arguably were really members of a different race and unquestionably had an ethnic distinctiveness that transcended that of the most exotic of the European nationalities, their presence triggered the first thoroughly nativist legislation since the short-lived Alien and Sedition laws of 1798. Under intense pressure from legislators from California, where most Chinese had settled, Congress passed the Chinese Exclusion Act in 1882. This legislation suspended all Chinese immigration for ten years, and in a devastating breach of the American assimilation contract, barred all Chinese—including those already settled in the United States—from achieving citizenship. Until the act's passage, several presidents, Congress, and the Supreme Court had strenuously resisted giving in to California's Sinophobia and repeatedly struck down state laws that aimed to discriminate against Chinese residents and exclude new Chinese immigrants.[31]

America's multiethnic stew took on new dimensions of alienness toward the end of the nineteenth century, when Italians and eastern Europeans streamed into the United States. Nativists had a field day organizing antagonism to these new aliens who were also Catholic (or worse, Jewish), spoke even stranger tongues than German, and were members of alien "races." Such language was not mere hyperbole; from the point of view of late-nineteenth-century American nativists, the despised Irish and stiff-necked Germans were at least "white," but Italians and Jews were not. As for Poles or Ukrainians, it was an open question.[32] It just goes to show how subjective and evanescent conceptions of "race" really are. When, as late as the 1910s and 1920s, nativists disparaged the desirability of southern and eastern European immigrant cohorts, they characterized them as being of alien—and inferior—racial stock. A 1912 article by Prescott Hall, one of the more respectable nativists, in the *North American Review* (a mainstream magazine), stated:

> The South Italian, which constitutes the largest element in our present immigration, is one of the most mixed races in Europe and is partly African owing to the negroid migration from

Carthage to Italy. The modern Greek is by no means the Greek of the time of Pericles, either in race or temperament. The Hebrew, which constitutes the next largest element of immigration, is still, as it always has been, an Asiatic race.[33]

The reminder that national and religious groups who now are unquestioningly accepted as white were once the objects of racial discrimination is especially relevant in the context of the current debate on immigration. Those who express alarm at the influx of racially alien Asians and Latinos and warn that the United States is in danger of becoming a nonwhite nation would do well to recognize that by nineteenth-century standards, the country already *is* a nonwhite nation.[34]

The Chinese Exclusion Act was, fortunately, only an island of restrictionism in the ocean of nineteenth-century laissez-faire immigration policy, but the sentiment to close America's borders was beginning to build. The year of the Chinese Exclusion Act, Congress also passed a general immigration law that set up an immigration-control process and barred "paupers." In 1887, the ownership of real estate was denied to noncitizens. The immigration law of 1891 strengthened the immigration-control process and provided for the deportation of illegal immigrants. A 1906 law made English-language proficiency a condition of citizenship. In 1907 Congress authorized the deportation of immigrants who went on welfare (such as it was in 1907). The Immigration Act of 1917 excluded illiterate immigrants and all other Asians besides the Chinese.

Thus, year by year, law by law, the restrictionist noose tightened as immigrants continued to come in ever-greater numbers. The noose was finally fully knotted and the chair kicked over in the Immigration Act of 1924. This legislation was the product of a decade's worth of highly unedifying debate about the purportedly inferior genetic and cultural attributes of America's most recent immigrants (the major focus was on Italians and Jews). Its most important feature was to restrict admission of immigrants by nationality. A complicated formula gave each European nationality a quota proportional to its share of the American population in 1890, with no quota exceeding 150,000. The year 1890 was purposely chosen to restrict stringently the entry of more southern and eastern Europeans, since most Italians, Jews, and members of other undesired groups entered the United States after that date. The combination of the 150,000 cap; the quota system, which kept out those who wanted to come; and the American Great Depression, which deterred those who were permitted to come, effectively stopped immigration dead in its tracks after 1929.[35] (See Table 2.)

Recurrent and nasty nativist reactions to perennially alien immigrants may be one leitmotif in the story of American immigration. But there is a much more important and positive one as well. This tidal wave of immigrants that kept washing up on American shores was, after all, integrated into American life with phenomenal speed and astonishing success.

The most incontrovertible part of this success story was economic. Most immigrants left the emotional security of their native lands to come to the United States because they were "seeking their fortune," as people used to say. For most immigrants and, more unequivocally, their children, the gamble paid off handsomely. But as Muller, Julian Simon, and other economists have convincingly documented, immigration paid off handsomely for native Americans as well.[36] American economic growth throughout the century of mass immigration was the highest in the world, averaging about 4.5 percent per year.[37] The American states with the highest percentage of immigrants were the most industrialized, the most urbanized, and, far and away, the most prosperous. The contribution of immigration to economic growth was certainly not lost on those Americans who were the most responsible for it: the political leaders and the "captains of industry."[38]

One reason the periodic bursts of nativism made so little legislative headway until the 1920s was that it was clear to many members of Congress and business leaders that immigrants were indispensable to America's economic progress. During the first half of the nineteenth century, when states set immigration policy, many states were eager to entice immigrants to join their workforces. Some, like Minnesota and Iowa, aggressively advertised in European newspapers, while others dispatched what one would

TABLE 2. IMMIGRATION, BY COUNTRY OF ORIGIN

Country	1820–60	1861–90	1891–1930	1931–70	1971–91
Ireland	1,956,000	1,528,000	1,084,000	112,000	48,000
Germany	1,546,000	2,958,000	1,402,000	1,010,000	177,000
Norway/Sweden	36,000	888,000	1,088,000	108,000	27,000
United Kingdom	794,000	1,962,000	1,479,000	588,000	313,000
Italy	13,000	375,000	4,263,000	525,000	226,000
Poland	2,000	67,000	330,000	89,000	137,000
Russia/Soviet Union	1,000	255,000	3,085,000	5,000	129,000
Other European	2,261,000	1,039,000	5,665,000	981,000	652,000
China	41,000	249,000	87,000	67,000	495,000
Other Asian	1,000	10,000	671,000	568,000	4,173,000
Canada	117,000	931,000	1,849,000	1,072,000	347,000
Mexico	18,000	9,000	729,000	837,000	3,244,000
Other American	47,000	57,000	484,000	1,319,000	3,305,000

Source: U.S. Immigration and Naturalization Service, *1991 Statistical Yearbook of the Immigration and Naturalization Service* (Washington, D.C.: U.S. Government Printing Office, 1992).

today characterize as "economic development" officials to recruit immigrant workers. Michigan, for example, had immigrant recruiters working the New York docks.[39] Later in the century, many of the rapidly expanding manufacturing firms sent recruiters abroad to staff their new factories.[40] After passage of the Homestead Act of 1862, the federal government extended an open invitation to potential European immigrants to settle the new lands of the western territories.[41]

While millions of immigrants settled in the rural lands of the Midwest and Plains States and many went to the hinterland as miners and railroad workers, the majority settled in the country's largest and fastest-growing cities. Indeed, it was the immigrants who made them grow. In his excellent 1993 book, *Immigrants and the American City*, Muller laid out the intimate connection between immigration and the rise of American cities.[42] As the country's largest city by far, New York was always the most obvious focal point of this connection. (Less obvious and often vehemently denied by other Americans is the close correlation of the immigrant-fueled economic growth of New York and the growing economic preeminence of the United States.)

After the Civil War, immigrants dominated the workforces (and politics) of New York, Chicago, Philadelphia, Boston, Milwaukee, Detroit, Pittsburgh, Cleveland, and St. Louis, as well as dozens of smaller cities. In the latter half of the nineteenth century, the United States was industrializing at a breathtaking clip, and the new factories were located in the cities (or cities sprung up around the factories), as were all the ancillary business and consumer services. The immigrants may have provided the lion's share of the workforce on the factory floor, but they also furnished a large proportion of the cities' merchants, salespeople, bankers, brokers, and civil servants.[43]

Immigrants were indispensable to America's economic growth for a number of reasons. The simplest is the matter of sheer numbers. The United States had a lot of land, it led the way in harnessing the latest in industrial technology, and world markets had an almost infinite appetite for its agricultural and manufacturing output. The opportunities for economic success in the United States under such circumstances were boundless—if, but only if, the country had sufficient manpower. But immigrants made ideal workers for other reasons: They were younger than native Americans, they worked longer and harder, and they accepted lower wages. Also, given the truncated economic opportunities of their homelands, those immigrants who decided to come to the United States were probably Europe's best and brightest.[44]

In a clear indication of how indebted the nation's economic well-being had been to immigrants, when America's immigration stopped, so did its prosperity. The Great Depression followed the effective date of the 1920s cutoff by only a few years. Economists lay the blame for the Depression on a variety of suspects: protectionism (imposed, incidentally, by the same political coalition behind the restriction of immigration), a tight monetary policy, and rampant stock speculation in the 1920s. But a growing number now unequivocally implicate the sudden dearth of immigrants after 1929. At the least, they believe, a continuation of immigration might, by increasing the demand for goods and services and the supply of cheap labor to produce them, have mitigated the Depression's length and severity.[45] Admittedly, the Depression was trans-Atlantic, but largely because America's economic collapse helped precipitate Europe's.

But the main point to be made here is that as the nation prospered, so did its immigrants. America's streets, immigrants soon found after they arrived, most certainly were not paved with gold. Life for new immigrants has always been almost unbearably hard. Days spent working in the coal mines, factories, and farmlands of nineteenth-century America were long, harsh, and dirty. Before the advent of unions, most workers—immigrants and natives alike—had to submit uncomplainingly to the stringent and unforgiving demands of their employers or risk losing their jobs. And then there were the appalling city slums where the immigrants lived, whose squalid and crowded quarters shocked middle-class Americans of the time and offered targets for turn-of-the-century muckrakers like Jacob Riis and reformers like Jane Addams.

But the very fact that immigration continued unabated indicates that the United States offered immigrants vastly greater economic gains than did the places they came from. The immigrant farmers at least owned their homesteads, and if they survived the harsh and unpredictable weather and the cyclical price swings of volatile agricultural markets, they often became prosperous. The southern and eastern European factory workers earned wages undreamed of in the countries they left behind. Many Jews and Italians were able to prosper as small businessmen. And, as far as the Jews were concerned, when they looked back on the pogroms of Russia and the ubiquitous anti-Semitism that prevailed in Europe, the United States was a veritable haven of tolerance. Immigrants prospered, however, not merely as producers, but as consumers. The whole point of America's rapid and technologically advanced industrialization was to turn out a cornucopia of inexpensive consumer goods, and immigrants constituted a large part of the market for these goods. As Max Lerner pointed out:

> The increase of immigration also meant more consumers as well as producers. The new machines cut production costs and prices, yet the steadily mounting millions of consumers kept big profits flowing into industry. And since the immigrants started on so little, their living standards kept steadily improving, and the home market grew not by arithmetical but geometrical progression.[46]

But the integration of immigrants into American life was not merely economic. Immigrants were also actively drawn into American politics, nowhere so assiduously as in the increasingly populous urban centers. The Irish, especially, had a legendary gift for politics, and after the Civil War, they used it to dominate the governments and hiring of most large northern cities. After decades of factory work, they took advantage of their newfound political leverage in the cities to get good (and unstrenuous) jobs as public employees.[47] The Germans, who had a broader geographic base, extending into the South, Midwest, and Great Plains, were also politically powerful and elected a sizable cadre of German American politicians. Carl Schurz, who became a U.S. senator just seventeen years after he arrived from Cologne in 1849, was perhaps the most famous, but also among the nationally prominent was German-born John Peter Atgeld, the governor of Illinois in the 1890s. In addition, countless German Americans served in local governments, state legislatures, and the Congress throughout the nineteenth century.[48] The political sensibilities of German and Irish

Americans were joined, in a manner of speaking, in the biting political cartoons of German-born Thomas Nast, who effectively caricatured corrupt Irish American politicians like Boss Tweed of New York's notorious Tammany machine. (Nast, incidentally, created the elephant and donkey symbols of the Republican and Democratic parties).[49]

But the other immigrants, though not as politically assertive, were eagerly courted by local political machines and both political parties nationally, and their votes were often decisive in determining political and governmental outcomes.[50] The Civil War and the antislavery sentiment that fueled it were heavily influenced by immigrant-based politics in the northern and midwestern states. Even though many Irish resented free blacks as economic competitors, the weight of Irish and especially German political action was against slavery and in support of Abraham Lincoln and the Union cause.[51]

Political participation not only bound immigrants to the most fundamental institution of American society and allowed them to shape local and national policies, it also integrated them into American life in other ways. The jobs that political influence gave them—as policemen, schoolteachers, and petty bureaucrats in regulatory agencies—made them enforcers of American values and protectors of the "American way of life." Becoming active in the political clubhouses gave immigrants an entrée into American social life. Seeing immigrants elected to office as mayors, governors, and congressmen gave immigrants prestige and raised their self-esteem and stake in American society.

Another reason immigrants were able to adjust so successfully to life in the United States was the ease and ubiquity with which social organizations sprang up in American communities, native and foreign born, to mediate between individuals and the larger society. Regarding those for immigrants, sociologist Milton Gordon wrote: "The self-contained communal life of the immigrant colonies served . . . as a kind of decompression chamber in which the newcomers could, at their own pace, make a reasonable adjustment to the [new American] society."[52]

Foremost among them were religious organizations. Early on, the American landscape was dotted with churches of every con ceivable Christian denomination. In the cities Catholics founded parishes for every nationality, and Jews organized congregations for every degree of orthodoxy. Maldwyn Jones catalogued the diversity of ethnic denominations besides the Roman Catholic church, which served most Irish, Italian, and German Americans: Lithuanian and Polish Catholic; Finnish Evangelical, Free Magyar (Hungarian) Reformed; Albanian, Carpatho-Russian, Assyrian, Greek, Romanian, Russian, Serbian, Syrian, and Ukranian Orthodox; Augustana Evangelical Lutheran (Swedish); Lutheran Free (Norwegian); and Missouri Synod, Evangelical Lutheran, and United Lutheran (all German). He went on to observe:

> It was in the immigrant churches, however, that [adjustment to American life] was most clearly evident. [Although] many American religious denominations have retained their ethnic character . . . these churches resemble each other, not only in having adopted the English language but in having taken on an American form of church life.[53]

The houses of worship were only the sacred representations of vast networks of other religiously affiliated social and charitable organizations. In the secular realm, immigrants and natives alike belonged to fraternal orders, service societies, labor unions, burial and gymnastic societies, study and self-improvement groups, organizations dedicated to political and social causes, and local civic associations.

In view of current hand-wringing about the prospects of living with today's new immigrants, the most important question is this: Why was America's immigration experiment so successful in the past? That the United States was able to absorb and integrate generation upon generation of immigrants from impossibly disparate ethnic backgrounds, while holding on to—indeed, strengthening—its fundamental liberties and principles, was a remarkable achievement, unreplicated in any other nation. But the experiment could, under the wrong set of circumstances, just as easily have gone awry. That it didn't was due, in no small measure, to natives and immigrants agreeing to subscribe to the three unities of the assimilation contract: the cultural unity imposed by uncompromised English-language dominance, the civic unity imposed by pride in being American and allegiance to the American Idea, and the unity of values imposed by adherence (in a one-third Catholic nation) to the Protestant ethic. It was especially important that immigrants and natives worked together to assimilate the immigrants' children and grandchildren.

Early in its history, the United States could have given in to the exigencies of bilingualism. During the decades of heavy German immigration, the German-speaking share of the American population was not much smaller than that of the French Canadians in Canada and was much larger than the United States' Spanish-speaking proportion today. In some states it was as high as 35 to 40 percent. And almost as insistently as French Canadians and more strenuously than Latinos today, German advocates of bilingualism demanded that their children be taught in their "mother tongue." The German-speaking community published German-language dailies like New York's *Staats-Zeitung*, sent its children to German-language schools, and belonged to German-speaking clubs. Nevertheless, in spite of their numbers and their political influence (Carl Schurz was an ardent advocate of bilingualism), they did not prevail. Every time it came up as a legislative issue at the national or state level (including as early as 1797, when it was proposed that federal laws should be published in German), efforts to institutionalize bilingualism were defeated as Americans steadfastly refused to condone bilingualism in the public domain.[54]

Even more critical to the assimilation of immigrants and their descendants was Americans' unwavering pride in the justice and liberty of their political system and the larger ideology that animated it. One cannot emphasize enough the importance of that ideology in providing a lodestar by which all American institutions and policies have navigated. As Lerner wrote forty years ago:

> For a century and a half the worship of the Constitution has been part of American traditional thought and emotion. It may have taken root as a way of giving Americans the sense of their place in the sun. Today it counts most as a symbol of the nontotalitarian way of living.[55]

Time and again, conflicts between immigrants and natives and between blacks and whites could be resolved peaceably because America's first principles could not, in the end, be denied. The American Idea not only motivated the abolitionists to launch a war against slavery, reconstructionists to solidify (briefly) the rights of freed slaves, and civil rights advocates in our time to demand an end to official racial discrimination once and for all; it gave them the institutional weapons by which they ultimately prevailed against racial bigotry in Congress and the courts. It was the American Idea that, in numerous congressional and courtroom battles, derailed nativist proposals to restrict immigration and deny immigrants' rights in the nineteenth century and that led to the liberalization of immigration policy in the twentieth century. Time and again, Americans learned to accept, socialize with, and eventually marry their immigrant neighbors because the American Idea made it the natural thing to do.

If the American Idea integrated immigrants on the higher plane of national first principles, the values of the Protestant ethic did so on the playing field of everyday life. Immigrants, whatever their native religions or cultures, eagerly responded to a society in which everyone was judged so heavily by their accomplishments. They were prepared to work hard, and many realized the fruits of their diligence. Despite enduring working conditions considered unacceptable today, most immigrants labored without complaint as they and their children struggled up the ladder of economic mobility. Welfare, as we know it today, did not exist, and (unlike workers in Europe at the time), few immigrants agitated to have it instituted. As Lerner pointed out, the legendary "self-made man" was usually an immigrant.[56] Regarding the Protestant ethic's noneconomic dimension, despite the rigors of their new home, most immigrants had little difficulty accepting personal moral responsibility and making sure that their children did so as well. The era of mass immigration was not free of crime, but crime was usually less violent than the present, and criminals were more apt to be "natives" than immigrants. Immigrants were intensely engaged in religious and other social organizations, and though they were, for the most part, poorly educated, their level of voting and civic participation would put contemporary Americans to shame. All in all, it was probably only the constant influx of non-Protestant immigrants that kept the Protestant ethic alive and well in the United States, since natives were continually tempted to abandon it, a point that is elaborated on in Chapter 7.

Citizenship and public education rounded out the assimilation process. Citizenship has always served as the indispensable proof to immigrants and natives that they are members of the same national family—a critical substantive and symbolic rite of passage. Citizenship has also offered immigrants the key to political participation. And the public schools have always served as the most universal assimilation training fields for immigrant children, immersing them in the precepts of the American Idea, a passing knowledge of American history, and daily social contacts with a cross section of schoolchildren of other ethnic groups.

This synoptic view of this country's immigration experience holds a number of important lessons for Americans today. Immigrants at all times have been good for America, and America has been good to them. Immigrants have always seemed alien initially, but Americans have always gotten used to them, and the experience has nurtured their tolerance and given them more cosmopolitan views. America's open economy, democratic politics, and dense social infrastructure have contributed to the integration of immigrants. But in the end national unity has depended, more than anything else, on the magic of assimilation.

It is only because of assimilation that the United States was able, despite periodic outbursts of nativism, to absorb—and make Americans of—the continuous stream of millions upon millions of immigrants. This project depended on accommodations by both "natives" and immigrants. Natives had to accept that they were living in a society that was in constant demographic and cultural flux. Immigrants had to learn a new language, adapt to an alien culture, and live by their adopted country's rules. In the spirit of a free and open society, both sides surrendered as little of their cultures as possible. The resulting formula of accommodation produced assimilation, American style.

How Assimilation
Actually Works

part II

3

Assimilation, American Style

For all of our enormous geographic range, for all of our sectionalism, for all of our interwoven breeds drawn from every part of the ethnic world, we are a nation, a new breed. Americans are much more American than they are Northerners, Southerners, Westerners, or Easterners. And descendants of English, Irish, Italian, Jewish, German, Polish are essentially American. This is not patriotic whoop-de-do; it is carefully observed fact. California Chinese, Boston Irish, Wisconsin Germans, yes, and Alabama Negroes, *have more in common than they have apart.* And this is the more remarkable because it has happened so quickly. It is a fact that Americans from all sections and of all racial extractions are more alike than the Welsh are like the English, the Lancashireman like the Cockney, or for that matter the Lowland Scot like the Highlander. It is astonishing that this has happened in less than two hundred years and most of it in the last fifty. The American identity is an *exact and provable thing.*

John Steinbeck, 1962[1]

Although assimilation, American style has, historically, proved to be an extraordinary success, the recent breakdown of the American consensus favoring assimilation can be traced, in large part, to the widespread misunderstanding of what the concept really means. Most Americans, both those who favor and those who oppose assimilation, believe that for immigrants to assimilate, they must abandon their original cultural attributes and conform entirely to the behaviors and customs of the majority of the native-born population. In the terminology of the armed forces, this represents a model of "up or out": Either immigrants bring themselves "up" to native cultural standards, or they are doomed to live "out" of the charmed circle of the national culture.

The notion is not entirely far-fetched because this is exactly what assimilation demands in other societies. North African immigrants to France are, for example, expected to assimilate by abandoning their native folkways with alacrity. Official French policy has been zealous in making North African and other Muslim women give up wearing their chadors and, in the schools, instilling a disdain for North African and Muslim culture in their children. To varying degrees, most European countries that have had to absorb large numbers of immigrants since World War II interpret assimilation this way. But assimilation as a repudiation of immigrant culture has not been the American approach at all. Assimilation, American style has always been much more flexible and accommodating and, consequently, much more effective in achieving its purpose—to allow the United States to preserve its "national unity in the face of the influx of hordes of persons of scores of different nationalities," in the words of the sociologist Henry Fairchild.[2] By contrast, assimilation, European style has promoted national and ethnic disunity.

A popular way of getting hold of the assimilation idea has been to use a metaphor, and by far the most popular metaphor has been that of the "melting pot," a term coined by David, the hero of Israel Zangwill's 1908 play of that name. In the play, David exclaims to his girlfriend Vera:

David: There she lies, the great Melting-Pot—Listen! Can't you hear the roaring and the bubbling? There gapes her mouth—the harbour where a thousand mammoth feeders come from the ends of the world to pour in their human freight. Ah, what a stirring and a seething! Celt and Latin, Slav and Teuton, Greek and Syrian, black and yellow—

Vera: Jew and Gentile

David: Yes, East and West, and North and South, the palm and the pine, the pole and the equator, the crescent and the cross—how the great Alchemist melts and fuses them with his purifying flame! Here shall they all unite to build the Republic of Man and the Kingdom of God.[3]

According to the melting-pot metaphor—the "melting" of each new immigrant's ethnicity and cultural peculiarity in the boiling "pot" of America—assimilation involved the fine-grained intermingling of diverse ethnicities and cultures into a single national "alloy." If taken literally, this metaphor implied two things. The point most commonly taken is that the new human products of the melting pot would, of necessity, be culturally indistinguishable. Presumably every piece of metal taken from a melting pot should have the same chemical composition. Less frequently understood is the metaphor's implication that natives and their indigenous cultural characteristics would also be irreversibly changed—blended beyond recognition—because they constituted the base material of the melting pot.

These two corollaries of the melting-pot metaphor have long invited criticism by those who thought they were inconsistent with the ethnic realities of American society. Critics of the metaphor have spanned the ideological spectrum and mounted several different lines of attack on it. One of the most persistent strains of criticism, first voiced by sociologist Horace Kallen, one of the most prolific American scholars of ethnicity, argued that it was not only unrealistic, but cruel and harmful, to force new immigrants to shed their familiar, lifelong, cultural attributes as the price of admission to American society. In place of the melting pot, Kallen called for "cultural pluralism."[4] In Kallen's words, national policy should "seek to provide conditions under which each [group] might attain the cultural perfection that is proper to its kind."[5]

Another, more contemporary critique has emanated from empiricists like Nathan Glazer and Daniel Patrick Moynihan, who, in *Beyond the Melting Pot*, merely submitted evidence that the melting pot wasn't working as predicted and concluded: "The point about the melting pot . . . is that it did not happen."[6] Both the cultural pluralists and the empiricists concentrated on the injustice or failure of the melting pot as it applied to immigrants. But there were also critics who understood the other corollary of the metaphor—that natives were changed by it, too—and saw no reason that native Americans should give up any part of their cultural attributes to "melt" into the alloy. If true assimilation were to occur, the criticism went, immigrants would have to abandon all their cultural baggage and conform to American ways. It is the immigrant, said Fairchild, representing the views of many Americans, "who must undergo the entire transformation; the true member of the American nationality is not called upon to change in the least."[7]

For all its somewhat ahistorical idealism, the melting-pot metaphor still represents the standard around which fervent proponents of assimilation have rallied over the years. The popularity of the metaphor for so many decades and the fact that assimilation cannot be discussed, even by scholars, without reference to it, testifies to Americans' enduring yearning for a "pure" vision of assimilation. Most Americans have wanted the melting pot to be true and have looked to it to resolve the country's persistent conundrum of how it might achieve national unity amid ethnic diversity. Indeed, during the United States' most aggressively assimilationist period, the "Americanization" movement of the 1920s and 1930s, Americans were capable of taking the metaphor literally. "On the stage" of Henry Ford's English school for immigrant workers

> was represented an immigrant ship. In front of it was a huge melting pot. Down the gang plank came the members of the class dressed in their national garbs and carrying luggage such as they carried when they landed in this country. Down they poured into the Ford melting pot and disappeared. Then teachers began to stir the contents of the pot with long ladles. Presently the pot began to boil over and out came the men dressed in their best American clothes and waving American flags.[8]

Ever since Zangwill coined the metaphor, those with empirical and ideological objections to the melting pot have tried their hand at alternative metaphors. One of the earliest antagonists of the melting pot compared America's diverse ethnic strains to strands of yarn in a woven cloth, with the process of assimilation likened to a "weaving machine." Civil rights activist Jesse Jackson suggested that Americans are members of a "rainbow coalition." Former New York Mayor David Dinkins saw his constituents constituting a "gorgeous mosaic." Former Congresswoman Shirley Chisholm characterized America's ethnic groups as being like ingredients in a "salad bowl."[9] Barbara Jordan, recent chairperson of the U.S. Commission on Immigration Reform, said: "We are more than a melting-pot; we are a kaleidoscope."[10]

These counter metaphors all share a common premise: that ethnic groups in the United States may live side by side harmoniously, but on two conditions that overturn both assumptions of the melting-pot metaphor. First, immigrants and black Americans should never have to (or maybe should not even want to) give up any of their original cultural attributes. And second, there never can or will be a single unified national identity that all Americans can relate to. These two principles, in turn, have become the foundations of cultural pluralism, the antithesis of assimilationism. Kallen, father of cultural pluralism, introduced the concept in 1916, only eight years after publication of Zangwill's *The Melting Pot*, determined to challenge that work's premises.[11] Cultural pluralism rejects melting-pot assimilationism not on empirical grounds, but on ideological ones. Kallen and his followers believed that immigrants to the United States should not "melt" into a common national ethnic alloy but, rather, should steadfastly hang on to their cultural ethnicity and band together for social and political purposes even after generations of residence in the United States. As such, cultural pluralism is not an alternative theory of assimilation; it is a theory opposed to assimilation. Cultural pluralism is, in fact, the philosophical antecedent of modern multiculturalism—what I call ethnic federalism. Kallen's views, however, stop significantly short of contemporary multiculturalism in their demands on the larger "native" American society. For Kallen, cultural pluralism was a defensive strategy for "unassimilable" immigrant ethnic groups that required no accommodation by the larger society. The multiculturalists, on the other hand, demand certain ethnic rights and concessions.

All these metaphors, although colorful ways of representing assimilation, don't go far in giving one an accurate understanding of what assimilation is really about. For example, across the ideological spectrum, they all invoke some external, impersonal assimilating agent. Who, exactly, is the "great alchemist" of the melting pot? What force propels the weaving machine, tosses the salad, or pieces together the mosaic? By picturing assimilation as an impersonal, automatic process and thus placing it beyond analysis, the metaphors fail to illuminate its most important secrets. Assimilation, if it is to succeed, must be a voluntary process, by both the assimilating immigrants and the assimilated-to natives. Assimilation is a human accommodation, not a mechanical production.

The metaphors also mislead as to the purposes of assimilation. The melting pot is supposed to turn out an undifferentiated alloy—a uniform, ethnically neutral, American protoperson. Critics have long pointed out that this idea is far-fetched. But is it even desirable? And if it is desirable, does it really foster a shared national identity? The greatest failing of the melting-pot metaphor is that it overreaches. It exaggerates the degree to which immigrants' ethnicity is likely to be extinguished by exposure to American society. It exaggerates the need to extinguish ethnicity. By being too compelling, too idealistic, the stirring melting-pot idea has inadvertently helped to discredit the very assimilation paradigm it was meant to celebrate. On the other hand, behind their unexceptionable blandness, the antithetical cultural pluralist metaphors are profoundly insidious. By suggesting that the product of assimilation is mere ethnic coexistence without integration, they undermine the objectives of assimilation, even if they appear more realistic. Is assimilation only about diverse ethnic groups sharing the same national space? That much can be said for any multiethnic society. If the ethnic strands of the fabric, the greens of the salad, the fragments of the mosaic, do not interact and identify with each other, no meaningful assimilation is taking place.

Perhaps a new assimilation metaphor should be introduced—one that depends not on a mechanical process (like the melting pot or the weaving machine) but on human dynamics. Assimilation might be viewed as more akin to *religious conversion* than anything else. In the terms of this metaphor, the immigrant is the convert, American society is the religious order being joined, and assimilation is the process by which the conversion takes place. Just as there are many motives for people to immigrate, so are there many motives for them to change their religion: spiritual, practical (like being married to a person of another faith), and materialistic (joining some churches can lead to jobs or subsidized housing). But whatever the motivation, conversion usually involves the consistent application of certain principles. Conversion is a mutual decision requiring affirmation by the convert and the religious order he or she wishes to join. Converts are expected in most (but not all) cases to renounce their old religions. But converts do not have to change their behavior in any respects other than those that relate to the new religion. They are expected only to believe in its theological principles, observe its rituals and holidays, and live by its moral precepts. Beyond that, they can be rich or poor, practice any trade, pursue any avocational interests, and have any racial or other personal attributes. Once they undergo conversion, they are eagerly welcomed into the fellowship of believers. They have become part of "us" rather than "them." This is undoubtedly what writer G. K. Chesterton had in mind when he said: "America is a nation with the soul of a church."[12]

In the end, however, no metaphor can do justice to the achievements and principles of assimilation, American style. As numerous sociologists have shown, assimilation is not a single event, but a process. In 1930 Robert Park observed: "Assimilation is the name given to the process or processes by which peoples of diverse racial origins and different cultural heritages, occupying a common territory, achieve a cultural solidarity sufficient at least to sustain a national existence."[13] More recently, Richard Alba defined assimilation as "long-term processes that have whittled away at the social foundations of ethnic distinctions."[14] But assimilation is more complex than that because it is a process of numerous dimensions. Not all immigrants and ethnic groups assimilate in exactly the same way or at the same speed. In *Assimilation in American Life* (1964), Milton Gordon suggested that there is a typology, or hierarchy, of assimilation, thus capturing some of the key steps that immigrants and ethnic groups go through as their assimilation—their cultural solidarity with native-born Americans, in Park's words—becomes more complete.[15]

First, and perhaps, foremost, natives and immigrants must accord each other *legitimacy*. That is, each group must believe the other has a legitimate right to be in the United States and that its members are entitled to pursue, by all legal means, their livelihood and happiness as they see fit. Second, immigrants must have *competence* to function effectively in American workplaces and in all the normal American social settings. Immigrants are expected to seize economic opportunities as they present themselves and to participate, at some level, in the social life of American society, and natives must not get in their way. Third, immigrants must be encouraged to exercise *civic responsibility*, minimally by being law-abiding members of American society, respectful of their fellow citizens, and optimally as active participants in the political process. Fourth, and most essential, immigrants must *identify themselves as Americans*, placing that identification ahead of any associated with their birthplace or ethnic homeland, and their willingness to do so must be reciprocated by the warm embrace of native Americans.[16]

The speed and thoroughness with which individual immigrants conform to these criteria vary, but each dimension is critical and interdependent with the others. The absence of legitimacy breeds ethnic conflict between natives and immigrants and among members of different ethnic groups. The absence of competence keeps immigrants from being economically and socially integrated into the larger society and breeds alienation among the immigrants and resentment of their dependence among natives. The absence of civic responsibility keeps immigrants from being involved in many crucial decisions that affect their lives and further contributes to their alienation. Having immigrants identify as Americans is, of course, the whole point of assimilation, but such identification depends heavily on the fulfillment of the other three criteria.

One of the most frequently overlooked dimensions of assimilation is the extent to which it depends more on the behavior of natives than of immigrants. Most conventional definitions and analyses of the subject assume that assimilation involves affirmative acts or choices that immigrants alone must make. But the real secret of American assimilation is that the native-born Americans—not the immigrants—have made it work. Since independence, a majority of Americans, all of whom once were immigrants themselves or the descendants of immigrants, have been instilled with the assimilationist ethos and have, in turn, instilled it in each new generation of immigrants.

Americans have accorded immigrants (and their children) their legitimacy. They have done so by letting them come, letting them quickly become citizens, according them a full complement of American civil rights, and treating them in myriad ways, both large and small, as equals. Americans, through their faith in individual achievement, have given immigrants the chance to prove themselves. They have employed them, let them buy homes in their neighborhoods, let them join their social organizations, and even let them marry their sons and daughters. (Regarding the latter point: Americans—and not all even today—have only recently grown so tolerant that they condone their children marrying immigrants of another race; but Americans have long surpassed the citizens of other nations in accepting interethnic marriages.) Americans have sustained a civic order and a civic ideology that values good citizenship and political participation by all residents. They have drilled the immigrants' children in the American Idea, actively encouraged immigrants to become citizens and to vote, aggressively appealed to them as political constituents, and let them run for political office. In short, Americans, by law, policy, and attitude, have actively encouraged immigrants to become fellow Americans in spirit as well in law.

The roots of Americans' predisposition in favor of assimilation reach deep into the American psyche. This predisposition is undoubtedly nourished by the personal and collective memories and aspirations of a nation of immigrants, but since other nations of immigrants (Argentina, Australia, Brazil, Canada, and New Zealand) have not been nearly as assimilationist, there must be some other explanation. American assimilation owes its power to four unique aspects of American society: (1) the liberal, universalist ideas embedded for all time in the U.S. Constitution; (2) the universal commitment to an economy built on market capitalism; (3) the density and redundancy of organizational life—governmental, political, religious, social, economic, and philanthropic; and (4) a persistent, society-wide, infatuation with modernity and progress. Each factor by itself is assimilationist. Together, they make assimilation irresistible.

America's political system has fostered assimilation in several ways. By blocking acts of discrimination against immigrants and ethnic minorities, it has given immigrants civil legitimacy, undermined the credibility of nativists, and prevented the buildup of unresolved ethnic grievances. In its machinery of political participation based on universal suffrage, it has further enhanced immigrants' civil status, offered appropriate forums for airing ethnic grievances, and provided an important entrée for involvement in American organizational life. One hundred years ago, political scientist Richmond Mayo-Smith observed:

> The exercise of political rights . . . makes [the immigrants] of importance to the political leaders. It gives them a higher position than they were accustomed to at home, and this naturally attaches them to the new country. However much our politics may suffer from the addition of this vote, much of it ignorant and some of it depraved, there is no doubt as to the educational and nationalizing effect on the immigrants themselves.[17]

By allowing all immigrants to become citizens after a brief residence and a painless apprenticeship, the United States has offered them formal membership in the American community. Finally, as the practical embodiment of universally cherished, if often breached, principles of civic idealism embodied in the "American Idea," the U.S. political system has served as a compelling philosophical rallying point for all Americans. The main features of the American political order are now staples of all Western democracies, but no other country has implemented them for so long, and no other people have so fervently embraced them as a "civil religion."

American capitalism has been nearly as important as its political institutions in fostering assimilation. As economist Thomas Sowell pointed out, by putting an economic premium on talent and effort, market capitalism makes any discriminatory, antiassimilation policies of natives or immigrants *unprofitable*.[18] Even an anti-immigration scholar like George Borjas noted in his 1990 book, *Friends or Strangers*: "Not only is economic mobility an important aspect of the immigrant experience, it is also sufficiently strong to guarantee that for most of their working lives, first-generation immigrants outperform natives in the American labor market."[19] Competition between natives and immigrants in most parts of the world has bred hostility and ethnic conflict. From time to time, it has done so in the United States as well, especially during economic downturns, but America's capitalist ethos has been so strong that inevitably the economic contributions of immigrants earn the grudging respect, rather than the envy, of natives. Once immigrants and natives work together and come to appreciate each other's economic value, it becomes much easier to form other kinds of interest-based relationships. Eventually, economic relationships lead to social ones, culminating in friendship and even intermarriage. At a deeper philosophical level, a society devoted to judging people mainly by their accomplishments is a society that, of necessity, places less stock on judging them by their ethnic, or even class, backgrounds. And yet, none of the world's other market societies has been so ideologically committed to capitalism and individualism that it has reflexively placed objective judgments of individual worth ahead of any subjective criteria like ethnicity, class, or family ties.

More than one hundred and sixty years ago Alexis de Tocqueville remarked about Americans' proclivity to join and participate in an array of organizational activities and saw that proclivity as one of the young nation's most stabilizing and heartening tendencies. The United States still leads the world in the density and profusion of organizations of every imaginable sort and the extent to which its citizens join them. Francis Fukuyama, in his 1995 book, *Trust*, thoroughly documented the importance of America's "intermediary" institutions in promoting the stability and harmony of American life, not the least in providing one of the most effective venues for the assimilation of generations of immigrants.[20] Even the formal governmental apparatus of this federated nation, which, in addition to the states, supports thousands of local and special-purpose jurisdictions, offers a vast arena for formal and informal participation by citizens. Leaving government aside, in even the smallest towns and neighborhoods, people have always belonged to an abundance of religious, fraternal, business, social, recreational, philanthropic, and single-purpose activist organizations.

Americans' active organizational life has greatly facilitated all aspects of assimilation. Civic organizations have given immigrants status and reinforced their civic assimilation. Other kinds of organizations have enhanced immigrants' competence and protected their economic interests, reinforcing their "structural" assimilation. From the beginning, ethnically based religious and social organizations have given aid and comfort to immigrants, which have greatly eased the immigrants' transition to American life and led inevitably to their participation in a wider social network. The historian Maldwyn Jones explained the paradox of how ethnic churches and ethnic celebrations actually worked to promote assimilation and "Americanization," as follows:

> Transplanted from Europe, where they had usually been part of the political structure, into the competitive American environment produced by church and state, the immigrant churches were forced to reorganize. . . . Shorn of their connection with the state, they have . . . metamorphosed into characteristically American institutions.
>
> This subtle yet profound type of alchemy provides the key not only to the immigrant contribution to American culture but also the paradox of immigrant loyalties. To some observers there has been an element of contradiction in the fact that immigrants assert their American patriotism as members of separate groups. But the contradiction is only superficial. When Polish-Americans observe Pulaski day, when Irish-Americans parade in honor of St. Patrick, when Italian-Americans gather to fete San Rocco or San Genaro, and even when Americans of Greek, Mexican or Armenian origin celebrate the old country's independence day, they are merely asserting their cultural distinctiveness, merely seeking to make clear their own identity in the larger American community. And even while doing so, they rededicate themselves to the common national ideals that bind them together.[21]

The most overlooked national attribute that has facilitated assimilation is Americans' enduring enthusiasm for "progress" and all things modern, what Max Lerner referred to as "the merging of the Constitution with the idea-of-progress strain in American thought."[22] A country that is in love with progress appreciates the potential contributions of immigrants and is eager to incorporate them. A country that is determined to be in the vanguard knows that antiassimilationist ethnocentricity represents a retrograde and outmoded way of thinking. A country that is always willing to embrace change is rarely daunted by the prospect of living with new and "exotic" peoples. Philip Gleason, in the *Harvard Encyclopedia of American Ethnic Groups,* pointed to the historic origins of American modernism and its inconsistency with ethnic consciousness:

> Newness was the second significant mark of American nationality [the first being Americans' distinctive political ideology]. Despite a long colonial past, the origin of the American nation could be definitively assigned to the Revolution and the establishment of a unified government in the 1780s, events that constituted a decisive break with the past. America had turned its back on Europe and proclaimed itself the new order of the ages, the model for the future. . . .
>
> Compared to the ideological quality, emphasis on newness, and future orientation, the ethnic element in American nationality was quite recessive in the first years of the republic.[23]

Over the United States' two centuries of existence, the tides of nativism have periodically advanced and receded with changing levels and national mixes of immigrants, the onset and conclusion of great wars, and the vicissitudes of the national business cycle. But they have never been strong enough to overwhelm the irresistible currents of America's bedrock political, economic, and social predispositions. These predispositions have reinforced the country's effective immigrant-assimilation paradigm, but they have also reinforced each other. It is the combination of these American predispositions and the assimilationist ethos they support that has made the United States, with all its problems and shortcomings, the most successful nation in world history.

One of the hallmarks of assimilation, American style is that immigrants are free to retain or discard as much or as little of their homeland cultures as they wish without compromising their assimilation. This is what sets assimilation, American style apart from assimilation anywhere else. This fact is rarely recognized, however, in most discussions of the subject, allowing a misperception to stand that severely distorts the American debate about assimilation's desirability and possibility. The conventional judgment as to whether immigrants or their descendants are assimilating is usually based on how much of their native cultural heritages they have discarded and how culturally "American" they seem. By this standard, a foreign-born teenager listening to rock music on his Walkman, wearing a baseball cap backward, and speaking accent-free English is "assimilated," whereas an Amish farmer is not. But the social characteristic being identified here is not really assimilation, but what Milton Gordon and other sociologists of ethnicity refer to as "acculturation."[24]

Acculturation may or may not accompany assimilation. Usually, immigrants who assimilate—or at least their children—become acculturated as well, but not always and not completely. Usually, acculturated people are assimilated, but again, not always. The distinction between assimilation and acculturation is crucial, and Gordon's decades-old insistence that acculturation is *not* synonymous with assimilation may be his greatest contribution to the theory of assimilation.[25] Except for the need to speak English, acculturation, in the American historical context, may be meaningless because the base culture to which immigrant communities may be expected to relate is so fluid. It is not clear what it is that immigrants should be acculturating to. As it turns out, the United States is actually much more of a melting pot, in Zangwill's original sense of the metaphor, than the critics were willing to concede. Notwithstanding the continuing predominance of English cultural and social influences, African American, Hispanic, Jewish, Italian, Asian and other ethnic influences are now deeply and ineradicably embedded in the national cultural mix, and new ethnic influences are changing that mix every day. Even international ethnic influences, detached from any immigrant cohorts, are at work changing the American "national" culture. The widespread appeal of Japanese products, architecture, and food is largely unrelated to the direct influence of the small cohort of Japanese American immigrants, and the large Italian American community has had little to do with the growing popularity of Italian furniture and crafts.

Acculturation, in the conventional understanding of the term, is largely irrelevant in a mass consumer culture to which the entire world is acculturating. Blockbuster Video stores, multiscreen cineplexes, and Burger Kings are scattered across the landscape from coast to coast. Housewives in a San Antonio barrio, a Detroit ghetto, and a Westchester County suburb watch Oprah Winfrey or the O. J. Simpson trial at exactly the same time. Youngsters from Watts or Chevy Chase or Hamtranck can all be found rollerblading in their cutoff jeans around the local shopping mall on a Saturday night. Virtually the entire American population (and a growing share of the world's) has made at least one visit to a Disney theme park. Americans of all ethnicities have never been more acculturated than they are today. If assimilation really was the same thing as acculturation, there might be nothing to worry about.

But because it is manifestly clear that people can be acculturated without being assimilated, there is a great deal to worry about. Indeed, in most of the world's hot spots of ethnic conflict, acculturation is not an issue, but assimilation is. Religion aside, Bosnia's Serbs, Croatians, and Muslims are acculturated to the same cultural base, as are Northern Ireland's Catholics and Protestants, but the ethnic conflicts of Bosnia and Northern Ireland transcend acculturation and religion and would not disappear even in the face of mass religious conversion. They owe their virulence to the absence of all the other aspects of the assimilation typology. Conversely, people can be assimilated without being acculturated. The strangely dressed Hasidim of Brooklyn, the devout Mormons of Utah, and the insular Chinese Americans of San Francisco's Chinatown are incompletely acculturated to contemporary American cultural norms, but they are very much assimilated. Not only is acculturation not synonymous with assimilation, it can dangerously distract attention away from the absence of true assimilation. That is why people in the United States, perhaps even people in the societies involved, cannot fathom the deep ethnic hatreds of a Bosnia or Northern Ireland today or the murderous anti-Semitism of Nazi Germany in the 1930s and 1940s that was unleashed against the most acculturated Jews in Europe.

One can see many examples of acculturation without assimilation in the United States itself. Several of the Arab-born perpetrators of the 1993 bombing of the World Trade Center in New York City were actually highly acculturated to American society. The sister of one of the ringleaders is quoted as saying about her brother:

"We always considered him a son of America. He was always saying 'I want to live in America forever.'"[26] Here, obviously, is a man who, though sufficiently acculturated, was thoroughly unassimilated. His unwillingness to identify with the United States *as a nation*, rather than as a culture, led him to participate in a murderous anti-American act. Even Timothy J. McVeigh, the perpetrator of the much more devastating bombing of the Oklahoma City federal office building, is, in his own way, an example of someone who is an acculturated but unassimilated American, even though he is the descendant of immigrants who came to the United States many generations ago. McVeigh claims that he is only antigovernment, not anti-American. But the research and testimony emerging since he was apprehended clearly show a man motivated less by libertarian or anarchic sentiments and more by hatred of America's ethnic diversity and of the American Idea's universalist principles that generated and legitimated that ethnic diversity.[27] McVeigh's case illustrates how national unity—the key output of true assimilation—depends on the commitment of natives, as much as immigrants, to what Gordon called "civic assimilation."[28]

On a much more mundane level and with fewer harmful consequences, one sees acculturation without assimilation among such immigrants as Dominicans in New York, who refuse to think of the United States as their permanent national home. Most Dominican youngsters in New York speak accent-free English and are very much at ease in the cultural matrix of New York and the United States. Their parents still speak accented English and Spanish among themselves, but they are far more acculturated than were the Jews and Italians on New York's Lower East Side a few generations ago. But as Luis Guarnizo documented in his study of the New York Dominican community, whether they are more acculturated or less acculturated, a disturbingly large number of Dominicans see New York and America as only a temporary way station—a place to make some money. They plan to return to their native Dominican Republic as soon as they have saved enough; in the meantime, they constantly travel back and forth.[29]

The confusion between acculturation and assimilation is no mere terminological quibble because the muddling of that distinction has been one of the most durable pegs on which the enemies of assimilation have hung their arguments for keeping the United States permanently divided along ethnic lines. In the thirty or so years since Gordon wrote *Assimilation in American Life,* there has been an explosion of studies on immigration, ethnicity, and assimilation in America. Many of the researchers of these studies have been dedicated to proving that assimilation isn't occurring, perhaps that it never did occur, and that such assimilation as may have occurred was a much more ragged and painful process than Gordon and other "theorists" of assimilation have laid out. By pointing to the supposed failure of assimilation, they have hoped to provide intellectual support for the antithesis of assimilationism, cultural pluralism, and political support for the policies of ethnic federalism.

But the revisionists have been wrong. By confusing assimilation with acculturation, they have missed two fundamental points. Ethnically diverse Americans do not have to be alike to be assimilated. And as the ethnic historian Stephen Thernstrom pointed out, "We can best appreciate the significance of assimilation in American history by taking as our standard of reference other multiethnic societies around the globe."[30] By that standard, assimilation in the United States has been a monumental triumph, which is clear in how successfully the United States has functioned, not just economically but socially. The interethnic amity of American society, enviable by world standards, sustained for centuries in the face of an ethnic diversity literally unmatched anywhere else, needs to be explained. The only plausible explanation lies in the United States' unique formula for assimilation.

4

Crucibles of Assimilation

The common school did not produce the harmony its promoters pro-
claimed for it; it did not eliminate all differences rooted in race, religion
or national origin. But it did embody a vision of cultural integration that
revealed the . . . aspirations and expectations of Americans. [It] is in the
educational programs that were designed to create Americans that the
meaning of Americanization becomes most clear.

Harvard Encyclopedia of American Ethnic Groups, 1980[1]

From the beginning, the major project of the public schools in
the United States was assimilation, rather than learning. I use the
word *assimilation* here to mean a comprehensive social and cultural unification of the American population, the breaking down not
only of ethnic barriers among American schoolchildren, but those
of class and region as well. Since the 1830s, when organized mass
public education was first introduced, the elites responsible for setting educational standards and those who implemented them
expressed a determination to use elementary and secondary schools
to promote national solidarity, democracy, and egalitarianism. But,
also from the beginning, there were deep divisions among
Americans as to what this project actually entailed and tragic dis-
crepancies between its lofty ideals and often unedifying practices. In
the end, the exceedingly bumpy road of assimilation—ethnic, class,
and regional—was somehow traversed. On the one hand, the fact

that many of the assimilationist objectives of American public education have been substantially realized seems to vindicate those
who, all along, promoted the assimilation ideal. At the same time,
there were enough departures from the ideal, especially when it
came to the treatment of ethnic and racial groups, that one must be
wary of losing sight of the many detours and dead ends that marked
that journey in a hazy mist of unjustified nostalgia.

All societies realize that the key to instilling society-wide values
is to make sure the values are instilled in their children. The United
States was ahead of its time, however, in organizing a system of
mass education to accomplish this goal—yet another instance of the
United States leading the world in fashioning modern institutions
that are now the staple of all highly developed nations. In Alexis de
Tocqueville's words, "It is the provisions for public education
which, from the very first, throw into clearest relief the originality
of American civilization."[2]

The seeds of universal, publicly funded education were planted
in American soil early in the seventeenth century, and by the middle of the eighteenth century, most of the thirteen English colonies
required individual townships to operate free or low-tuition "district" schools open to all local children from the age of six to the
early teens (after which the children were expected to work full
time).[3] The French de Tocqueville, visiting America in the 1830s,
was in awe that systems of universal and compulsory education—
only a distant hope in France—had been established there a century earlier:

> Provisions follow [a religious preamble] establishing schools in all
> townships, and obliging the inhabitants, under heavy penalty of
> fines, to maintain them. In the same way, high schools are found-
> ed in the more densely populated districts. The municipal officials
> are bound to see that parents send their children to the schools
> and can impose fines on those who refuse to do so; if the parents
> remain recalcitrant, society can take over the charge of the chil-
> dren from the family.[4]

After independence, the district school system was firmly
entrenched in most of the new states and was especially well devel-

oped in the major states of Massachusetts, New York, and Pennsylvania. The typical district school was small—the legendary one-room schoolhouse—and classes spanned broad (or all) age groups. The curriculum was basic as well—the equally legendary "three Rs." This approach to mass education persisted well into the mid-nineteenth century. It was primitive, but because of it, the United States educated a far higher share of its youths than did any other society of the time, and Americans had unrivaled rates of literacy and mathematical competence. By 1815, nearly 50 percent of all American children had had some schooling.[5]

By the 1830s, this bare-bones approach to elementary education came under attack by the reformers of the "common-school" movement, whose most notable spokesman was the Massachusetts clergyman and educator Horace Mann. The objectives of the common-school reformers were threefold: to make at least elementary education universal, to make it mandatory, and to make it much better. The reformers also advocated the establishment of separate secondary schools and wanted states to establish uniform statewide standards.

Since education, then as now, was entirely under the discretion of the states, the movement had to gain converts state by state. The first state to implement a comprehensive, free, and compulsory system of local common schools was Massachusetts in 1852, with New York quickly following suit in 1853.[6] The cities, however, often led their states in establishing modern school systems. New York City had a free universal system by 1832, Buffalo in 1838, and Rochester in 1848.[7] By the onset of the Civil War, all northern states and territories had instituted similar common-school systems. After the Civil War, so did the states of the former confederacy, but mainly for whites. The Reconstruction era Freedmen's Bureau eagerly established new common schools in the South for black children, and other northern efforts of the time sought to have all southern children—black and white—attend integrated, national-quality schools. But after the end of Reconstruction in 1877, most southern states wasted little effort or money on the education of poor white children, and even less on blacks.[8] And the Supreme Court's 1896 decision in *Plessy* v. *Ferguson* extinguished the prospects for integrated schooling in the South for six decades.

Despite their halting and decentralized march to universal, free, public education, from the first days of the nineteenth century, Americans led the world in the amount of schooling they had and what they spent on it. As early as 1830, nearly three-quarters of all Americans under age nineteen had attended school, a proportion not seen in any European country. Between 1840 and 1860, spending for American schools quadrupled as the nation's population only doubled. By the time of Abraham Lincoln's election, white Americans had a literacy rate of 90 percent, matched only by Germany. Educational scholar Albert Fishlow estimated that by 1860 the United States devoted nearly 1 percent of its gross national product to education, far exceeding France, which committed 0.4 percent, and England, which spent even less.[9]

The common-school movement was driven by several compelling objectives, all of which resonated well with Americans. In the spirit of American exceptionalism, the schools were to be the forges in which an "American personality" was to be molded. The curriculum of these schools would turn out graduates dedicated to appreciate and uphold the new nation's democratic institutions and to embody the personal attributes of individual achievement and high moral character. In tune with Americans' aspirations for a high standard of living—what de Tocqueville described as their "love of comfort"—and rapid economic growth, the new public schools were to make sure that all American children would grow up to be not only literate but masters of a variety of economically "practical" subjects. Finally, to fulfill American hopes that the United States would be a beacon of universalism and egalitarianism in an intolerant and class-ridden world, the public schools were to instill ethnic tolerance and egalitarianism both by exhortation and by direct social experience.[10]

The 1830s, when Horace Mann and other proponents of common schools wrote, also marked the beginning of the long nineteenth-century period of mass immigration, with thousands of poor Irish immigrants inundating the cities and towns of New York and New England. Thus, the early school reformers were not only aware that a large proportion of their school clientele would be immigrant children, but they were committed to using the schools as the nation's frontline institutions of assimilation. New York's

Public School Society (roughly equivalent to today's Board of Education) made this intention explicit in one of its promotional documents) in the 1830s:

> [Because of] sympathy for the oppressed of other lands, who seek an asylum in this [country], . . . [we] act under a firm conviction that the sooner such persons abandon any unfavorable prejudices with which they may arrive among us, and become familiar with our language, and reconciled to our institutions and habits, the better it will be for them, and the country of their adoption. The best interests of all will be alike promoted by having their children mingle with ours in the public seminaries of learning.[11]

Thus, from the outset of America's mass-education experiment, all the issues raised by immigration and assimilation came to be more pertinently and urgently addressed in the public school arena than in any other institutional setting. However, although the need to educate immigrant children and the desirability of assimilating them were clear and universally agreed upon, what these ideas actually meant in practice were matters of contentious disagreement throughout the nineteenth century and well into the twentieth.

One area in which, by general consensus, public schools first promoted assimilation in a concrete—and relatively uncontroversial—form was in the language curriculum. The issue was not English-language instruction, per se, since all children were expected to learn and speak English in school. The issue was the kind of English. Even before independence, Americans were painfully aware of the linguistic basis of class distinctions. Henry Higgins's trenchant observation in the 1956 musical *My Fair Lady* (based on George Bernard Shaw's 1912 play, *Pygmalion*) that "an Englishman's way of speaking absolutely classifies him; the moment he talks he makes another Englishman despise him,"[12] was well recognized even by eighteenth-century Americans. In 1789, Noah Webster wrote, "A sameness of pronunciation is of considerable consequence in a political view. Thus small differences in pronunciation at first excite ridicule . . . and without respect friendship is a name, and social intercourse a mere ceremony."[13]

Therefore, Americans were determined to develop a unique

American idiom, in vocabulary and accent, and to ensure that it would be universally applied. According to Robert Church: "As Americans believed that their nation was morally and politically superior because it was free of class differences, they felt concern for eliminating linguistic evidence of class distinctions. If all Americans could read, write, speak and spell in the same way, it would demonstrate beyond doubt how equal in station they were."[14]

The key to making sure that all Americans grew up speaking the same way, as well as to all other aspects of the public education system's determination to graduate as classless and assimilated a student body as possible, was to make sure that all children attended the same schools. In the early nineteenth century, this was a radical idea on a number of counts. First, at that time in all nations, including parts of the United States, only a minority of children went to school at all. Second, such education as existed was highly stratified. Upper-class children were often educated at home. Children of the upper middle class and of the most upwardly mobile members of the middle class were sent to select private schools, for which their parents incurred heavy costs. Some lower-middle-class children attended religious schools. And poor children usually did not go to any school.

In this context, the attempt to institute universal, free, and mandatory education was a breathtaking experiment. In one stroke, the reformers believed, the great American universalist paradigm could be realized. By going to the same schools, all young Americans would get to socialize with others from different backgrounds—ethnic, religious, and class—and the experience would make them respect each other and erase the social barriers that separated their parents. Being taught in the same classrooms by the same teachers, learning the same subjects, and reading the same books, all children would begin their vocational careers from the same educational starting gate. And speaking and hearing the same version of English, they would never again be distinguished—like their former English countrymen—by invidious differences in speech or accent.

Having all schoolchildren attend the same classes in the same schools was not as easy an objective to achieve as it might seem. It required another great American educational innovation: the avoidance of the stratification of public school students by ability. No European country has ever had a system of public education so uniform and so ability ungraded as that of American schools. To implement this objective, American educators put a lot of effort into developing common teaching materials, common curricula, and common methods of instruction. America's "normal schools" (teachers' colleges) were launched in the mid-nineteenth century as the world's first institutions of higher education devoted primarily to training teachers.[15] Some recognition had to be taken of students' differential abilities, but the methods that were favored to do so, like keeping slow students back for one or more grades, still did not violate the inclusionist paradigm.

Putting all American schoolchildren in the same school settings and asking them to learn roughly the same lessons for most of their elementary and secondary school careers advanced assimilation (in terms of class even more than ethnicity) in several ways. Because differences in the academic abilities of schoolchildren invariably reflect differences in the class of their parents, such a policy supplemented and reinforced the linguistic program to erase or minimize class distinctions. It also preempted the antiegalitarian impulses the schoolchildren might display after they grew up and found themselves in radically disparate occupational and income statuses as adults. Such an egalitarian approach to public schooling exacted a price, however, that Americans are still paying today. The paradigm demanded that the academic standards of the public schools could not be too demanding, so that the academically least talented would not fall hopelessly behind. It is this particular aspect of American public education that, as much as any other factor, accounts for the relatively low academic standards of U.S. public schools today.

The broad consensus in favor of universal, assimilation-favoring, public education that has prevailed over nearly two centuries, has nevertheless masked many points of disagreement—among educators, between educators and parents, and among members of different ethnic groups. One of the key points of disagreement over the years has been the definition of assimilation itself and, hence, how it was to be achieved. The great public school assimilation project went through a variety of distinct phases and approaches. In

the early decades of universal public education, schools implemented a fairly passive model of assimilation. Assimilation was to be
achieved by placing all schoolchildren—natives and immigrants
alike—on a level playing field. All children learned roughly the
same subjects, including American civics, and socialized with each
other, both in and out of the classroom. The foundations of
Americanism—democracy and capitalism—were inextricably
embedded in the curriculum and were to be absorbed by a kind of
intellectual osmosis. This was the public school prototype of assimilation, American style.

As the numbers of immigrant schoolchildren grew during the
nineteenth century, educators and lay members of school boards,
most of whom were drawn from the ranks of the Protestant upper
middle class, were increasingly disturbed by the immigrant parents'
cultural attributes, beginning with those of the Catholic Irish.
Therefore, immigrant youngsters were encouraged in school to disregard as much of their parents' linguistic and other cultural features as possible. Whereas Irish schoolchildren were expected to
change their accents and attitudes, later immigrant children were
actively discouraged from speaking their parents' native languages
at home or observing their parents' customs.[16]

By the turn of the century, when legions of Italian and Jewish
immigrants prompted the previously restrained nativist impulse to
turn rancorous and racist in the political arena, the assimilationist
paradigm of the schools also took some unfortunate detours because
educators feared they were faced with a considerably more alien and
intractable cohort of immigrant children than before. The more
benign of these detours was the so-called Americanization movement, dedicated aggressively to turning immigrant schoolchildren
into Americans. At its most innocuous, this movement merely
"attempted to provide patriotic indoctrination and to exclude foreign influences. The daily flag salute and observation of national
holidays became widespread."[17] Only in its last and most extreme
phase in the early twentieth century did some of the more zealous
public schools "Americanize" their immigrant pupils by disparaging
and ridiculing their parents' ethnic and cultural traditions.
Nevertheless, the United States has not entirely put aside the bad
memories of the Americanization campaign, and these memories are

among the many factors at work in discrediting assimilation today.

A much more malignant response by public school educators (and, more pertinent, lay members of local school boards) at the end of the nineteenth century to the challenge of accommodating growing numbers of increasingly alien schoolchildren was to reject the assimilationist paradigm and shunt such students into nonacademic programs.[18] This was an especially popular approach in dealing with Asian (mainly Chinese, but also some Japanese) children. California was the epicenter of this racist, antiassimilation practice that so incensed Asian parents that they sued their school districts in state and federal courts and appealed to diplomats of their native countries for assistance. To avoid serious foreign policy disputes with China and Japan, federal officials stepped in and made local schools allow Asian students into their academic programs.[19] The Asian cases were the most extreme, but all over the United States, from about 1880 to 1930, many American school districts had a hard time applying the traditional American paradigm of assimilation to the most ethnically exotic schoolchildren. These children were either subject to insultingly intolerant programs of "Americanization" or, under the specious rationale that they lacked academic aptitude, were directed to ghettos of vocational training.

Immigrants' reactions to the programs of aggressive assimilation were mixed. Some immigrant parents were pleased that their children were quickly becoming Americans and counted on their children's education to help in their own adjustment to American society. The Jews, especially, found that compared to the virulent anti-Semitism of Eastern Europe, with its pogroms, residential and occupational segregation, and absence of civil liberties, Americans' eagerness for immigrant children to "Americanize" was a positively benevolent gesture. Also, Jews were among the immigrants who were the most alert to the benefits of an Americanizing public education in opening the doors of economic and social opportunity for their children.

Another exceedingly important segment of the immigrant community, the Catholics—especially the Irish Catholics and their clergy—found the aggressive assimilation paradigm, or its ostracizing counterpoint, demeaning and threatening. However else their constituents might adjust to American society, the Catholic leadership also wanted to ensure that their parishioners' children succumbed neither to the Protestantism of the majority nor to the secularism of the rapidly industrializing and territorially expanding society. So, to rescue them from the clutches of bigotry and sin and to help them escape the psychic blows of a demeaning brand of assimilation, the Catholic clergy, as early as the 1840s, organized systems of Catholic schools throughout the urbanized areas of the United States. Catholic education got its biggest boost, however, after 1884, when America's Catholic bishops, with papal blessing, decreed that every parish in the nation was to operate a parochial elementary school.[20]

The Catholic schools, especially once they were well established and recruited a large share of immigrant children, caused great consternation among advocates of public schools and the Protestant majority. But over time, the dual school systems of America's large cities came to be an accepted feature of both popular education and urban life. Until the practice was outlawed by the courts in 1948, many Catholic schools even received public funding. More to the point, the Catholic schools were fully on board in promoting assimilation. Except for the limited time they devoted to religious instruction, most Catholic schools cast themselves in the mold of public schools and were just as eager as their secular counterparts to promote such assimilationist themes as the virtues of American democracy, the need to achieve economic advancement, and the importance of inculcating high standards of moral character.[21]

If the enrollment of immigrant children in Catholic schools represented one kind of challenge to the public school model of assimilation, the defection of some members of the upper middle class, especially in the Northeast, represented another. Not wanting their children to have schoolday contact with poor, and perhaps rowdy, immigrant youngsters, many sent their children to private day and boarding schools. At no time in U.S. history did more than a small fraction of American children actually attend such schools. Yet both the Catholic school movement and the rise of private schools represented serious departures from the ideal of universal education and assimilation.

*   *   *

When one looks at public education today, the threats to assimilation posed by Catholic or private schools no longer appear all that ominous. But other developments do. If Americans were persuaded to undertake the revival of assimilation, American style, there would be no better place for the project to begin than in the country's public schools. Public schools, which educate 85 percent of the nation's youths, are the most universal and comprehensive American institution. Public schools have been the places where previous generations of immigrant children were assimilated. Public schools have also been the main forums in which faith in other seminal American values—egalitarianism, democracy, capitalism, and (tempered by a strong dose of peer pressure) individualism—has been instilled. By their very nature, public schools should be ideal settings for unifying the youths of America; that is, if we let them be.

A casual look at contemporary public schools and a casual assessment of immigrant children may suggest that promoting assimilation should be a piece of cake. Never before have the schools of the United States been so superficially uniform. Generations of teachers across the country have graduated from teachers' colleges and educational programs with nearly identical training. State-mandated licensing, certification, and curriculum requirements are strikingly similar from state to state. Uniform standards for the sizes of classrooms, schools, and districts are well established from coast to coast. In the past two decades, even disparities in levels of school funding among states and districts within states have narrowed appreciably. From Maine to California, from Texas to Michigan, American public school classrooms, and what goes on inside them, are now as alike as the fast-food restaurants on America's highways.

Immigrant children themselves are well positioned to make assimilation easy. Almost every study of their attitudes and performance when they begin school paints a picture that supports assimilation. In just about every subject, most immigrant children outperform native children of the same economic background. Immigrant children are generally conscientious about doing their school- and homework and are usually encouraged by their parents to do well in school. If they are made to do so, immigrant children quickly learn English. Even if they are not, they usually want to learn English because they also want to be as American as possible, even though they may not understand what being American really means. In other words, immigrant children—today as much as in the past—are putty in the hands of public school educators.

The sad truth, however, is that in spite of the national homogeneity of the public school environment and the educational malleability of immigrant schoolchildren, a number of factors increasingly stand in the way of assimilation. One of them is the increasing geographic isolation of immigrant children. Immigrants today are concentrated in only a handful of American states and within these states, in a handful of metropolitan areas. Even more important, however, is that within these metropolitan areas, immigrants are concentrated in a growing, but limited, number of neighborhoods. The concentration of immigrants is nothing new. Previous immigrant cohorts—the Italians and Jews at the turn of the century and the Irish in the mid-nineteenth century—were also highly concentrated geographically. But the earlier assimilationist drive in the larger society was strong enough to overcome at least some of the resistance posed by spatial isolation. Today, the spatial isolation of immigrant schoolchildren strongly reinforces whatever antiassimilation tendencies are at work.

The other major factor is the antiassimilation mood itself. There can be no doubt that the ideological tide of official sentiment in the educational establishment in recent decades has been antagonistic to assimilation; more precisely, it is antagonistic to the curricular and educational policies that might make assimilation succeed. As the brief review of the history of public education for immigrants revealed, the misalignment of official policy and immigrants' aspirations is not unprecedented. Only the motives of the educators are different. One hundred years ago, the American paradigm of assimilation was violated by public school educators who, believing that immigrant children were uneducable, shunted them into vocational education or believing that these children's home cultures were barbaric, made the children renounce their ethnic heritages. Bad motives and bigoted sensibilities drove bad policies. Today, benign motives and enlightened sensibilities drive equally bad policies.

Today's antiassimilationism in the public schools rests on three misguided initiatives: bilingual education, "multicultural" curricula, and the disparagement of American traditions—a striking repudiation of all three clauses of the nineteenth-century assimilation contract. Unquestionably, these initiatives were initially undertaken with the best intentions and with entirely plausible rationales. Bilingualism has been promoted, from its inception, as merely a transitional method of acclimating immigrant children to English—something more humane than the rude shock of instant immersion in English. Multicultural curricula have some unsavory educational and ideological wellsprings, but compared to the unconscionable (and antiassimilationist) turn-of-the-century attempts to discredit immigrant cultures in the public schools, they seem enlightened. As for American traditions, we all know enough of American history, hypocrisy, and general human frailty to understand how they may easily be disparaged. But the sum of these well-intentioned efforts has had the effect of undermining assimilation in the very environment in which it is most easy to promote and among the very subjects who could most easily profit from it.

Of the three antiassimilationist initiatives, bilingualism is the most firmly entrenched and the most insidious. It is also the hardest to justify, even on its own terms. The concept behind bilingual education is laudable: that foreign-language children need a gradual transition to English-language courses and that it is cruel and subversive of learning to place them in English-speaking classes as soon as they enter the school system because they will flounder academically and be subject to ridicule and other assaults on their self-esteem. This view gained enough adherents throughout the 1960s that by the end of the decade, Congress passed the Bilingual Education Act of 1968. In 1974 the Supreme Court lent its authority to the bilingual cause by ruling, in *Lau* v. *Nichols*, that school districts must offer special language programs to all non-English-speaking students.

But bilingual education is, in the eyes of its most vehement supporters, not just an educational tool or the means for implementing a particular educational philosophy. It is an antiassimilationist ideological cause masquerading as pedagogy. In an unpublished study of New York City's controversial bilingual program, urban planner George Gonzalez wrote: "Many in the Latino community view bilingual education as an important benefit won for the empowerment of the community. Attacks on bilingual education are likely to be classified as racist and labels of 'uncle Tom' are certain to follow."[22]

As it turns out, bilingual education has also been a monumental failure even on its own pedagogical terms. It has largely failed in its avowed objective of speeding English-language proficiency and helping limited-English students master other academic subjects. Linda Chavez in *Out of the Barrio*, Rosalie Pedalino Porter in *Forked Tongue*, and other Hispanic analysts have argued that bilingual education visits the greatest harm on the children of its most forceful advocates, America's Latinos.[23] In New York State, the Hispanic advocacy group ASPIRA won a court-imposed consent decree in 1974 mandating bilingual education in every New York school district. Since 1989, the New York State Education Department has ruled that all students who test under the fortieth percentile on an English proficiency test must be enrolled in bilingual programs. As a result, 15 percent of all New York City schoolchildren, 65 percent of them Latino, are in bilingual classrooms at a cost (in 1994) of $300 million.[24] Yet, even for its ostensible constituents, ASPIRA won a hollow victory. In 1994, a coalition of parents in New York City, most of them Hispanic, sued the city's Board of Education because their children were, in the language of the suit, "imprisoned" in New York's bilingual programs.[25] They lost their suit, but they were right to bring it—especially since often the criterion for placing children in bilingual programs is their surname rather than their English-language proficiency.

A large number of studies have now documented that immigrant children enrolled in bilingual programs fall far behind their counterparts who are taught in English in all subjects. In New York City, 90 percent of bilingual students fail to enter regular classes within the three-year transitional time frame. Even among first to third graders, who traditionally have the least difficulty learning new languages, three-quarters fail to meet the target deadline.[26] Perversely, bilingualism most egregiously fails Spanish-speaking students, for whom most bilingual programs were initially established. These children learn English later and with less proficiency, and they test more poorly in other subjects as well. Making matters worse, many children entering bilingual programs are more proficient in English than in their putative "native" language and lose their fluency after years of "transitional" instruction. So, after years of "imprisonment" in bilingual ghettos, immigrant children are doubly victimized. They are denied competence in academics, and they are denied access to one of the key elements of the assimilation paradigm.

Even if bilingualism was innocuous, it would be unnecessary for most children. Linguists have documented the ease with which all children under age twelve can quickly acquire any language without an accent if they are immersed in its environment.[27] English was not my first language or that of my wife. My entire generation of immigrant children consists of people who learned to speak, read, and write English flawlessly after a brief—and admittedly sometimes traumatic—school-based encounter with the language in schools that offered neither bilingual nor other English-transition programs. They, like many of their nationally prominent immigrant forebears in business, politics, and the arts, benefited from the ostensibly harsher linguistic approach to assimilation that preceded the advent of bilingualism.

In any case, bilingualism is not the only way to help less-English-proficient children adjust to America's English-speaking environment. The major pedagogical competitor of bilingual education is what is called teaching English as a second language (ESL). Under ESL, children who speak foreign languages but not English take courses that are explicitly devoted to English-language instruction (much like the foreign language courses that English-speaking students take) while they take subject-specific courses, such as mathematics and science, with other children in the mainstream program. ESL instruction has proved to be much more effective than bilingual programs in instilling English proficiency in immigrant children. In a study commissioned by New York City schools chancellor Ramón Cortines in 1994 that compared outcomes for non-English-proficient schoolchildren who entered either bilingual or ESL programs in kindergarten, it was found that 79 percent of the ESL students versus only 51 percent of the bilingual students passed English proficiency tests within three years.[28]

As the historian Arthur M. Schlesinger, Jr., noted, "Bilingualism shuts doors. It nourishes self-ghettoization, and ghettoization nourishes racial antagonism."[29] Schlesinger also cited the Mexican American writer Richard Rodriguez, who stated: "Those who have the most to lose in a bilingual America are the foreign-speaking poor. . . . Only when I was able to think of myself as an American, no longer an alien in a *gringo* society, could I seek the rights and opportunities necessary for full public individuality."[30]

Multiculturalism is not yet as universally entrenched and officially institutionalized in the public schools as is bilingualism, but it is rapidly becoming so, and it is much more explicitly antiassimilationist. A case in point is the new multicultural curriculum developed by the New York State Social Studies Review and Development Committee in 1991 for adoption by all New York school districts, which inspired Schlesinger to write *The Disuniting of America*.[31] This excerpt from the committee's report helps one understand Schlesinger's concern:

> Much of the heat of the debate concerning the importance of valuing cultural difference in the schools arises from divergent opinions on whether preparing students to become members of U.S. society necessarily means assimilation. *While the goal of assimilation has historically been relatively explicit in American schooling, in recent years many thoughtful writers and educators have argued against assimilation . . .* [italics added]. *Education must respond to the joint imperatives of educating toward citizenship in a common polity while respecting and taking account of continuing distinctiveness* [italics in original]. Even more . . . the perspectives of a number of major groups in American society must be recognized and incorporated. Nor is assimilation essential to educate citizens who . . . participate in [this country's] polity and economy.[32]

The inherent contradiction between assimilationism and multiculturalism could hardly be made more explicit. But what exactly is multiculturalism anyway, especially as it affects the public school curriculum and other aspects of the educational enterprise? And why should one object to it? Taken at face value, the term is broad, vague, and inherently unexceptionable. As the journalist Richard Bernstein noted:

> Multiculturalism and its rhetorical sidekicks, diversity and inclusion, represent, at least in theory, a sensibility of openness to the enormous cultural difference that has always existed in American life, but whose fullness has been suppressed by the might of the dominant European culture. . . .
>
> In other words, multiculturalism is good, unobjectionable, virtuous. It is like Liberty, Equality, Fraternity, like economic justice for the working class and an end to exploitation.[33]

The typical mandated multicultural public school curriculum imposes a new lens through which many ordinary subjects are to be viewed. The subjects usually affected are American and world history, geography, social studies, and literature, although some aspects of science can also be given a multicultural gloss. The directives from state education departments demand that instruction and materials for these subjects be shorn of their "Eurocentric" and "monocultural" biases and replaced with a heightened appreciation of non-European influences and contributions. For American studies, it means greater attention to the contributions of—in the correct multicultural terminology—Native Americans (a.k.a. American Indians), African Americans, and Latino Americans. Rarely does the rubric include the later European immigrants: Jews, Italians, and eastern Europeans—or, for that matter, even Asian Americans.

Why would anyone object to such a broadening of public school students' educational horizons? The reason people like Schlesinger (who was a dissident member of the New York State committee) and a growing number of other "thoughtful writers and educators," in the committee's words, object is that behind its bland facade, multiculturalism in the schools promotes an agenda of ethnic grievances, and the delegitimation of the prevailing national culture. For example, in a typical multicultural history course, historical relations between the "dominant" Anglo and European cultural figures and members of the newly highlighted minority ethnic group are almost never presented in a neutral, dispassionate way. There are always "good guys" and "bad guys," and it is the Anglos and other northern Europeans who are invariably cast as the bad guys. In multicultural social studies classes, discussions of ethnic relations in an urbanizing and industrializing America eschew objective assessments of prevailing economic and social forces and instead place most events and trends in the context of greed and injustice, racism and exploitation. Again, people who inhabit the expanded multicultural horizons—ethnic minorities almost exclusively—are portrayed as the victims, and representatives of the "dominant" Anglo and white culture are portrayed as the victimizers.

The explicit and implicit ground rules of multiculturalism discourage a balanced and complex presentation of American or world society and make it unthinkable ever to reverse the good guy, bad guy roles. Lessons on the slave trade, for example, assiduously avoid discussing the black Africans who sold their "ethnic" brethren into slavery. As the journalist Robert Hughes observed: "Afrocentrists [in the schools] wish to invent a sort of remedial history in which the entire blame for the invention and practice of black slavery is laid at the door of Europeans."[34] In *Dictatorship of Virtue*, Bernstein described a world history course in Brookline, Massachusetts, that, according to one local parent, "was all to set up the villainy of the West. All of the case studies were presented as instances of western colonialism oppressing Third World peoples."[35] As Bernstein pointed out, the multicultural treatment of world history emphasizes the outrages of British and other European colonialism, but steers clear of such unwholesome non-European customs as precolonial East Indians' burning widows on funeral pyres; the Muslims' stoning to death of adulterous women; or the still-widespread practices of genital mutilation, polygamy, and slavery—yes, slavery—going on in the "exploited" but otherwise blameless third (that is, "ethnic") world today.[36] In a similar vein, multicultural American history courses will accurately note how American Indians were driven off their lands and subject to many other injustices at the hands of white settlers, but never remind students of the Indians' many—by nineteenth- and twentieth-century American standards—cruel and primitive practices. In the multicultural canon, cruelty is the exclusive preserve of

Europeans and white people, and words like *primitive* or *barbaric* are unacceptably value-laden Eurocentric and Anglocentric terms.

Multiculturalism taught at the college level is not identical to that of the public schools, but it responds to the same general directives. Two recent examples from Hunter College, where I teach, are illustrative of the multicultural mindset. After a new curricular initiative in 1992 required students to take a specified number of "pluralism and diversity" courses to graduate, each department was invited to present courses to the curriculum committee that might meet the criteria for diversity. My department (Urban Affairs and Planning) identified a number of courses that dealt extensively with race, immigration, and other ethnic issues in urban America. These courses were quickly rejected for inclusion in the diversity curriculum because they focused too much on the "problems" of minorities and insufficiently on the "contributions." In another Hunter College example, a part-time professor of history was dismissed because, in his vivid presentation of the historical encounter between Pilgrims and Indians in seventeenth-century Massachusetts, he painted an unflattering portrait of the Indians as he imagined the settlers saw them.

Notwithstanding the lofty claims for multicultural education made by state education administrators (like New York State Commissioner of Education Thomas Sobol, who asserted that such courses would help students "understand our complex society . . . and the history and culture of its major ethnic and cultural components"),[37] multicultural initiatives are not designed merely to breed a cosmopolitan appreciation of ethnic diversity in the United States and the world. Multiculturalism is explicitly and self-consciously directed toward building "self-esteem" and nurturing an acute sense of ethnic grievance and victimization among the children of ethnic minorities, with ethnic minorities narrowly defined as encompassing only blacks, Latinos, and American Indians. In the multicultural world, Jews, Italians, and other ethnic groups, who were thought to be members of distinctive "races" less than a century ago, are lumped with descendants of the English, Scots, and Germans. Even Asians—one of America's most truly victimized ethnic minorities—barely qualify. The overwhelming preoccupation of multicultural courses with the negative aspects of mainstream American culture and the victimization of ethnic minorities and their questioning of the civic and economic morality of the majority of "nonethnic" Americans can only divide American schoolchildren along ethnic lines and have a profoundly antiassimilationist impact. And if the quoted passage from the New York State report is typical of multicultural efforts in other states, that is exactly what they are meant to do.

However, the most harmful aspect of the multicultural enterprise is the disparagement, if not outright demonization, of America's history, its civic institutions, and its great political and civic leaders. Contrary to the assertions of many proponents of multiculturalism, the traditional history courses in American public schools of the recent past were not content just to record the progress and enlightenment of the United States and the West. Even in the small and unexceptional New Jersey towns in which I went to school in the 1940s and 1950s, teachers documented the problems and depredations of the United States and European nations. But they also helped students appreciate the civic wonder of American institutions, and this had a strong culturally unifying impact on me and my "ethnically diverse" classmates. Today's multicultural classes in American and world history and social studies aim to replace that sense of wonder with one of guilt and shame. Take Christopher Columbus, for starters, who may not have been an American, but was given a lot of credit in the elementary schools of my youth for having "discovered America." That harmless bit of pop history and mythology cannot be allowed to stand—even symbolically—in today's multicultural classroom. First, children are told that Columbus didn't "discover" America at all; it was already there. True enough, but that's a fine semantic distinction for first graders. Much worse, children are told that Columbus was guilty of "genocide," not so much because he and his men killed many West Indian natives (which they did), but because they devastated the natives with European diseases for which they had no immunity. There goes Columbus Day, whose celebration is now largely devoted to an exegesis of Columbus's wickedness (except among Italian Americans, who resolutely cling to it as a commemoration of *their* ethnicity).

More seriously, the multicultural revisionism of the schools also deprecates the U.S. Constitution, as well as America's political and civic leaders, westward expansion, technological progress, foreign policy, and military engagements. Not even George Washington is spared. In its most benign form, multicultural courses slight the American Idea and its progenitors by ignoring them in favor of the more important historical milestones of ethnic minorities. Bernstein described a Minneapolis school in which Washington and the events of the Revolutionary War are taught as a footnote, but Zuni poems, the Ojibwa language, and the origins of slavery are central; moreover, the Constitution is presented as a document that was plagiarized from the Algonquins. But when traditional American institutions, events, and icons are not neglected, they are vilified. Schoolchildren are taught that Andrew Jackson caused the Cherokee Trail of Tears and that Washington was just a rich slave owner. An occasional word of praise for Abraham Lincoln constitutes ideological balance.[38]

Some of the fiercest anti-American fire of the multicultural curriculum is aimed at traditional justifications for American foreign policy and participation in wars. Even when I went to school, we learned that the Spanish-American War was an imperialist venture and that the western frontier advanced at the expense of the American Indians, the Spanish, and the Mexicans. But we were also taught about the idealistic and universalist strain in American foreign and military policy, the fundamental decency that motivated our participation in the two world wars, the real threats posed by Hitler and Stalin, the magnanimity of the United States toward its former enemies, and the role of the United States in establishing international organizations and alliances dedicated to furthering world peace. You would never recognize this America in the social studies classes of the multicultural curriculum. As one Massachusetts parent told Bernstein: "For weeks my daughter was devastated about how evil the U.S. was, what a terrible country we were," after her child learned that (but not why) the United States bombed Hiroshima and Nagasaki.[39]

The multiculturalist trashing of America should concern Americans not just because it is one-sided, ideologically motivated, and often factually wrong. It should also concern us because it robs our children—indeed an entire impressionable next generation of Americans—of their most precious birthright: a justifiable pride in the American Idea and the generally enlightened and idealistic trajectory of America's domestic and foreign policies. "The genius of America," Schlesinger said, "lies in its capacity to forge a single nation from peoples of remarkably diverse racial, religious, and ethnic origins. It has done so because democratic principles provide . . . the philosophical bond of union."[40] If he is right, then multiculturalism's systematic discounting of those principles and delegitimating of the American figures of the past who designed, implemented, and fought for them will undermine, in the name of ethnic diversity, the only thing that holds this ethnically diverse nation together.

Even as I write, a contingent of American soldiers is patrolling and rebuilding war-torn Bosnia. This expedition can be seen as a fitting refutation of multiculturalist assumptions and teachings on four counts. First, Bosnia should serve as a powerful object lesson of where the cultivation of ethnic differences can lead. Second, the United States committed itself to end the Bosnian conflict not out of any narrow self-interest, but in fulfillment of its historic dedication to furthering world peace and order, its determination to be—in the best sense of the term—the world's policeman. Third, it is a tribute to how seriously the world takes America's devotion to universalist principles that only America, in the Dayton peace accords of 1995, had the moral stature to end this war—something that eluded the major western European nations for four years—and that only America was trusted by all belligerents to enforce the peace fairly. Finally, the twenty-thousand-person cadre of young Americans in Bosnia is more "ethnically diverse" than the troops of any other nation.

The publication in the past few years of books like Schlesinger's *The Disuniting of America*, Sowell's *Inside American Education*, Bernstein's *Dictatorship of Virtue*, and Charles Sykes's *Dumbing Down of America's Kids* testifies to the backlash against multiculturalism and America bashing in the public schools that is building both at the grass-roots level and among a growing segment of America's intellectual leadership.[41] But can the multiculturalist genie be put back in the lamp? Perhaps. It was, after all, only a small contingent of liberal advocates and educational officials who conjured it up in the first place. And as in the case of bilingual instruction and the Latino community, the demand for multicultural education does not originate with the parents of ethnic minority children. As Sowell noted: "Perhaps the most tendentious aspect of the claim that ethnic diversity requires multicultural education programs is the assertion that this demand comes from the various ethnic groups themselves—as distinguished from vocal activists."[42]

Until multiculturalism came along only a few decades ago, the public schools of the United States—the country's most broad-based and universal institution since they were established a century and a half ago—had, after some regrettable lapses and detours, settled on a highly successful formula for reconciling the ethnic diversity of their charges with the cultural unity of the nation. That formula allowed the children and grandchildren of immigrants to become Americans without denying them their ethnic heritages. It did so by exposing them to a common curriculum, instilling in them a common appreciation of America's civic culture, and nurturing their proficiency in English—in a common accent (with some regional variations), no less. But the most important thing America's public schools used to do was to make most schoolchildren, regardless of their own religious, racial, or national backgrounds, feel they were the same. By word and deed, the schools emphasized the children's commonalities, not their differences. That was assimilation, American style, and it did more to protect America's ethnic diversity than multicultural education ever can.

5

Assimilation's Anglo Base

[Although] the people of the United States, considered as a whole, are composed of immigrants and their descendants from almost every country . . . the English language is almost wholly used; the English manners, modified to be sure, predominate, and the spirit of English liberty and enterprise animates the energies of the whole people. English laws and institutions, adapted to the circumstances of the country, have been adopted here . . . The tendency of things is to mould the whole into one people, whose leading characteristics are English, formed on American soil.

Jesse Chickering, 1848[1]

One of the central points of assimilation, American style is that for all its ethnic diversity, for all the waves of immigrants that have landed on its shores, the United States is one of the most culturally unified societies on earth. It is unified by language. It is unified by the devotion of all its people to a singular, centuries-old set of political principles embedded in a rich civic culture. It is unified by a mass popular culture. As the historian John Keegan observed:

[T]he supreme triumph of the American people is to have created the largest homogeneous cultural unit on earth. Neither Russia nor China, comparable though each is in extent and population, can claim that the official language of the state is understood from border to border or that the values that obtain among the governing and intellectual class of the capital are the raw material of public life in the remotest province.[2]

America's three cultural unifiers are so powerful, in fact, that their influence is growing throughout the world, as each year more of the world's people learn English and consume American popular cultural products, and more of its nations adopt democratic institutions. Nevertheless, America's cultural unity is subject to two important qualifications. One is that American culture is not static, but a work in progress, continuously transformed by influences imported through immigrants and other external sources. The other is that America's unified culture is sufficiently varied and flexible enough to permit Americans to conform to as little or as much of it as they choose. As educator Diane Ravitch puts it, "the United States has a common culture that is multicultural."[3]

But however changeable and flexible it may be, American culture does have a distinctive base, and that base, from the nation's beginning, has been English. The most visible ingredient of this base has been the English language. In its role as the medium of communication and of literature, language defines and limits culture in important ways. At a minimum, people who speak the same language are able to communicate with one another to accommodate all the human interactions of work and trade and daily living. Beyond the narrow arena of day-to-day functioning, people who speak the same language experience a sense of kinship and social solidarity. They read the same newspapers, books, and magazines; watch the same movies and plays; and laugh at the same jokes. Because of its importance, language is the one feature of American culture that is not optional, even under America's flexible rules of assimilation. All immigrants are expected, sooner or later, to learn and be able to function in English, and their children must do so almost as soon as they set foot on American soil. On this point, social commentators across the spectrum of cultural ideology, from Jesse Jackson to Jesse Helms, from Norman Mailer to Norman Podhoretz, agree.

According to linguists, many immigrants may even consider themselves better off in the process. Compared to most foreign languages, English has a simpler syntactic structure and a more malleable and easily expanded vocabulary, with fewer irritating linguistic features, such as cases, declensions, formal and informal modes of address, gender-specific articles and nouns, and agglutinated strings of adjectives. That is the reason why English text takes up 20 to 50 percent less space than do texts of other languages in multilingual publications. Americans have a language uniquely suited to their national spirit: direct and efficient, egalitarian and democratic. They also have one that a growing number of people throughout the world are eager to learn.

But the English language is only the tip of this country's cultural inheritance from England, which permeates American political institutions, values, social customs, traditions, festivals, holidays, and general outlook on life. It is the nonlinguistic manifestation of English cultural influences, what critics have called America's Anglocentrism, that arouses controversy. Over the years, many members of the nation's intellectual and institutional leadership have openly questioned the legitimacy of the Anglocentric base of American culture, asserting that it is nothing more than cultural imperialism, the consequence of American WASPs imposing their culture on the rest of the country's ethnically and culturally diverse population. Eighty years ago, Randolph Bourne complained of "English snobberies, English religion, English literary styles, English literary reverences and canons, English ethics, English superiorities" and that Anglo-Americans were "guilty of just what every dominant race is guilty of in every European country: the imposition of its own culture upon the minority peoples."[4] More recently, sociologist Andrew Greeley noted disapprovingly that ethnic Americans must engage in "Anglo-conformity" to be accepted into the elite and implied they should not have to,[5] and Norman Podhoretz made a similar point when he referred to the "brutal bargain" (the exchange of their ethnicity for Anglo-conformity) exacted from ambitious Jews.[6]

This view was most clearly spelled out by the social commentator Benjamin Schwarz in a 1995 article in the *Atlantic Monthly*. According to Schwarz, America's ethnic pluralism and tolerance are a "myth," and its unity is only a product of unadulterated cultural imperialism:

[L]ong before the United States' founding, and until the 1960s, the "unity" of the American people derived not from their warm welcoming of and accommodation to nationalist, ethnic and linguistic differences but from the ability and willingness of an Anglo elite to stamp its image on other peoples coming to this country. That elite's religious and political principles, its customs and social relations, its standards of taste and morality, were for 300 years America's, and in basic ways they still are.[7]

The eminent social historian Michael Novak covered nearly identical territory twenty-three years earlier in *The Rise of the Unmeltable Ethnics*: "English conceptions of order, decorum, social planning, the free marketplace (of goods and ideas), friction-free consensus, etc. dominate American life so thoroughly that most WASPs seem unaware of them as ethnic preferences. . . . For years WASPs could comfortably comment on the distant progress of others in 'Americanizing' themselves, that is to say, in making themselves into WASPs."[8] The corollary of this argument is that, as the product of a WASP hegemony that is clearly fading, America's Anglocentrism should now be overthrown. Novak closed his argument by observing: "All [other ethnic groups] acceded far too long to the pressures of Americanization—which was really WASP-ification. . . . it is the cumulative power and distinctive styles of the WASPs that the rest of us had to learn in order to survive. WASPs have never had to celebrate Columbus Day or march down Fifth Avenue wearing green. Every day has been their day in America. No more."[9]

In several short logical leaps, doubts about the legitimacy of Anglocentrism lead inevitably to doubts about the legitimacy of a unicultural vision for the United States and ultimately to doubts about the legitimacy of assimilation itself. Thus, those who would promote assimilation and defend a unified national culture need to engage the Anglocentric issue head-on. I propose to do so by asserting five propositions. First, although the United States' English foundations cannot be denied, American culture has evolved independently of Britain's for centuries and, from a social and political base already substantially differentiated from Britain's at independence, American society has traveled on a cultural trajectory that has made it less English with each passing year. Second, the whole notion of WASP hegemony is a myth. Third, those English influences that have survived America's independent development are overwhelmingly benign. Fourth, the majority of Americans clearly prefer a unified national culture—even an "Anglocentric" one—to the paradigms of ethnic diversity that, it has been proposed, should take its place. Fifth, for most American ethnic groups, any particular "ethnic" culture has no more authentic a claim on their allegiance than does America's Anglo uniculture.

How English is American culture once one looks beyond the surface of a common language? Not very. One hundred and fifty years ago, Alexis de Tocqueville spent a better part of *Democracy in America*, written when America's divorce from Britain was still fresh, laying out all the ways in which American society and the American people differed profoundly not just from Europe and Europeans, but from England and the English. In a typical expression of his surprise at this fact, he observed: "That two peoples, sprung so recently from the same stock, should feel and talk in ways so diametrically opposite is in itself remarkable."[10] Those differences, Tocqueville observed, went back to the earliest days of American colonial settlement.

America's cultural roots were planted by settlers—mostly (but not exclusively) from England—who first left Europe more than 350 years ago, and the society that grew from these roots was only fitfully nourished by the British motherland during the century and half of colonial rule. Throughout the colonial period, English traditions were continuously transformed in the New World by the exigencies of carving a civilization out of the wilderness and by Americans' ever more radical political and social ideas—ideas that may have had their basis in English laws and customs, but that even in the seventeenth century had been pushed far beyond their English origins. The War of Independence was not just about the tax on tea and the tyranny of King George. It welled up out of deep-seated social, political, economic, and even spiritual differences that distinguished Americans as a "race" apart. Both before and after independence, most immigrants, even those who came to America only for its economic opportunity, were well aware of the uniqueness of American culture and American values. Few felt oppressed by them; few took them as manifestations of English hegemony.

And those Americans who were the most Anglophobic, the most keenly intent on forging a distinctive American culture, were the members of the leadership class who actually had English ancestors. In *The Disuniting of America*, Arthur M. Schlesinger, Jr., pointed out: "As Anglocentric myths grew, they had at times to be protected against the British themselves. Anglophobia died slowly in the United States; and, despite the current theory of an Anglo-Saxon cultural conspiracy, American WASPs from the Adamses in the eighteenth century to the Lodges in the twentieth, were always among the leading Anglophobes."[11]

As Americans were differentiating themselves from their nominal or actual English ancestors in the realm of ideas, attitudes, and values, whatever remained of English cultural influences was also being progressively diluted by their contact with an ever-expanding array of non-English peoples. First, the European settlers were changed by contact with the real "native" Americans—the American Indians—who introduced them to new foods, new arts and crafts, new modes of shelter, new strategies for survival in the wilderness, and perhaps even some important civic principles.[12] From the time that the first slaves were brought to America in 1619, American culture borrowed liberally from African Americans (who were 20 percent of America's population in 1790) as it evolved distinctive American traditions in music, art, language, and modes of thought. Then, throughout the nineteenth and twentieth centuries, the flood tide of immigrants introduced myriad intellectual and social elements in literature, scholarship, the arts, and popular culture that transformed American society beyond recognition. As the social historian Philip Gleason put it:

> As the years went by, American nationality became more a reality and less a project for the future because of the accumulation of lived experience by people who thought of themselves as Americans. If the original mix in the population had continued without change, if there had not been massive immigration of culturally variant peoples, the original consciousness of kind of

the core group would presumably have coalesced with American nationality.[13]

Schlesinger wrote eloquently about the way Americans have transcended and enriched their English cultural base as it has been "reconstituted by transfusions from other continents and civilizations" and how "the ethnic transfusions affect all aspects of American life—our politics, our literature, our music, our painting, our movies, our cuisine, our customs, our dreams."[14]

Thus, American culture, for all its having been shaped by, and developed from, deeply embedded English traditions, has become profoundly non-English, a fact wryly noted by George Bernard Shaw in his statement that the United States and England are "two nations divided by a common language."[15] On the one hand, English influences are pervasive enough so that Americans—even those who are foreign born—often feel an instant sense of kinship when they watch English movies or visit Great Britain, a bond that even the most familiar cultures of other European nations cannot arouse. Yet, Americans—of all classes and all ethnic origins—don't imagine for one moment that they are like the English. They know how different their society is, in hundreds of ways, both large and small, from England's, a truth long chronicled, often satirically, by American novelists like Mark Twain, Henry James, and Sinclair Lewis or English ones like Charles Dickens and Evelyn Waugh. The differences are fundamental, and they go back hundreds of years. Whereas the English are profoundly class conscious, Americans are egalitarian. Whereas the English are reserved, Americans are informal. Whereas the English keep religion in the background, Americans are openly and aggressively devout. Whereas the English are fond of understatement, Americans are inclined to exaggeration and hyperbole. Whereas the English admire idiosyncrasy, Americans are conformist. Whereas the English worship the anachronistic, Americans enthusiastically embrace modernity.

These differences are not just matters of custom or habit. They are grounded in a matrix of disparate institutions. Britain is still a monarchy, with an aristocracy more vital than any in continental Europe. Britain has no formal constitution or the equivalent of the U.S. Bill of Rights. Britain's political leadership is parliamentary, whereas the United States' is presidential. Britain's governmental powers are highly centralized, whereas the United States' are decentralized, diffused, and redundant. Britain has a single official religion—the Church of England—whereas the United States maintains a wall of separation between church and state. In the realm of lesser institutions, English upper-middle-class parents send their children to private schools, whereas most Americans send theirs to public ones. Even after nearly twenty years of Tory government, the British choose to rely on a comprehensive social welfare system while Americans viscerally disdain a dependence on the government.

In any case, contrary to conventional wisdom, the United States has long ceased to be a WASP society (if it ever was one) in both senses in which WASP hegemony has been alleged: that WASPs are a majority of the American population and that a WASP elite sets the nation's sociocultural agenda. In the spirit of Voltaire's acid comment about the Holy Roman Empire being neither holy, nor Roman, nor an empire, most so-called WASPs, though admittedly white, are often neither Anglo-Saxon nor Protestant. In terms of numbers, at no time after the 1820s have the majority of Americans been able to trace their primary ancestry to England. Throughout most of the country's history, more Americans have claimed German descent (half of them Catholic) than any other. The next most dominant ancestral strain is Irish. English is a distant third. And those who are Protestant hardly share a common cultural heritage, belonging as they do to dozens of theologically distinct denominations. The widespread application of the WASP label to just about any American of a generally northern European aspect is simply a great misnomer.

In any case, the acronym WASP is of recent vintage and, when first introduced, was meant not to describe a dominant cohort of the national population, but a tiny elite. The earliest record of its appearance is ascribed to Andrew Hacker in a 1957 article in the *American Political Science Review* entitled "Liberal Democracy and Social Control." In that article, he wrote: "These 'old' Americans . . . are WASPs—in the cocktail party jargon of sociologists. That is, they are white, they are Anglo-Saxon in origin, and they are

Protestant (and disproportionately Episcopalian). To them WASPishness should be added to the tendency to be located on the Eastern Seaboard or around San Francisco, to be prep school and Ivy League educated, and to be possessed of inherited wealth."[16] By so defining the WASP, Hacker offered a narrow specification, indeed. At no time in American history could many Americans possibly have simultaneously met all these criteria.

If the demographics of the general population contradict the hegemony of Anglo-Americans as a whole, the demographics of the supposed WASP elite make their hegemony even more implausible. In 1994 the entire Ivy League graduated fewer than 12,000 people (less than 1 percent of American college graduates that year); one hundred years ago they graduated even fewer. The subset of Ivy Leaguers that also went to prep school, possessed inherited wealth, lived on the East Coast, were Protestant, and had predominantly English ancestors has always been minuscule. It is absurd to believe that such a finely dimensioned elite could ever have dominated the cultural, social, or political agenda of as vast, populous, dynamic, and heterogeneous a country as the United States. Nevertheless, the myth of WASP hegemony is a popular one, promoted most assiduously by members of the WASP elite themselves. A recent case in point is Joseph Alsop's 1991 book, *I've Seen the Best of It*, in which the author both celebrated and disparaged what he called "the WASP ascendancy," referring, essentially, to the same upper-class cohort as Hacker did. When Alsop wasn't being self-serving and self-aggrandizing in exaggerating the importance of WASPs (and his own as a premier member of this group), he conceded that WASP influence has long been in a state of irreversible decline.[17]

Critics may wish to challenge me for being too literal. Everyone knows, they will say, that the acronym is not to be taken at face value. When many of my Jewish and Italian friends use the acronym, they really mean any American of generally northern European aspect. After all, isn't Ireland close enough to England to be almost Anglo-Saxon? Don't Germans and Scandinavians share England's Teutonic culture? The answer to both these rhetorical questions is a resounding no! During the era of mass Irish and German immigration, those Americans who really were WASPs, in the literal sense, complained bitterly of the cultural incompatibility of the Irish and the Germans. The P (for Protestant) in WASP is no incidental modifier. The fact that all the Irish and about half the Germans were Catholic immediately disqualified them for cultural brotherhood with Protestants of English descent. Either WASP means precisely "white, Anglo-Saxon Protestant" or it means nothing.

This is no small point. General acceptance of the paradigm of assimilation may depend on it. As Americans debate and deconstruct the roots of American culture and as the voices of multiculturalism become ever more shrill and insistent, the ethnic basis of the national culture will take on a real significance and the issue of WASP hegemony will matter. And if WASP hegemony matters, the issue of "who are the WASPs?" matters as well. If the WASPs are an actual ethnic group, then we are asserting that they are engaging in ethnic politics and cultural imperialism. If, by WASPs, we are just talking about people, regardless of their actual ethnic origin, who share a common culture and a common point of view, we are asserting something else entirely. In the latter case, we are merely agreeing with the major premise of this chapter: that most Americans are members of a unified national culture that happens to have an English base.

Even if the United States has evolved from its English origins and the notion of WASP hegemony is a hoary myth, American society still embodies, in its political and governmental system, an inheritance of English institutions and English traditions. Rather than resent this fact, all Americans, regardless of their own ethnic heritages, should be grateful that some English elements have survived in American society because these elements represent the best part of the nation's English heritage. The essence of American cultural development has been to discard the most undesirable English traditions and to keep the best. Early on, Americans rejected England's aristocratic privileges and rigid class distinctions. Yet, in forming a society dedicated to protecting basic human rights, built on the supremacy of law and the love of justice, governed by the consent of its citizens, they borrowed heavily from their English patrimony. As Gleason observed in his essay on American identity, the United States is indebted to "the English tradition of liberty that stressed self-government, institutional limitations on the power of the sovereign, and procedural safeguards in law for a person accused of a crime."[18] The particular American genius was to blend these English concepts with broader notions developed by Enlightenment philosophers and universalize them. As the historian Hans Kohn put it: "The historical birthright of Englishmen became in America, under the influence of eighteenth century ideas, the natural right of man . . . the birthright of mankind."[19] Indeed, it is only America's English heritage that enables its non-English citizens to disregard that heritage as they assimilate to a transcendent national identity because, according to Gleason, "In establishing American nationality on the basis of abstract social and political ideas, Protestant Americans of British background had in fact committed the nation to a principle that made it inconsistent to erect particularistic ethnic criteria into tests of true Americanism."[20]

Whether they ponder these "abstract social and political ideas" or not, most Americans, according to the results of surveys, would rather live in a unicultural United States, even one with an Anglocentric core, than subscribe to any of the models of cultural pluralism being offered as an alternative. According to Malcolm Jones, Jr., in a recent *Newsweek* story supported by data from a poll, the ascendancy of cultural pluralism is causing a majority of Americans to worry that they are losing their "national character." This perception is buttressed by the results of another recent poll that half those surveyed were so turned off by ethnocentric cultural demands that they wanted the government to stop collecting *any* information on race and ethnicity.[21]

Cultural pluralism comes in two distinctive guises. Anti-Anglocentric "moderates" would like the government to recognize and promote a national "polyculture" that blends as many cultural influences as possible, drawn (or imagined) from Americans' diverse ethnic backgrounds—what I would characterize as American culture: the culture of many lands. This is the popular cultural vision in American elementary schools today. It is the vision of most American churches. It is the vision of television in its balanced news teams, sitcoms, and variety shows. It is the vision of the *New York Times* and other progressive newspapers.

The more aggressive enemies of Anglocentrism—Afrocentrists who believe that "it [is] impossible for a black person to be whole in a predominantly white culture"[22] and Latino activists who refuse to "put up with educators who promote a monolingual, monocultural society"[23]—would like the United States to be hospitable to a fragmented "multiculture" in which each ethnic group is actively encouraged to practice its own homeland culture and to protect it from the pernicious influence of Anglocentrism. This view seems to follow naturally from the vociferous complaints of African American and Latino leaders, and even those, like Novak, who speak for white ethnics, who believe that non-English Americans have long been compelled, by public school education and the pressures of social conformity, to betray or hide their indigenous ethnic heritages and habits and assume an insincere and synthetic posture of WASPishness. With the overthrow of Anglocentrism, they would be free at last to be true to their ethnic selves. Under either model everyone would continue to speak English (in the case of polyculture, liberally mixed with non-English words and expressions), but in the world of multiculture, those whose "first" language was foreign would do so grudgingly; English—not Spanish, Chinese, or Russian—would be their "second" language.

As African American, Latino, Asian, and a handful of Italian American ethnic advocates, joined by state education commissioners, university presidents, and foundation executives, promote multiculturalism, ordinary citizens un-self-consciously behave "like Americans." They are acting on the presumption that America's English-derived culture is the only authentic culture the country has. In the marketplace of ideas, entertainment, and voluntary organizations, most Americans stay away from the products and associations that are trying to market a bland polyculture. And only a small, and dwindling, set of Americans would ever be content to be permanently marooned on their isolated islands of multiculture in the vast American unicultural sea. This isn't just the view of "middle Americans" (referring to those who are white, middle class, native born, and probably suburban). The existence and durability of a unified American culture is taken for granted by most immigrants—even the most alienated and embittered Latinos and African Americans. In a *Newsweek* story on immigrant writers,

Malcolm Jones quoted Haitian American Edwige Danticat as saying, "When I'm [back] in Haiti, I am an American," and noted that
Cuban American Perez Firmat is amazed when he finds himself
singing the American national anthem "with feeling and conviction" and asking himself, "How can I feel at home in North
Carolina, given my heritage?"[24] According to Schlesinger, James
Baldwin discovered, after he arrived in Europe, that he was "as
American as any Texas G.I."[25] The reality of American culture is
taken for granted, above all, by people all over the world who know
something about life in the United States and are eager to import
as much of it as they can into their own countries and by those who
aspire to be Americans themselves one day.

Finally, to the degree that Americans give in to the demands for
cultural pluralism, they are surrendering their cultural ground to an
illusion. Most immigrants do not come to the United States with
an ethnic culture any more "authentic" than America's English-
based one. For example, the largest group of recent immigrants—
the Latinos—identify with cultural traditions inherited not from
their actual (often Indian or African) ancestors, but from countries
whose cultures bear exactly the same relationship to their former
colonial sponsor, Spain, as the United States' does to England.
Indeed, Spanish customs and traditions underwent considerably
less transformation in Latin America than English ones did in the
United States. Even as indigenous Indian groups in Mexico and
Central America are asserting their linguistic and cultural independence, those among their American immigrant compatriots who
advocate cultural pluralism promote a more-or-less pure (linguisti-
cally and otherwise) Spanish culture. Jewish immigrants have, historically, been amenable to assimilation, but their descendants have
often been the harshest critics of WASP hegemony. Yet they must
be aware that much of the culture their immigrant forbears brought
to the United States at the turn of the century had little to do with
their ostensible Levantine religious and ethnic roots, but was actually the product of Poland, Russia, and the other countries whose
persecution and poverty they fled. Some of the most vociferous
proponents of cultural separatism are "Afrocentrists" like City
College's notorious Leonard Jeffries, yet according to Schlesinger,

"Unless one believes in racist mysticism, [African Americans] belong far more to American culture than to the culture of Africa. Their history is part of the Western democratic tradition. . . . No one does black Americans more disservice than those Afrocentric ideologues who would define them out of the west."[26]

One of the most unfortunate consequences of demands for institutionalized cultural separatism under the banner of multiculturalism or cultural pluralism—and in opposition to America's European and English traditions—is that it furnishes powerful ammunition to the enemies of further immigration. Cultural separatism is Exhibit A for neonativists, such as Peter Brimelow, John O'Sullivan, and Laurence Auster, in their argument that the United States will risk ethnic dissension if it admits more immigrants from countries whose cultures diverge radically from the English.[27] Such immigrants, they allege, will never be able or willing to conform to America's Anglo-based culture and thus, are unassimilable. This is actually an old argument. It was made by nativists in the early nineteenth century who were contemplating the arrival of the Irish and Germans. It was made by racist Americans in the late nineteenth century, who were referring to the arrival of the Chinese. It was made by Nordic supremacists at the turn of the century in relation to the hordes of newly arrived Italians and Jews. The most eloquent rebuttal to both the multiculturalists and the nativists may be Gleason's, written in 1980:

[An] American nationality does in fact exist. That it seems necessary to make such a statement indicates the degree to which the rhetorical imbalance of the . . . discussion of ethnicity has created a situation in which very basic matters related to American identity appear questionable. For that reason it may be redundant to add that American nationality is not Anglo-Saxonism or WASP ethnicity . . . Rather it is a distinctive sense of peoplehood. . . . To affirm the existence of American nationality does not mean that all Americans are alike or must become uniform. . . . It simply means that a genuine national community does exist and that it has its own distinctive principle of unity, its own history, and its own appropriate sense of belongingness by virtue of which individuals identify with the symbols that represent and embody that community's evolving consciousness of itself.[28]

Americans without a drop of English blood should feel at home in the United States, not just in spite of, but in large measure *because* of, its English traditions. This proposition may be obvious or a matter of little interest to most Americans, but it enrages a small but influential cadre of ethnic advocates, intellectuals, and institutional leaders who vehemently object to "forcing" Americans into "Anglo-conformity." What the cultural pluralists need to understand is that there is no inherent contradiction in the United States having a legitimate, distinctive, and unified culture, one that members of any ethnic group can participate in without "betraying" their ethnic heritage and the American culture's English foundation. If one accepts this fundamental cultural fact, it follows that in the course of assimilation, no immigrants, regardless of their original nationality, can escape its pervasive "Anglocentric" influence nor should want to. Americans, whatever their ethnic heritages, enjoy the best of all cultural worlds. America's English traditions have given them their language and their freedoms, while America's ethnic diversity—and the right of each American to be as ethnic as he pleases—has made them part of the most cosmopolitan and universal culture on earth.

6

Americans United by Myths

America is a memory—a memory of the lives and actions, the beliefs and efforts, of millions of human beings who have lived in American spaces, participated in an American social world, and died Americans. The memory is contained in American names—of people, of places, of events and institutions. The memory is contained in stories Americans tell one another—in poems and histories, in speeches and broadcasts, in shows and pictures, in jokes and obituaries. It is contained in the ways Americans behave and in their expectations of behavior; it is contained in the rituals Americans perform and in the games they play; it is contained in American social groupings, and in the political, economic, and religious institutions Americans maintain.

In the American memory are contained many of the truths which are self-evident to Americans, which help them understand their country, and to explain their lives.

James Oliver Robertson, 1980[1]

Assimilation in the United States depends on all Americans—immigrants and natives and members of all ethnic groups—sharing a strong and unified national identity. In other countries people acquire a shared identity from ethnic and historical bonds—tribalism elevated to the level of the nation state. (Or they don't, as in Yugoslavia, Lebanon, and even Canada, and the result is tribal warfare, hot or cold, within the confines of the nation state.) In the

United States, a country marked by exceptional ethnic diversity and a relatively brief history, national unity is grounded, instead, in a majority of Americans sharing the same conception of who they are, what they believe in, and how they are different from the people of other nations. America is, perhaps, unique in the intensity and eagerness with which its people have been psychically invested in a singular national mission and a singular collective self-image.

At first glance, it would seem unlikely that the citizens of the United States should have come by a shared identity. Ours is a vast continental nation, with enormous regional variations in topography, climate, and economic conditions and with strong regional traditions. Its population, one of the largest in the world, encompasses members of innumerable occupations, religions, and ethnicities living in every conceivable setting, from teeming cities and leafy suburbs to rural villages and isolated farms. Clearly, Americans are too varied and numerous to have achieved their shared identity by negotiation, as if such a thing could ever be negotiated anywhere. In some countries, like Britain, a national identity is derived from a monarchy and the traditions of a powerful elite, but the American people have always been far too egalitarian and pluralistic to submit to a shared identity imposed from above. Yet, almost miraculously, the shared identity is there, and it has been an essential ingredient in the maintenance of national harmony and the overcoming of national differences for over two hundred years.

The American identity emerged from a compelling national mythology. Since independence, the most essential ideas and images that unify Americans have been elevated to the status of myths. Myths are not mere fantasies or untruths. Myths are exaggerated or simplified representations of human traits and situations, paradigms of society and morality, that are based on some underlying truth. The word *myth* is often used in a narrower and more superficial sense to disparage a commonly held view and to dismiss it as false or mistaken, as in the common formulation "the myth and reality of. . . . " I even used the word that way in Chapter 5, when I discussed the *myth* of the WASP. In this chapter, however, I refer to myths in their deeper and broader meaning, as popular images that help to unify a society by creating, in the words of this chapter's epigraph, the ingredients of a collective memory and a collective self-image. Most people believe them to represent if not actual reality, then a kind of idealized reality.

What distinguishes myths from mere propaganda is that they are communicated and diffused throughout society in an entirely natural, un-self-conscious way. They have no single source or any particular venue; rather, they infiltrate a vast cross section of institutions and media. Whenever and wherever they crop up, people just presuppose their inherent validity. Even the sophisticated and the skeptical do not reject myths outright; they accept them as metaphors, reflections of reality. The only explicit antagonism to societal myths comes from individuals and groups that reject the myths' fundamental premises and wish to replace them with their own countermyths.

America's myths have been essential to the country's great project of assimilating its immigrants and maintaining social harmony. They made it easier for native Americans to accept the arrival of immigrants, to live sociably with them, and even to feel a kinship with people so radically different from themselves. They made it easier for immigrants to feel at home in their new country, to accept the legitimacy of its institutions, and to understand their new countrymen's mores and values. Myths made it possible for native-born Americans and immigrants to share lands and resources, laws and institutions, even ancestors and traditions.

Americans are especially well disposed to share a national mythology. As I discussed in Chapter 4, Americans attained high (and standardized) levels of mass literacy and education sooner than just about any other national population. Already by the middle of the nineteenth century, 90 percent of the American population could read and write and three-quarters had some formal education.[2] And they have been plugged in longer to a more extensive and redundant network of communication than have citizens of any other nation: The United States was the home of the first mass-market newspapers and magazines, the first mass-market cinema, and the first mass-market radio and television broadcasts. It was easy for ideas and concepts with popular appeal to spread quickly across the United States and to acquire a transcendent mythic status.

The mythic poems of Henry Wadsworth Longfellow and Walt Whitman and the mythic novels of James Fenimore Cooper, Bret

Harte, Mark Twain, Horatio Alger, and Zane Grey became best-sellers. Norman Rockwell's covers on the *Saturday Evening Post* became emblems of harmonious and egalitarian small-town life from coast to coast. Political heroes like George Washington and Abraham Lincoln and inventors like Alexander Graham Bell and Thomas Edison were mythologized in elementary school texts read by a majority of American schoolchildren. American values were mythologized in the editorials of mass-circulation newspapers, political speeches, religious sermons, and commencement addresses. Notions and symbols of American myths were expropriated by commercial products and widely disseminated in their advertisements. But perhaps the most powerful generators of myth were the twentieth-century innovations of radio, television, and the movies. Hollywood, especially from the 1930s through the 1950s, was self-consciously dedicated to mythmaking on a grand scale.

While the myths of other countries revolve around ethnic bonds, ancient traditions, triumphs of the battlefield, or the universal dilemmas and paradoxes of human existence, America's are obsessed with articulating the ingredients of a unique American identity. While the myths of other countries have no comprehensive focus, Americans' originate in a few basic ideas, beginning with America's master myth: *America as the land of the new beginning*. When the sociologist Seymour Martin Lipset called the United States "the world's first new nation,"[3] he gave voice to a conviction that Americans, from colonial times to the present, have fervently held about their country. In one way or another, all the ingredients of American mythology come back to that single powerful concept. America was not simply *there*, it was *created*. It was created by men and women who turned their backs on the wicked and backward *Old* World (Europe) and who were determined to make the *New* World (America) a far better place. America was to be an exemplar to the rest of the world of what a free people (in many senses of that word) could accomplish: the place where the most just principles of social organization and political governance would reign, where the most useful products of human ingenuity would be applied, and where the noblest traits of human character and the highest aspirations of the human spirit would flourish. As Oscar Handlin, the leading historian of immigration, noted, "The image of the city on the hill persisted since the days of the first settlers; and the events of the revolutionary period only confirmed the certitude that a great destiny awaited the Republic."[4] Americans especially enjoyed having their mythic self-conception confirmed by Europeans, hence the enthusiastic reception in the United States of Alexis de Tocqueville's *Democracy in America*. But few Europeans expressed the myth more lyrically than did the English poet Percy Bysshe Shelley:

> That land [America] is like an Eagle, whose young gaze
> Feeds on the noontide beam, whose golden plume
> Floats moveless on the storm, and in the blaze
> Of sunrise gleams when Earth is wrapped in gloom;
> An epitaph of glory for the tomb
> Of murdered Europe may thy fame be made,
> Great People! as the sands shalt thou become;
> Thy growth is swift as morn, when night must fade;
> The multitudinous Earth shall sleep beneath thy shade.[5]

Immigrants were always central characters in this master myth, and their assimilation was always one of its central premises. As the land of the new beginning, America had no choice but to be made up of immigrants. That was the whole idea. People would leave their old, unsatisfactory homelands and join together to create this more perfect nation. As social commentator James Oliver Robertson put it: "The society immigrants left behind was corrupt, decadent, tyrannical, or at least inferior. American society is new and superior."[6] Woodrow Wilson expressed the immigrant's aspiration more grandly: "America lives in the heart of every man everywhere who wishes to find a region where he will be free to work out his destiny as he chooses."[7] Seen in this light, the ethnic heterogeneity of the immigrants was a positive—even essential—feature because if the immigrants were merely a nation transplanted, they would find it harder to abandon their discredited institutions, anachronistic customs, and invidious status distinctions. Better yet, people from many lands would complement each other as they harvested the best traits of each constituent culture and discarded the worst. The notion of immigrants creating the New World is enshrined in two of the most familiar and compelling American mythological stories (each celebrated by a national holiday): Christopher Columbus's voyage of discovery and the Pilgrims' flight from persecution to establish a free and moral society in the New England wilderness.

There was another way in which immigrants were essential to America's master myth. A steady flow of immigrants served to validate America's superiority. From the beginning, Americans have been firm believers in markets, and immigration has been the supreme market test of national superiority. Each new wave of immigrants attested to America's enduring desirability. America was a club (or a religion) that was perpetually pleased to enroll new members. Under this formulation, it was not immigrants who were privileged to be allowed to settle in America; it was America that was privileged because it was chosen by immigrants, from among all the nations of the world, to be their new homeland. As the historian Henry Steele Commager noted: "The American cherished an uncritical and unquestioning conviction that his was the best of all countries, and every emigrant who crossed the Atlantic westward—few went the other way—confirmed him in his assumption that this fact was everywhere acknowledged."[8] Even today, practically the first question a native American asks of a newly encountered immigrant is: "How do you like the United States?" If the answer, as expected, is enthusiastic, the American feels fulfilled; if it is critical, the American is crushed.

Assimilation, American style follows naturally from this conception of the immigrant in the land of the new beginning. In the traditional view of assimilation (assimilation, European style) there is an established society to which immigrants must assimilate. Under such circumstances, immigrants are expected to shed all their "alien" cultural features and conform as closely as possible to the characteristics of their adopted country. In the land of the new beginning, there is no firmly established society. A new society is being created, and it is being created by immigrants. American society and American culture are works in progress, and immigrants are the artisans who are fashioning those works. Thus, the ethnicity of immigrants and any cultural baggage the immigrants bring along as a result of that ethnicity are irrelevant to their new status as Americans. By virtue of the act of immigration itself, immigrants have enrolled in the project of building their new nation and have turned their backs permanently on the imperfect societies they left behind. Whatever cultural habits immigrants may want to retain from their former homelands are thus viewed by "natives" as mere idiosyncratic vestiges, markers of individual differences in a new society that, among its many unique values, is supremely tolerant of individual differences. In Robertson's words:

> Americans were people who came here and committed themselves to America, or they were people who were born here and belonged here. They were not Creoles or colonials, or provincials; they were not exiles, not English or Scots or Irish or German; nor were they "natives." [America] made them free of all such identities.[9]

The most assimilationist aspect of America's master myth is the conviction that in the process of creating a new country, the immigrants have re-created themselves. In other words, the new land is populated by a "new man." Few passages of American social history have been as frequently reprinted as this excerpt from Hector St. John de Crevecoeur's *Letters from an American Farmer*:

> What, then is the American, this new man? . . . He is an American, who, leaving behind him all his ancient prejudices and manners, receiving new ones from the new mode of life he has embraced, the new government he obeys, and the new rank he holds. He becomes an American by being received in the broad lap of our great Alma Mater. Here individuals of all nations are melted in a new race of men, whose labors and posterity will one day cause great changes in the world. . . . The American ought, therefore, to love this country better than that wherein either he or his forefathers were born.[10]

This concept of Americans constituting an entirely "new race" distinct from any particular ethnic stock is the bedrock of assimilation because it so completely contradicts the ethnic particularism that is assimilationism's great enemy. If the mere act of joining the American nation makes immigrants, regardless of where they come from, members of the American "race," then ethnicity (including race), in its traditional sense of connoting some immutable biological or otherwise hereditary state, is explicitly superseded. Two hundred years after de Crevecoeur, this idea is alive and well. Few Americans would disagree with Patrick J. Buchanan's assertion during the 1995–96 Republican presidential primary campaign, apropos America's troubled black-white relations, that "there is only one race in this country, the American race."[11]

America's master myth has, since independence, inspired the unique institutions, activities, and personality traits that characterize Americans, which, in turn, have generated a host of subsidiary myths that keep reminding Americans of who they are, what makes them different from the peoples of other nations, and the scope and grandeur of their shared national project. Only a few of these myths revolve around immigration per se, but most have some particular relevance to the status of immigrants.

The American Idea is the oldest and most powerful of these mythic concepts, and rightly so. As the ideological foundation on which national unity rests, it has generated a mythical idiom from which most other national myths derive. John Gunther said, "Ours is the only country deliberately founded on a good idea."[12] The substance of the American Idea is enshrined in three universally revered texts: the Declaration of Independence, the Constitution, and Lincoln's magnificent Gettysburg Address. Although the Constitution, specifically its first ten amendments (the Bill of Rights), is the living, breathing official document that transforms the American Idea from myth into concrete reality, it is the soul-stirring language of the Declaration of Independence and the Gettysburg Address that gives the American Idea its mythic status:

> We hold these truths to be self-evident; that all men are created equal; that they are endowed by their Creator with certain inalienable rights, that among these are life, liberty, and the pursuit of happiness; that, to secure these rights, governments are instituted among men, deriving their just powers from the consent of the governed.[13]

*   *   *

Fourscore and seven years ago our fathers brought forth on this continent a new nation, conceived in Liberty, and dedicated to the proposition that all men are created equal.

Now we are engaged in a great civil war, testing whether that nation or any nation so conceived and so dedicated can long endure. . . .

. . . We here highly resolve that this nation under God shall have a new birth of freedom; and that government of the people, by the people, for the people, shall not perish from the earth.[14]

These words, memorized by every American schoolchild (as well as by millions around the world) form the inspirational seal of the American people. Indeed, I was deeply moved myself as I committed them to paper. Here we find all the key precepts of the American Idea: the supremacy of the individual, the equality of men, the guarantee of liberty and other fundamental human rights, the rule of law, and government by consent of the people. What lifts the American Idea from the plane of reigning political orthodoxy to that of mythology are three things: its moral grandeur, its presumed immutability, and its function as the great unifier of the American people. It is mainly the American Idea that makes America and Americans different from all other people on earth (even if an increasing share of that polity is cribbing important parts of it). It is mainly the American Idea that vanquishes ethnic particularism and ethnic prejudice. It is mainly the American Idea that places the United States on the moral high ground that has allowed it to dominate world geopolitics. It is mainly the American Idea that enables Americans to resolve the recurring conflicts and challenges of modern society. Beyond its symbolic manifestations, the American Idea, in its full mythological majesty, has been continually invoked since independence to inspire and motivate Americans to feel good about themselves and to do the right thing. Politicians wrap their own personae and programmatic ideas in its precepts. The correct resolution of every philosophical controversy among Americans is adduced from it. All aggrieved individuals and groups—above all, black Americans—appeal to its guaranteed civil rights and liberties. It is the American Idea that, from the beginning, has given Americans their most precious gift: a sense of moral superiority over the people of every other nation. It is this moral superiority that led labor leader Meyer London to say: "To me Americanism means . . . an imperative duty to be nobler than the rest of the world."[15] As Commager put it:

> The moral superiority of his country was . . . axiomatic to the American. The assumption of superiority was accompanied by a sense of destiny and mission. . . . Successive generations were equally eager to spread the American idea over the globe and exasperated that foreign ideas should ever intrude themselves into America.[16]

Just as the American master myth—America as the land of the new beginning—is assimilationist to the core, so is the American Idea, its purest submyth. The American Idea furnishes the philosophical rationale for admitting immigrants. More important, it offers the moral justification for treating them as equals after they arrive. It provides a noble and stirring platform for a shared national identity. Its rules and concepts offer a basis, both idealistic and pragmatic, for resolving disputes among immigrants and natives and among members of diverse ethnic constituencies. In other words, if you believe in the American Idea, then assimilation is easy.

All myths need human incarnations, especially heroes. The American Idea is personified by the heroic Founding Fathers: the simple men of incomparable wisdom who devised it and who fought the War of Independence against great odds to make it the charter of the land of the new beginning. And looming heroically above the rest of the Founding Fathers is the Father of Our Country, George Washington. Much of the mythology of the American Idea is wrapped up in the larger-than-life portrayals—in schoolbooks, children's literature, plays, and movies—of George Washington and the other revolutionary heroes: Thomas Jefferson, Benjamin Franklin, Alexander Hamilton, John Adams, James Madison, and others. The other key mythic figure of American history is Abraham Lincoln, the martyred president who arose providentially from the most humble beginnings to keep his countrymen true to the American Idea and who had to fight a war to make it prevail against the dark forces of sectionalism and immorality.

Lincoln has sparked an even richer and more voluminous mythological literature than the somewhat distant heroes of the revolutionary era.

The American Idea has depended heavily, for its mythic promotion, on the efforts of public institutions. Schools have been its
primary marketplace, backed up by museums, libraries, public
events, monuments, and, of course, holidays. The American Idea is
celebrated directly on the Fourth of July and on Washington's and
Lincoln's Birthdays (recently combined in Presidents' Day) and
indirectly on Veterans Day and Memorial Day (honoring those who
fought and died for the American Idea). The American Idea is the
staple of political speeches and schools' commencement addresses.
But it has not lacked for fictional validation. A few movie classics
like *Abe Lincoln in Illinois* (1939), *State of the Union* (1948), and
1776 (1972) engaged it directly, and it forms the implicit subtext in
political movies like *The Best Man* (1964), *Seven Days in May*
(1964), and the musical *Of Thee I Sing* (1931). In *Mr. Smith Goes
to Washington* (1939), a classic of this genre, Jimmy Stewart saves
the American Idea, as embodied in the day-to-day workings of congressional politics, from the subversive forces of political cynicism.
Many war movies, especially those made about the two world wars,
such as *Sergeant York* (1941), *Sands of Iwo Jima* (1949), and
Command Decision (1948), revolve around the American Idea as
the raison d'être for American involvement in the conflicts and the
selfless heroism of the main protagonists.

As the American Idea gives Americans a way to view their society,
the other myths give Americans a way to view themselves, especially in comparison with the lesser mortals of other societies.
These myths persuade Americans that they are pioneers, rugged
individualists, people who rise by achievement, people in the vanguard, people of justice and principle, and people of tolerance.
And just as the American Idea provides the larger rationale for the
United States being perpetually a nation of immigrants, these
subsidiary myths give natives and immigrants the day-to-day
rationale for living together. The mythic celebration of the individualist makes it easier for natives to tolerate newcomers, however strange. The mythic celebration of achievement makes it eas-

ier for them to tolerate immigrant competitors in the workplace. The mythic celebration of progress and enlightenment makes it easier for both immigrants and natives to accept change, to abandon traditional customs and occupations, and to move on to common new ones.

As the American Idea itself has been mythologized mainly in the public arena of textbooks, museums, holidays, and speeches, its subsidiary myths have been conveyed mostly in the world of fiction: novels, plays, movies, and television.

One of the richest troves of American mythology is the most popular of American fictional genres, the Western. Stories about the settlement of the West (every place west of the Mississippi) have loomed large in both popular and serious literature: James Fenimore Cooper's *The Prairie* (1827), Bret Harte's *The Luck of Roaring Camp* (1868) and *The Outcasts of Poker Flat* (1869), Owen Wister's *The Virginian* (1902), Zane Grey's *Riders of the Purple Sage* (1912), and Willa Cather's *O Pioneers!* (1913). But most Americans have been steeped in the mythology of the Western by the movies—hundreds of them. Westerns may span a variety of subgenres, but each shares certain paradigmatic plot structures and characters. The main protagonist is a heroic figure, who comes out of nowhere and rides into a newly settled town on horseback. (Subtext: The hero is an immigrant, an American "new man.") He comes by himself, usually without family or friends. (Subtext: He is a rugged individualist.) He either has a specific mission that brings him to this place or is passing through and discovers a mission. The most common mission is to save the townspeople from some greedy and immoral villains. Here we have a profusion of mythic subtexts. The townspeople represent the faces of American progress. They, too, are immigrants, at least figuratively, sometimes literally, dedicated to building a modern society in the prairie or the wilderness. They are extending American civilization and the values of the American way, but as a collectivity they are weak. They need our hero, the rugged individualist, the superior American, to secure their new world. The villains, usually corrupt local businessmen or marauding lawless bands, represent the Old-World forces of darkness. They are the un-Americans, the ever-present agents of anti-democracy against whom true Americans must continually do battle with steadfast courage and vigilance. Americanism in a wicked world is under constant attack.

Beneath the surface of their main plots and key characters, Westerns illustrate a host of American mythical ideas. One evident idea is the categorical rejection of class distinctions. The hero is always classless, perhaps even uncouth. He is often romantically linked with a local woman (often the person who is the most directly endangered), who is invariably better educated—but this does not matter. Any people in the frontier town with class pretensions are ridiculed or come to grief. The good guys and the bad guys are judged only by their actions and achievements, not by their wealth or breeding.

Nevertheless, in the classless society of the West, the pursuit of wealth, if undertaken honestly, is admirable. In spite of the surface turbulence of good guys fighting bad guys, there are enormous opportunities for economic advancement and upward social mobility, which illustrate another staple of American mythology. Messy as they are, the frontier territories of the West are booming. Formerly penniless settlers get rich operating ranches; panning for gold; and opening general stores, hotels, and even saloons and brothels. It is the job of the hero to protect this spirit of enterprise. The saloons and brothels, and their owners and patrons, are usually portrayed indulgently, illustrating the uneasy tension between what today would be called "family values" and a libertarian tolerance of petty vice. This tension itself is built into American mythology. Free men (and women) are presumably free to do anything, even to sin, if others are not harmed in the process. But the libertarianism of the American Idea is implicitly grounded in a higher morality that demands that Americans display personal virtue and self-restraint. Just as real-world American society has never resolved this tension, neither have the mythical Westerns.

The Western mythologizes the irrelevance of ethnicity in American life. Neither American nativity nor national origin make any difference with regard to the characters, both good and bad, although ethnicity may show up as a mark of picturesque individuation, for example, in portrayals of "the Frenchie" or "the Swede." Even blacks are usually portrayed with respect in Westerns and are generally found in the entourage of the good guys. The case of the

Indian is problematical, but in a way that does not really contradict the mythic paradigms. There are good Indians and bad Indians. The familiar Western slogan—"the only good Indian is a dead Indian"— is not really an accurate statement of the way Indians are perceived. There *are* good Indians; they are the ones who throw in their lot with the good Americans, serving as workers, scouts, or allies. Perhaps the most famous good Indian is the Lone Ranger's sidekick, Tonto. By abandoning their ethnic compatriots, Indians, like all other immigrant "new men," are on their way to becoming Americans. The bad Indians—the ones who can be killed with impunity—are the ones who insist on maintaining not so much a separate ethnic identity as a national one. (In a popular Lone Ranger joke, Tonto says, in response to the Lone Ranger's description of some presumably shared danger, "What do you mean 'we,' white-man?") In the mythology of American identity, this is the unforgivable sin.

What I have described is the classic, pre–1960s Western. Like assimilation itself, the Western genre has been subject to revisionism, a revisionism explicitly aimed at overturning the classical American myths and replacing them with countermyths. The best movies of this revisionist genre include *Hang 'Em High* (1967), *McCabe and Mrs. Miller* (1971), and *Unforgiven* (1992). In these films and many others, the hero, although still a loner, is a man of highly ambiguous character. (Subtext: America has a dark past.) He still arrives alone, but he regrets his solitude. (Subtext: Individualism is lonely and unsatisfactory.) The townspeople are also portrayed much more ambiguously. The lawmen— legitimate lawmen, not to be confused with the explicitly wicked ones in some classic Westerns—dispense arbitrary and unfair justice. (Subtext: The American Idea is often perverted.) The town's development is chaotic and unsatisfactory; the ranches are ruining the unspoiled natural environment. (Subtext: Capitalism and progress are not all they are made out to be.) Movies like *Little Big Man* (1970) and *Dances with Wolves* (1990) introduce the most radical revisionist idea, one that most subverts the myth of ethnic universalism: recasting the status of Indians. Not only is the oppression of Indians now seen as profoundly immoral, the good Indians are the ones who stick by their independent nationhood, and the bad ones are the ones who betray their tribes and join the white man. And the best white men are the ones who throw in their lot with the Indians. (Subtext: Indians should not assimilate and the officially sanctioned ethnic federalism built into the Indian treaties and reservations is a model for ethnic relations in the larger society.)

If American mythical concepts have been amply illustrated in the realm of popular culture by the Western genre, they have been reinforced by parallel works of literature and drama appealing to middle- and highbrow tastes. Just about every giant of American literature has touched on one or another of these mythic themes. James Fenimore Cooper, in *Leatherstocking Tales: The Deerslayer* (1841), *The Last of the Mohicans* (1826), and *The Pathfinder* (1840), was the first major author to chronicle the lonely frontiersman bringing civilization to the wilderness. His hero, Natty Bumppo, or "Leatherstocking," anticipating the Western hero by half a century, is a classless individualist. His mission is to be a herald—a pathfinder—of modernity. Mythical themes animated the works of the transcendentalists, whether essayists like Ralph Waldo Emerson and Henry David Thoreau or novelists like Nathaniel Hawthorne and Herman Melville, as they celebrated individualism and rationality (a surrogate for modernity). And in his poems, Whitman was directly engaged in advancing American mythology, as in this passage from *Leaves of Grass* (1855):

> How America is the continent of glories, and of the triumph of freedom
>   and
> of the Democracies, and of the fruits of society, and of all that is begun,
>   . . .
> Of seeds dropping into the ground, of births,
> Of the steady concentration of America, inland, upward, to impregnable
>   and
> swarming places, . . .
> Of mighty inland cities yet unsurvey'd and unsuspected,
> Of the new and good names, of the modern developments, of inalienable
>   homesteads,
> Of a free and original life there, of simple diet and clean and sweet blood,
> Of litheness, majestic faces, clear eyes, and perfect physique there,
> Of immense spiritual results future years far West, each side of the
>   Anahuacs,
> Of these songs, well understood there. . . . [17]

These works have lent plausibility and nuance to the myths of the migrant, the pioneer, the principled individualist, the rugged capitalist, the classless society, the march of progress, the evil of racism, and the nobility of immigrants. Immigration and assimilation are addressed explicitly in only a limited corner of this literature. But they are addressed implicitly in much of the rest because the mythical traits and institutions these works glorify, advertently or not, flatter immigrants and support assimilation. The works that romanticize Americans who migrated across the continent implicitly romanticize those who migrated across the world. The works that glorify the lonely individual making his own way implicitly glorify immigrants who were determined to be masters of their own destiny. The works that satirize snobbery and class pretensions implicitly legitimate the status of lower-class immigrants. The works that celebrate upward mobility implicitly endorse the economic success of immigrants.

Important as American literature has been in developing the tapestry of American mythology, no medium has been so instrumental to this purpose as film. As the pop artist Andy Warhol put it:

> It's the movies that have really been running things in America ever since they were invented. They show you what to do, how to do it, when to do it, how to feel about it. Everybody has their own America, and then they have the pieces of a fantasy America that they think is out there but they can't see.[18]

Given the seminal importance of movies in solidifying American mythology, it is noteworthy that most movies, especially those of the 1930s, 1940s, and 1950s—the ones with the greatest mythical resonance—have been made by immigrants or the recent descendants of immigrants, notably Jewish Americans. Not only were owners of the great studios of the mythmaking era immigrants or, at best, first-generation natives, so were most of the directors, screenwriters, and actors. So here we come full circle. American mythology secures a place for immigrants at the American social table. Immigrants repay the debt by becoming the most effective promoters and disseminators of that mythology.

A cursory review of the Academy Award winners since 1930 imparts the flavor of American mythology as portrayed in film. Not every award-winning film has had mythic significance, and many of the mythic messages have been muddled or blurred, but through it all, certain themes pertaining to American identity and the collective American self-image have appeared again and again. In the 1930s, a period of great economic hardship and great inequality of income and wealth, movies like the "screwball" comedies of such directors as Frank Capra, Preston Sturges, and George Cukor painted a mythic picture of class relations and class attitudes. Typical of these movies were *It Happened One Night* (1934), *Holiday* (1938), and *The Philadelphia Story* (1940), in which dashing, impecunious, highly individualistic male heroes woo and win spoiled rich girls. The rich girls' wealthy families are the heavies, not because they are rich, but because they are stuffy and snobbish. The hero either comes from a modest background or rejects his wealthy one. In addition to his romantic appeal, he is a man of boldness, vision, and accomplishments. He pries the heroine loose from her stifling upper-class roots and gets her to join him in the pursuit of his own quintessentially American dream. Several myths come together here: America as basically egalitarian and classless despite its vast income disparities (but also tolerant of those wealth and income disparities); the lonely, but ultimately triumphant, individualist hero; his dogged upward mobility; and the bridging of class (and, implicitly, ethnic) barriers. Other Oscar-winning movies of the period, like *You Can't Take It With You* (1938), developed similar themes.

After World War II, when prosperity had returned and Americans needed to ponder the significance of the war, movies turned their mythic lens on reaffirming the universalism of the American Idea. *The Best Years of Our Lives* (1946) mythologized this universalism, both in celebrating the heroism of American soldiers who fought for it in the war and in depicting the painful postwar adjustment that allowed Americans to live and work together despite their class and ethnic differences. *Gentleman's Agreement* (1947) was a hard-hitting attack on "un-American" ethnic discrimination (in this case, anti-Semitism), made all the more universal an American issue because the crusading hero was a Gentile.

In the 1950s and early 1960s, movies like *On the Waterfront* (1954), *Marty* (1955), and *A View from the Bridge* (1962), made in the then fashionable mode of gritty social realism, for the first time tackled the significance of immigration and assimilation directly as they portrayed first- and second-generation immigrants' painful—but ultimately successful—adjustment to American society. They presented a naturalistic image of life in America's urban ethnic enclaves in stories that pit the protagonists' aspirations for upward mobility and social assimilation against the un-American and antiassimilationist forces holding them back, namely, corrupt unions (read un-American socialism) and tradition-bound families and friends.

Since the late 1960s, Academy Awards have been given to movies that have taken cinematic mythology sharply off its historic trajectory into revisionist countermythology. *Midnight Cowboy* (1969) stood many earlier myths on its head. The two individualist protagonists, a drifter from the Southwest (the locale of the former Western hero) and a derelict in New York, are no longer heroes; they are losers. The message seems to be that individualism definitely does not pay. New York City, the movie's setting, is no longer a site for upward economic and social mobility with some understandable urban rough edges but a swamp of irredeemable pathology; thus, if you live in New York City, you can forget about the American Dream. The Oscar-winning *Godfather* movies (1972 and 1974) discredited New York as well, and by glorifying the Mafia, they cynically discredited Americans' mythic assumptions about upward mobility, the virtue of the entrepreneur, and the justice of the American civic order. *One Flew Over the Cuckoo's Nest* (1975) parodied American myths: The heroic individualist was really mentally ill, and the societal establishment (the management of a mental institution) was evil. *The Deer Hunter* (1978) portrayed the injustice of the Vietnam War, puncturing Americans' mythic pretensions regarding the universalist values driving its foreign policy, and depicted life in ethnic Pittsburgh as singularly bleak. No upward mobility or assimilation was to be found there.

And so it goes. *Ordinary People* (1980) showed the hollowness of the American Dream, even for Americans who have achieved it. *Dances with Wolves* (1990) and *Unforgiven* (1992) were textbook examples of the revisionist Western, in which American soldiers and men on horseback were the villains while the Indians who maintained a separate tribal identity and women were the victims. *Pulp Fiction* (1994) satirized and inverted the typical crime adventure story; the "heroes" were two thugs who literally got away with murder but were supposed to engage our sympathy as they contemplated their unsatisfactory lives with mock-maudlin philosophizing. Almost without exception, the Oscar-winning movies after the late 1960s not only have repudiated Americans' cherished myths, but they have pessimistic and cynical endings. The happy endings of American movie classics (as well as most mythic fiction) were not mere concessions to the tastes of an immature and naive audience, they were metaphors of general societal optimism. Americans fighting for American values and displaying American virtues always faced tough fights against cunning and determined adversaries, but they always prevailed, meaning that American values and American virtues prevailed. In the more recent countermythology, corrupted or disillusioned Americans, pursuing unworthy and selfish objectives, either overcome their blameless victims or lose out against adversaries even more wicked than themselves; either way, injustice triumphs and American society stinks.

This critique of cinematic mythological revisionism does not mean to suggest that traditional American mythology was insensitive to America's manifest contradictions and imperfections. On the contrary, the best of America's mythological fiction, whether in the works of its great novelists or in the best of its plays and movies, clearly recognized all the betrayals of American values and inconsistencies in American behavior that accompanied the pursuit of American ideals. Cooper's classical mythical individualist pioneer, Natty Bumppo, clearly understood the tragic dimension of the American settlers' confrontation with the Indians, that American progress and civilization were being imposed at the expense of an ancient and worthy culture, and he was troubled and ambivalent about it. Novels set in America's rapidly industrializing and urbanizing post–Civil War era, such as those of William Dean Howells, Frank Norris, and Theodore Dreiser, may have portrayed the daring and ingenuity of America's quintessential self-made men, but they also depicted their cruelty and ruthlessness; they presented a panorama of rising prosperity and general upward mobility, but also the harsh and unforgiving attributes of urban and industrial life. The finely nuanced novels of social behavior by Henry James and Edith Wharton presented their American characters in a profoundly ambivalent light: on the one hand, innocent, optimistic, venturesome, and idealistic but on the other hand, naive, crude, and unsophisticated. James and Wharton seemed never quite sure whether Europeans were, in the end, a far superior and more civilized breed. Sinclair Lewis portrayed the paradigmatic successful middle American of the 1920s as a blinkered Philistine and the quintessentially wholesome American small town as a wasteland. Novelists of twentieth-century urban life like John Farrell, Henry Roth, and Saul Bellow, writing about the children of turn-of-the-century immigrants in their ethnic ghettos, painted a decidedly mixed picture of American locales as full of pitfalls as they were of promise.

Nevertheless, even as they presented American life as it was, warts and all, America's serious novels, plays, and movies contributed to American mythology in two important ways. First, their heroes and heroines often embodied, in relatively unequivocal terms, mythic American virtues: rugged individualism, devotion to progress and modernity, and aspirations of personal advancement and mobility. Also, their story contexts usually exemplified paradigmatic American settings and themes: the frontier, the developing city, the modern workplace, the ethnic ghetto, or the mythic farm or small town. Second, like the ancient myths grounded in human frailty, the very complexity and ambivalence of their portrayals deepened, rather than undercut, their mythic resonance. By highlighting America's flaws, this literature developed a profoundly mythic paradigm: Americans seek desperately to build their new world in the land of the new beginning and to build it on the new and idealistic American principles—the American Idea and its subsidiaries—but as they do so, they often lose their way. They lose their way either because many American ideals are inherently contradictory (liberty and virtue, equality and merit, the natural and the modern, country and city) or because Americans are only human. But their attempts are nevertheless heroic; there is nobility in trying, in pursuing the vision and the ideals, even if they must often be betrayed.

These powerful ideas anticipate the angry charges of hypocrisy that have been leveled against the American belief system by the young and the disillusioned since the 1960s, poisoning the national dialogue, including its dialogue about assimilation. The best works of America's mythology supply an answer to those who claim that traditional American aspirations are all a fraud. American aspirations are not a fraud, but in an imperfect world they can only be imperfectly realized, and it is far better to dedicate oneself and one's society to an ideal, even if it cannot be achieved, than to accept an imperfect world cynically and fatalistically. Without their myths, Americans can never remain a truly unified people, no matter how common their consumer culture. Without their continued mutual dedication to a unified national mission and a unified national self-image, Americans will not only be unable to bring the newest immigrants into the national fold, they will no longer be able to get along with each other.

7

Americans United by the Protestant Ethic

Freshly wrested from the frontier wilderness, the American land was a living reminder of the relation between work and survival; and as America grew in wealth it was a reminder also of the relation of work to its immediate rewards.

And to ultimate rewards also, for the religious spirit of America's Protestant sects reinforced the practical reasons for work by bringing God's reasons to bear as well. The American bourgeois spirit, which existed in its purest form where economic man met religious man, regarded idleness as sinful and the way of work as the good way. In the whole calendar of economic virtues . . . work was the primal source of all the others.

Max Lerner, 1957[1]

Nothing has so united immigrants and natives in America over the years as the world of work and the work ethic. It is work, after all, that has brought immigrants and natives together in the first place. Most of the 87 million immigrants who have entered the United States since 1820 have come seeking economic opportunity, which, of course, has meant different things to different immigrants. For those without jobs, like the Irish after they were pushed off their ancient homesteads by expropriation and famine, the United States has offered the opportunity to work; for those who were used to working for practically nothing, like the Chinese laborers who helped build the American railway system, the opportunity to earn decent pay; for those stuck in the lowest rungs of their occupations, like skilled German artisans, the opportunity of career mobility; for those with an entrepreneurial spirit, like the Italians, Jews, and Scandinavians, the opportunity to own their own businesses or farms. Over the long term, the immigrants' bet on America's economic opportunity paid off. By 1869, the United States had achieved the highest per capita income and gross economic product in the world and has remained in first place ever since.[2] America overtook every advanced European country to become the world's richest nation, even though it drew most of its workers from among the ranks of Europe's poorest classes.

Balancing the immigrants' quest for economic betterment and making it possible has been native Americans' pursuit of economic growth. Immigrants have offered a way of rapidly expanding the workforce; they have contributed new or formerly scarce skills; and, most important, they have always been willing to work very hard— much harder than most natives. In referring to the great wave of nineteenth-century immigrants, social commentator Max Lerner observed:

> Whatever one may say of the importance of America's natural resources, the richest resource was manpower: without the immigrants America could not have found quickly enough the manpower to build the railroads, mine the coal, man the open-hearth steel furnaces and run the machines. Moreover, while most of the immigrants were pushed into the unskilled, backbreaking jobs, enough of them were skilled . . . so that the Great Migration was not only one of people but of talents, skills, and cultural traditions.[3]

Through most of America's history, this symbiotic relationship between immigrants and natives, centered on work, became one of the cornerstones of assimilation, one of the three clauses of the assimilation contract. This linkage of assimilation and the work ethic is not automatic or inevitable; it is a uniquely American phenomenon. There is plenty of evidence around the world that mere mutuality of economic interest between natives and immigrants does not necessarily advance assimilation. On the contrary, in most countries that have admitted a large number of immigrants—even when the arrangement has been economically advantageous—interactions of immigrants and natives in the labor market have generated bitter rivalry, retarded assimilation, and promoted interethnic conflict. Whether one looks at the historical experience of immigrants like the East Indians in Africa, the Chinese in Southeast Asia, the Palestinians in the Persian Gulf, or the Turks in northern Europe, the phenomenon of immigrants and natives mixing in the workplace has rarely made immigrants eager to seek assimilation or encouraged natives to let it happen.

Only in America, then, have immigrants gained acceptance and been encouraged to assimilate because of, rather than in spite of, their dedication to the work ethic. Indeed, the reason that the work ethic has been so deeply embedded in America's assimilation contract is because it is even more deeply embedded in America's broader social contract. An old aphorism of the French, in comparing themselves with Americans, has it that "the French work so they may live; Americans live so they may work." True enough, America *is* about work, about economic advancement for individuals, and about economic growth for the larger society. And it was always so. Throughout its history, America has been the country most enthusiastic about unbridled capitalism, not because the market made people rich, but because it (theoretically) encouraged people to work hard and rewarded them for doing so. In 1837 the Viennese immigrant Francis Grund observed:

> There is probably no people on earth with whom business constitutes pleasure, and industry amusement, in an equal degree with the inhabitants of the United States of America. Active occupation is not only the principal source of their happiness, and the foundation of their national greatness, but they are absolutely wretched without it. . . . Business is the very soul of an American: he pursues it, not as a means of procuring for himself and his family the necessary comforts of life, but as the fountain of all human

felicity. . . . It is as if all America were but one gigantic workshop, over the entrance of which there is the blazing inscription, "*No admission here, except on business.*"[4]

The secular appeal of the work ethic for Americans can be traced to its powerful religious endorsement. In the sixteenth century, Calvinism, the religion of the rising Protestant merchant class of post-Reformation Europe, considered personal economic success a sign of God's grace. According to the Calvinist doctrine of predestination, prosperity (unblemished by other sins) was a sure sign that a person was a member of the elect, entitled to pass through the gates of Heaven. To prosper, one had to succeed in work. To succeed in work, one had to labor long and hard and save the fruits of one's labor. As the sociologist Daniel Rodgers characterized it: "At the heart of Protestantism's revaluation of work was the doctrine of the calling, the faith that God had called everyone to some productive vocation, to toil there for the common good and His greater glory."[5] The sociologist Max Weber, coining one of social science's most famous concepts, called this belief system the Protestant ethic.[6] (He should have called it the Calvinist ethic because it did not really apply to Lutherans or Anglicans.) Most early Protestant settlers of New England (including the Pilgrims and the Puritans) were Calvinists, as were a majority of those who later settled along the rest of the eastern seaboard north of Virginia. By independence, their religious values had become the secular values of most newly liberated Americans, regardless of religion. And by the end of the era of mass immigration, a century and a half later, the Protestant ethic had come to be as much the operative ideology of immigrant Catholics and Jews as of native Protestants. According to Rodgers: "Most emigrants, finally, brought with them not only ambition but some measure of faith in toil itself. [Their] work ideals lacked the sharp, driving edge of the American work ethic, but [they also accepted] the health-giving and useful powers of labor."[7]

The Protestant ethic has served America well. The behaviors it encouraged—diligence in work, thrift, self-discipline, and ingenuity—were ideally suited to the economically and geographically expanding United States of the nineteenth century, and they are still of great economic and social benefit today. The Protestant ethic was, of course, equally relevant to an economically expanding and modernizing Europe, but in Europe the dead hand of history and deeply entrenched antithetical traditions—hereditary aristocracies, a hostile Catholic clergy, and a semifeudal peasantry—fought the Protestant ethic and the capitalism it fostered every inch of the way. In the United States, the Land of the New Beginning, these ancient anticapitalist traditions had never gained a foothold. Among America's manifold novelties, it was the one country in the world where the Protestant ethic could prevail unchecked.

The Protestant ethic was not just good for America, it was extremely good for immigrants and their descendants. If the American Idea provided the philosophical rationale for admitting immigrants, the Protestant ethic provided the economic rationale. Americans may have always subscribed, in the abstract, to Jefferson's assertion that "all men are created equal," but an abstract commitment to human equality was not enough to promote America's unusually high level of social harmony and national unity; it needed confirmation in the concrete world of human achievement.

If Americans had not worshipped for so long at the altar of economic growth, not nearly so many immigrants would have been welcomed. As Oscar Handlin noted: "The unrestrained flow of people across the Atlantic, rising with demand during prosperity . . . relieved every American entrepreneur of concern about this element [labor] in the productive system."[8] Then, by elevating the work ethic to primacy in the catalog of personal virtue and by making work-based success the hallmark of personal status, the Protestant ethic created a social playing field in American society on which immigrants could not only join in the game but could often win. Since people in any society will socialize with, and accept as worthy fellow citizens, only those they respect, economic success became the basis of this respect. The Protestant ethic helped make the United States a country in which respect could not be earned by mere membership in a hereditary class, by mere enrollment in a particular religion, or even by mere descent from a particular nationality. But it could be earned by work—minimally by demonstrating extraordinary diligence, substantially by displaying exceptional talent and competence, and unquestioningly by amassing a great fortune. This is a wonderful basis for assimilation because it is the only thing immigrants—or disadvantaged natives for that matter—can actually do something about.

Because of the Protestant ethic, immigrants to America, unlike their counterparts in just about every other country of the world, entered a new society that would judge them favorably for the very traits in which they could excel. Whereas the native workers of other societies usually hated immigrants for setting higher standards of diligence or competence, American workers (often grudgingly) admired them for it. Whereas the artisans of other societies often hated immigrants for their skills, American artisans admitted them to their guilds. Whereas the employers of other societies discouraged immigrants from showing initiative, American bosses gave them raises and promotions. Most tellingly, whereas the upper classes in other countries permanently barred upstart immigrant nouveau riche from crashing the gates of "society," American social arbiters (after a discreet interval) welcomed them. The reason: In America money became the primary criterion of social acceptability, ranking well ahead of such traditional Old-World criteria as education, breeding, or "superior" hereditary bloodlines.

As a key social criterion, money has, from the beginning, distinguished Americans from Europeans. Alexis de Tocqueville was the first of a long line of Europeans who have accused Americans of being too materialistic, too obsessed with making money, too quick to venerate those who made a great deal of money, and too ready to equate virtue and success with high income and great wealth. Yet, what Europeans have seen as one of America's great defects may actually be one of its great virtues. In the end, money is a far more democratic basis for respect and social status than is any other standard. Immigrants and upwardly mobile natives can obtain money much more readily than they can any of the traditional, subjective, and ethnically biased criteria that would be its most likely alternatives. Education takes great time and effort. Breeding takes generations. An acceptable ethnicity cannot be attained at all. And although Americans undoubtedly have been—and continue to be—materialistic, their respect for wealthy people has not really been driven by materialism, but by their search for a simple measure of a person's fulfillment of the Protestant ethic. Henry Grunwald, a former editor of *Time* magazine (himself an immigrant), observed, "In one sense the faith in money is pure: it need not, as it does in so many older societies, apologize for its existence. Money is what it is—good in its own right, a sign of success, if perhaps no longer of divine grace."[9]

The real magic of the Protestant ethic in the United States is not that it has provided an opportunity or an incentive for immigrants to succeed by working hard. That can happen anywhere, and does. The real magic is that it has led members of the host society to admire immigrants, rather than despise them, when they have succeeded by working hard. Well before the era of mass immigration had ended, the immigrant in America was not only accepted—and assimilated—as an exemplar of American virtues, but he was seen as embodying the promise of America. Americans loved the notion of immigrants "making it" and becoming hugely successful; it was the ultimate proof of America's superiority. According to Lerner:

> The immigrant's obsession with rising living standards was something he gave to American life as well as something he took from it. He was a man in a hurry, not only to make money but to show he had made it, not only to sow the crop of his labor and ingenuity but to reap the harvest of his success. The stories of the "self-made man" that caught the American imagination were in many cases the Horatio Alger rags-to-riches stories of immigrant boys who rose to the top of the heap. . . . He was full of a sense of promise and possibility which renewed the pioneer spark.[10]

The Protestant ethic also has its downside, however, one that has affected immigrants as well as natives. A place where people are judged and rewarded by their success and where success is grounded in work is inevitably a place with a great deal of income and status inequality. People vary enormously in their natural intelligence and talent; in their physical strength and muscular coordination; in their stamina and endurance of hard work; in their charm, ambition, and especially in their luck; and, of course, in how they relate to the swings of national business cycles. If the good news of

America is that anybody can get ahead, the bad news is that anybody can fail. This situation creates a real dilemma for a country that so fervently cherishes equality of status, a country where "all men are created equal."

During most of American history, much of the hard edge of the Protestant ethic has been blunted by the country's high rate of economic growth. From 1820 to the present, the per capita gross product of the United States has grown at an average rate of over 20 percent a decade.[11] The rising tide of a high-growth economy usually raised all workers' boats, and, switching metaphors, a growing economic pie usually offered larger slices even to those who were entitled to the smallest shares. Nevertheless, the normal workings of any national economy inevitably creates a class of economic losers, and America's has been no exception. The class of economic losers may be of a tolerable size during good times, but it can grow intolerably large during the inevitable "panics," recessions, and depressions, especially when the Protestant ethic mixes with capitalism to generate the widest possible income disparities between winners and losers. (A recent international study documented that the United States today has the highest level of income inequality among the seventeen most industrialized Western nations.)[12] At the same time, the harsh logic of the Protestant ethic denies the economy's losers even the kind of sympathy they might be entitled to elsewhere because it ascribes their ill fortune not to bad luck or a bad system, but to divine disfavor or an absence of diligence.

Nevertheless, most American workers have accepted the existence of economic inequality and periodic economic hardship with surprising equanimity. This is one of the most striking things that has set the United States apart from other highly industrialized nations, especially during the era of rapid industrialization. American workers' equanimity has been rooted in their near universal internalization of the Protestant ethic and their faith in America's intrinsic economic openness and equality of opportunity. The sociologist Seymour Martin Lipset pointed out:

Because equality and achievement have been linked throughout America's development as a nation, the concept of equality has a special character. . . . the American concept of equality, which focuses on opportunity and the quality of social relations, does not demand equality of income. The focus on the ideology of equal opportunity for each individual has made Americans relatively insensitive to gross inequalities of income and wealth in their country.[13]

The Protestant ethic's double-edged sword has had a profound impact on immigrants' relations with other Americans in several ways. As I just mentioned, in times of prosperity (which has prevailed through most of American history), the Protestant ethic has greatly speeded immigrants' assimilation and given them a valued place in the American economy and an honored status in American society. In contrast, during economic downturns or in places where a large number of immigrants have competed for work with native Americans, it has not always protected them from the envy and loathing of their unsuccessful native American competitors in the labor market. American workers may not have blamed the economic system for their misfortune, but they have not shied from blaming someone other than themselves, immigrants being the most appealing scapegoats. Just about every one of America's intermittent bouts of nativism—including the current one—has been fueled by the disappointments of American workers who have looked to find a cause for their economic misery. This was as true 150 years ago when "native" workers (the children of earlier immigrants) attacked the newly arrived Irish under the banner of the Know-Nothing Party for taking their jobs, as it is today in the high-unemployment area of southern California, where economically insecure "neonativist" voters (including many recent Hispanic and Asian immigrants) recently endorsed the most draconian sanctions against the newest immigrant workers.[14]

Although immigrants may have been the Protestant ethic's greatest beneficiaries, the Protestant ethic's disappointments often made them the most conspicuous institutional antagonists of America's corporate employers and of free-market capitalism in general. From the earliest days of industrialization, immigrants or their children were usually the most aggressive organizers and members of labor unions. As early as the 1860s, Irish workers organized themselves for better pay and working conditions, and after World War I, the Irish were joined by the Jews, with strong reinforcement from Italians and eastern Europeans, in establishing a full-fledged American labor movement. Nevertheless, many times immigrants found themselves on opposite sides of labor issues. Older immigrants like the Irish looked to unions not only to protect their interests against the harsh demands of their employers, but to shield them from the labor competition of newer immigrants, who were often—especially when they were newly arrived—employed as scabs.

Immigrants were also America's only standard-bearers of socialism, most broadly defined as a philosophy that would distribute societal rewards on the basis of criteria unrelated to the work ethic (need, social benefit, compassion, and so forth). After the turn of the century and through World War II, it was mainly immigrants and the children of immigrants who made up the backbone of the most radical political parties, including the Communist Party. Here too, immigrants were divided, with radical politics appealing primarily to the more educated members of the Jewish and Irish working class (or their children) and shunned by most other Irish, Italian, and non-Jewish eastern European workers. Nicola Sacco and Bartolomeo Vanzetti, two avowedly anarchist Italian immigrant laborers who became a left-wing cause célèbre after they were executed for murder in 1927 (perhaps unjustly, because of their radical political beliefs), were not typical of the Italian working class. As an alternative to radical politics, in the teeming cities of the late nineteenth and early twentieth centuries, immigrants practiced a brand of municipal socialism, earning social and employment benefits by cooperating with the political machines of cities. And since the New Deal, immigrants—and the children and grandchildren of immigrants—have been the most steadfast supporters of the Protestant ethic's persistent nemesis, the welfare state. New York City, throughout its history America's most populous bastion of immigrants, has always been the place most committed to socialist and welfare-state ideology.[15]

The apparent paradox of the Protestant ethic's greatest beneficiaries assaulting its institutional foundations is not surprising, given the historical context. Almost all immigrants arrived in the United

States dirt poor. Although many prospered and some even achieved great wealth, many did not. They worked in America's new factories, where labor unions and radical politics were the by-products of mass industrialization and the factory system. The factories and sweatshops of the late nineteenth and early twentieth centuries, with their miserable working conditions and long hours, could try the patience of the most dedicated adherents of the Protestant ethic. Under such circumstances, it is no wonder that immigrant workers found attractive those organizations and parties dedicated to improving their working conditions, increasing their pay, and giving them a social insurance safety net. In this regard, they were not so different from their working-class counterparts in Europe. In fact, they often had firsthand experience of European working-class movements.[16]

But in the end, American immigrants behaved differently from their European peers (and relatives), and this difference can be traced to the enduring hold of the Protestant ethic on the American imagination. As members of the American working class, immigrants never embraced socialism fully, and they didn't embrace it for long. Even at their most militant, they were narrowly intent on improving their working conditions and their pay and, when it came to governmental programs, advocating income support only during old age and spells of unemployment. American immigrants usually vociferously rejected appeals to labor-management or interclass warfare. Most rejected any notions of working-class solidarity and shunned the explicitly socialist parties. Norman Thomas's American Socialist Party and the Communist Party never enrolled more than a tiny fraction of the electorate—even in New York City—and the highest elective office any Socialist or Communist ever attained was congressman. And as soon as immigrants and their children achieved a modicum of personal economic security or entered the world of white-collar work, they abandoned any socialist notions or organizations altogether. The Democratic Party, the main repository of America's residual and denatured brand of socialism since the turn of the century, has always adamantly repudiated the socialist label. Today it repudiates even its weak euphemistic surrogate, "liberal." Even so, the last remaining descendants of the European immigrant working class have been deserting the Democratic Party. American labor union membership, at 11 percent of the workforce in the private sector, is not only lower than that of any other industrialized country, it is lower than it has ever been in this century. Only the Jews, by far the most successful of all the immigrants, still cling to vestiges of the socialist impulse—not to help themselves, but to help their lower-income successors—and still vote Democratic. Even so, most Jews today offer at least, in the words of neoconservative editor Irving Kristol, "two cheers for capitalism."[17]

Does this mean that the Protestant ethic reigns triumphant? Maybe not. On the one hand, Americans today remain the hardest-working people in the West. Compared to the workers of other major industrial countries, American workers have the shortest vacations, the least number of holidays, and the longest workweek and spend more years in the workforce—all of which is truer of those at the well-paid top of the market than of those at the hard-pressed bottom. The recent study by the social psychologists Adrian Furnham, Michael Bond, and Patrick Heaven, which compared beliefs in the work ethic in thirteen countries, found that American workers had by far the greatest attachment to work-ethic values.[18] Another recent survey of Americans' and Canadians' attitudes toward the work ethic found that Americans have a significantly greater commitment to work and less attachment to leisure than do Canadians.[19] In his book, *The New American Poverty*, liberal author Michael Harrington observed ruefully: "Most American working people will do almost anything to avoid welfare. They believe with a deep passion in the Protestant work ethic."[20]

Yet many Americans also express ambivalence about the Protestant ethic, especially as it may apply to the young, the poor, and the unemployed. The situation seems to be that even though they are challenged by corrosive contemporary mores and the temptations of a consumer society, most Americans still live by the Protestant ethic (or at least its work-ethic core) but are ashamed to admit it and reluctant to instill it in those who don't. Since the 1960s, this orientation has been especially true of America's opinion leaders. America's "best and brightest"—intellectuals, public officials, university administrators, heads of foundations and philanthropies, mainstream clergy, and media commentators—have either avoided discussing the Protestant ethic or denounced its application to contemporary Americans (specifically the poor) when others have brought it up. The term itself is seen as suspect, except when spoken in derision, because it implies foisting culturally suspect "middle-class" values on Americans in an era when they are supposed to be free to live by any values they choose. It also suggests a callous "social Darwinism" that would doom individuals of limited ability or training to poverty, perhaps even starvation, if they refused to apply themselves. Explicitly, when they argue with "cultural conservatives," and implicitly, when they make policy, members of the opinion elite give the Protestant ethic little credit for the successes of the successful and categorically reject it as an antidote for the failures of the unsuccessful. The theologian Dennis McCann's critique of organized Protestantism's disavowal of the Protestant ethic applies equally to the rest of the opinion elite:

> When was the last time you heard about the Protestant work ethic in church? Its theological affirmation of our worldly vocations these days tends to get dismissed as "old hat." . . . The work ethic is regarded as more a part of the problem than part of the solution. The Protestant work ethic thus is but the most pernicious expression of the Western will toward economic domination.[21]

But the issue is not just theoretical. The best educated and most highly respected Americans have allowed their contempt for the Protestant ethic to ripple through the institutions they influence or control, the very institutions that America counted on in the past to instill its values. These contradictory trends have important implications for the assimilation of the country's most recent immigrants—members of what economist Thomas Muller called "the fourth wave."[22] These new immigrants' exemplary embrace of the traditional values of the Protestant ethic should be a major factor in speeding their assimilation and integration in American society, just as it was for generations of their immigrant predecessors. But Americans' current diffidence in openly promoting the Protestant ethic runs the risk of sending the immigrants a contradictory message and, far more seriously, driving a wedge between immigrants and the native American poor.

This anti–Protestant ethic orthodoxy remained largely unchallenged until the most recent cohort of immigrants grew so large and its members' success so conspicuous that they could not be ignored. Hail a taxi in New York, Washington, or Los Angeles, and the odds are ten to one that the driver will be an immigrant, and usually one who hasn't been in the country very long and who has only a limited command of English (and of the local geography). That immigrants would want to drive cabs doesn't seem very strange on the face of it, since driving a cab is an occupation that requires minimal training, is in high demand, and pays reasonably well. What is strange is that so few native workers are driving cabs. The cities awash in immigrant cabdrivers are the same places that have armies of unemployed young men, most of them native born and poor. Cab driving would seem to be an ideal occupation for energetic people with limited skills and a lot of time on their hands. The taxi industry is only one small example of a phenomenon that is becoming increasingly characteristic of American big-city labor markets: In places where generations of experts on urban affairs and advocates of the poor have said there are no jobs for the unskilled and poorly educated, immigrants seem to be working, challenging the conventional wisdom that the economy of the modern American metropolis has no room at the bottom.

That immigrants are working in the inhospitable economic jungles of large American cities while native Americans languish in idleness and dependence on welfare is a huge embarrassment for America's opinion and policy leadership; it reproaches them for their loss of faith in the Protestant ethic. They had convinced themselves and many other Americans that in a "high-tech," "information age," "postindustrial" economy, the Protestant ethic no longer had any relevance, that with the decline of manufacturing, unskilled workers in an urban service economy were doomed to suffer long bouts of "structural" unemployment. Former New York City budget director Edward Hamilton's remarks at a 1974 symposium of leading public officials and scholars at the Lyndon B. Johnson School of Public Affairs, University of Texas, aptly summarizes the prevailing view:

[C]ities are centers for jobs for which most of their citizens cannot qualify. The influx of people of limited education creates a labor force weighted . . . toward low-skilled entry-level jobs. Meanwhile [cities have lost] the labor-intensive manufacturing enterprises which have been the traditional source of such jobs. . . . We may be faced with incontrovertible evidence of structural unemployment, that is, a national inability to absorb all of the willing labor force in what the market determines to be "gainful" employment.[23]

In a similar vein, a recent sociology text blamed poverty in cities on the lack of economic opportunity because "blue-collar industries which have traditionally provided jobs to the working class and the poor of the inner-city, have moved out of the inner cities in record numbers."[24] According to this diagnosis, the only remedy for poor, often minority, city dwellers who are facing such structural unemployment lays in programs of job training, day care, and "work-readiness," and until such programs are implemented and effective, the stopgap has to be welfare. Imagine, then, the blow to this thesis by the fact that millions of immigrants from Latin America, Asia, and the Caribbean—dirt poor, uneducated, unproficient in English, maybe even illiterate—have found work and gotten ahead.

How can we account for the divergent employment prospects of immigrants and native workers in cities? It cannot be the structure of the urban economy because immigrants are proving there are jobs to be had in the service sector or in such manufacturing as remains in cities. It cannot be racial discrimination because many of the new immigrants who are finding jobs are blacks or other racial minorities. (According to a New York City analysis of 1990 census data, 82 percent of foreign-born black men were working or looking for work compared to 68 percent of the native born, and 83 percent of foreign-born Hispanic men were in the labor market compared to 69 percent of the native born.)[25] It cannot be skills and education because studies by the economist George Borjas and others have documented that most new immigrants are less skilled and educated than are natives.[26] It cannot be proficiency in English because most new immigrants speak English poorly.

What really distinguishes immigrants from natives in the urban labor market is immigrants' willingness to work—what economists call their "labor force participation rates." By willingness to work, I mean not a vague predisposition to work at a "good" job at "good" pay, but a gritty determination to work under almost any circumstances—to work long hours at rock-bottom wages in jobs that are physically strenuous, dirty, and even hazardous. Many unskilled American-born workers, regardless of race or ethnicity, have been conditioned by unions, the specifications of governmental job programs or contracts, an awareness of the higher standards that prevail in many occupations, and perhaps by the alternatives of welfare or crime to disdain "dead-end" jobs, hard work, extended workdays, and low pay. Economic studies have long shown that unskilled men in inner cities reject work that pays less than a hoped-for, but economically unrealistic, "reservation wage."[27] Immigrants, on the other hand, have been conditioned by the harsh and low-wage labor markets of the countries they come from to embrace uncomplainingly jobs that are in the basement of the American economy. Simply put, in the urban economy where both immigrants and the poorest native Americans share a labor market, immigrants have demonstrated that the Protestant ethic still pays off.

Perversely, many Americans today are not prepared to praise the immigrants for their dedication and success (and, incidentally, the urban economy for its newfound resilience); instead, they are apt to condemn them and those who employ them. Poor native Americans at the bottom of the American labor market are, perhaps understandably, resentful of the immigrants' success. But the sternest criticism of hardworking immigrants comes from academics, public officials, institutional leaders, and shapers of public opinion. Academic analysts discount the immigrants' success as being grounded in unfair advantages—high savings rates, sharing savings with fellow ethnics, and finding work though ethnic networks (as if natives couldn't do the same).[28] The most widespread critique faults immigrants for accepting poor working conditions and substandard pay and making their children work.[29] Economists refer disparagingly to the low-wage and unappealing jobs that immigrants take as a "secondary" labor market—as opposed to the good jobs at good pay which make up the "primary" labor market—barely acknowledging that without it the day-to-day needs of America's cities and farms could not be met. (Actually, the boundary between primary and secondary labor markets is decidedly fuzzy, and not all secondary labor market jobs are bad or even poorly paid. It includes not only apparel-manufacturing sweatshops, frenetic restaurant kitchens, and varieties of household drudgery, but a lot of self-employment in retail and service enterprises.) Unions are bitterly opposed to the kinds of jobs; working conditions; and, most adamantly, the pay that immigrants are willing to accept. Politicians and public officials indignantly assert that no Americans should take "dead-end" jobs or work under "Third World" conditions. And ordinary Americans, while happy to reap the fruits of the secondary labor market, from inexpensive nannies and housekeepers to affordable gardeners, will reflexively condemn "exploitation." The bottom line seems to be: Americans will tolerate immigrants working hard, but refuse to give them much credit for it and are highly reluctant to make native Americans follow their example.

That reluctance might sensibly be overcome if Americans understood how the so-called secondary labor market has actually functioned for immigrants and when they realistically considered the work options available to unskilled natives. It turns out that in spite of the rigors of the secondary sector, immigrants—especially legal ones—are doing a lot better than one might expect and a lot better than unemployed Americans. The grueling working conditions at the bottom of the American (usually urban) labor market represent a transitional phase for most immigrants. Immigrant families have fashioned a successful strategy for upward economic mobility. All family members who can work do so, and they put in long hours (even low wages mount up when multiplied by enough hours). Living conditions are spartan and cheap. Money is saved. Investments are made in education and training for the younger family members, in business opportunities (buying a cab or opening a newsstand, gas station, or restaurant) for the older ones. After spending a decade or so in the United States, the average immigrant household has an income rivaling that of a typical American family. A widely cited study by economist Barry Chiswick found that, when education, age, and other characteristics are held constant, immigrant men who begin their American work history earning 15 percent less than native Americans catch up with them in about fourteen years and earn 10 percent more after thirty years. [30]

While immigrant families painfully climb the lower rungs of the secondary sector's ladder of upward mobility, native workers who hold out for employment on acceptable terms languish in idleness or, what is more likely, succumb to the self-destructive temptations of the inner city: unwed motherhood, criminal activity, and drugs. The lessons to be learned from these disparate outcomes are compelling. First, when the national economy is not in a deep recession, anyone who is determined to work should be able to find a job, even in the center of a typical large city. Second, there are really no dead-end jobs. Even the most menial, lowest-wage jobs develop necessary work skills and habits; many actually have career ladders (even burger-flipping can lead to a supervisory job and perhaps the ownership of a franchise); all work promotes upward economic mobility. Third, there is an intimate connection between "family values" and economic success.

As remarkable as the differences in work profiles between immigrants and natives are the differences in family profiles. Foreign-born men and women, regardless of race or ethnicity, are much more likely to be members of traditional families. Thus, immigrant men and women, including blacks and Hispanics, who are parents are far more likely to be married than are natives of the same ethnic groups, and immigrant children are far less likely than those with American parents to be raised in female-headed families or to be born out of wedlock. In New York, for example, a black or Hispanic child whose parents are American is twice as likely as a child of black or Hispanic immigrants to live only with his or her mother, and a white child with American parents is ten times as likely to do so as one born to immigrants. Some immigrant groups display an unusually strong attachment to family values; for example, female-headed families are practically unknown among Asians.

The higher rates of labor participation and traditional family structure to be found among immigrants are inextricably related. Immigrant men are determined to work, even under unfavorable conditions, because they must support their families. Immigrant women expect their men to work and usually work as well. The children see all the adults around them—parents, uncles, cousins, older siblings—working and thus are deeply imbued with working role models at an early age. As soon as they are old enough, they go to work, too. A strong work ethic and strong family structures reinforce each other. Family responsibilities make people work. Families with many working members are successful economic units that are much more likely to stay together.

Among native-born Americans living in the poor neighborhoods of the inner city, on the other hand, an entirely different relationship between work and family induces a vicious, negative cycle that undermines the work ethic and family values at the same time. Many women are prepared to bear children and raise them without marrying their fathers and don't expect the fathers to contribute much financial support. Given these expectations, many fathers don't feel compelled to work. The prevalence of unemployed men in the community convinces women that the men are not worth marrying and that asking for financial help is futile. Many children grow up in fatherless homes, where the role models for girls are single mothers who are dependent on their own sources of income from work or welfare and those for boys are absent or fitfully encountered fathers and other irresponsible men, most of whom are idle and many of whom commit crimes or are serving time for having committed them. (Recent data show that one-third of all African American males aged 16 to 25 are under the supervision of the criminal justice system.)[31] Attenuated but positive work and family values are imparted to girls, and negative work and family values are instilled in boys.

This vicious cycle, more than anything else, is responsible for urban poverty in America, and immigrants have demonstrated the most effective way to break the cycle. Even Louis Farrakhan, head of the Nation of Islam, recognizes this fact and, along with his noxious anti-Semitism and promotion of the worst kind of ethnic federalism, preaches that African Americans should emulate immigrants and adopt his own peculiar version of the Protestant ethic. This is also the context of Congress's recently enacted radical changes in the welfare system. Meanwhile, many liberals dismiss the possibility of restoring the values of the Protestant ethic among the poor. They oppose welfare reform's rigid work requirements and cutoff of benefits for unwed teenage mothers, arguing that these measures will doom inner-city minority and other poor households, especially their children, to certain destitution. In an unacceptably large number of cases, they say, neither women nor men will go to work when welfare is cut because there are no jobs; neither women nor men will change their sexual or family-forming behaviors because these behaviors are now an indelible feature of their culture, resistant to economic disincentives.

To counter such arguments, it may no longer be fashionable or persuasive for public officials and others who are intent on ending the cycle of urban poverty to invoke the Protestant ethic, but they can point to the immigrants' example. The successful economic and family outcomes of immigrants are built on a foundation of highly functional and responsible personal behavior, including an unconditional willingness to work. That behavior may be nothing more than a response to the stringent and unforgiving economic conditions immigrants have had to face in their native lands and in the United States, but it has been demonstrably beneficial. No one can say for certain how long it may take for welfare reform's bracing economic discipline to instill functional and responsible behavior in the dependent American-born poor people who lack it, or even whether welfare reform is the right means to instill such behavior. The immigrants demonstrate, however, that the expectation of such behavior is not entirely fanciful, that the Protestant ethic can still pay off—for them, for the poor in general, and for society.

The major point to be made here is not merely that immigrants still display the virtues of the Protestant ethic and natives do not or even that poor native Americans would do well to emulate the immigrants. It is, rather, that Americans should stop being so ambivalent about the Protestant ethic and begin to send the right messages to immigrants and poor natives alike. To immigrants, they should send their warmest congratulations for working so hard and their acknowledgment that the Protestant ethic is still one of the most effective pathways to assimilation, American style. To the native poor, they should send the message that promoting the Protestant ethic is neither "racist" nor "blaming the victim" but, rather, the most solid and time-honored basis for their own upward mobility, their own "assimilation," American style.

8

Americans United
but Living Apart

Even today, much of Chicago is a patchwork quilt of ethnic enclaves. On
the North Side, for example, driving west on Peterson Avenue from Lake
Michigan, one passes the offices of *India Weekly* and, a bit further on, of
the Seoul Travel Service, before coming to a distinctly Polish, and then a
Jewish, neighborhood. . . . A bicyclist in Chicago can easily have a multicultural experience, overhearing conversations in rapidly alternating
Spanish, German, Swedish, Greek and African-American street English, as
he crosses a series of intersections. The dividing lines may be as stark as an
expressway or as imperceptible as the beginning of a school-district zone,
but everyone who lives in each neighborhood knows where the boundaries are.

Sanford J. Ungar, 1995[1]

Assimilation, American style has never demanded that immigrants or their descendants "melt" into the general population or
that they become indistinguishable from the mass of other
Americans. Even as they assimilated, the various nationalities have
maintained their distinctive customs and cultures, their manners
and dress, and often live apart from other Americans. Not only have
immigrants settled in ethnic enclaves immediately upon their arrival

in the United States, but they have maintained those enclaves for generations. Even after their children and grandchildren have become more fully integrated into American society economically and socially and have moved out of their parents' ethnic neighborhoods, they still have not settled randomly in the cities and towns of America and they have not given up their membership in a rich variety of ethnic associations. They have created new ethnic social colonies in the outer neighborhoods and the suburbs of American cities. Even today, ethnic traditions and ethnic social networks maintain a strong hold on a large proportion of non-English-descended Americans (which happens to be the majority of all Americans) many generations beyond the arrival of their first immigrant ancestors. Indeed, most Americans, both native and foreign born—including those of English descent—give themselves ethnic identities. A 1980 survey by the National Opinion Research Center, which asked respondents their ethnic backgrounds—and specifically permitted them to choose "American only"—found that nearly 90 percent identified a specific ethnicity.[2]

Seeing so many of their countrymen hanging on to their ethnic identities and living in ethnic communities for generations has often confused Americans and led them to draw the wrong conclusions. As explained by an entire school of sociologists or described in influential popular books like Nathan Glazer and Daniel Patrick Moynihan's *Beyond the Melting Pot*[3] or attacked in the anti-immigrant polemics of nativists, this phenomenon has led many Americans mistakenly to fear that certain immigrants and certain ethnic groups were not assimilating and, indeed, that these groups could not assimilate. But that fear, grounded in the notion that assimilation requires the literal "melting" of ethnic distinctions, the obliteration of ethnic identities, is, as I argued in Chapter 3, one of the great fallacies of the immigration debate. Immigrants of America's second (Irish, German) and third (Italian, eastern European) waves unambiguously assimilated without melting, and unless contemporary American attitudes and policies stand in the way, so will the newest immigrants of the fourth wave.

Getting this notion straight is critical today, as a growing number of Americans come to view the new immigrant colonies in their midst with increasing alarm, fearful that the Mexicans, Cubans, and Dominicans; the Haitians, Jamaicans, and Nigerians; and the Chinese, Filipinos, and Vietnamese who are colonizing ever larger slices of New York, Los Angeles, Chicago, Miami, and scores of other large- and medium-sized cities will never assimilate. Americans are actually of two minds on the subject. When they read heartwarming accounts of these enclaves—the eager striving of their immigrant residents and their picturesque folkways—in journalistic stories and books, such as Sanford Ungar's *Fresh Blood*,[4] many Americans are reassured that this is just another chapter in the American Dream. But on other days, Americans—perhaps a majority—are easily convinced by neonativist works like Peter Brimelow's *Alien Nation* and grim newspaper accounts of "the dark side of the dream" that the inhabitants of the new immigrant ethnic enclaves, because of their distinctive racial characteristics, languages, and religions, will prove to be impervious to Americanization, that they are too "alien" to assimilate and are inherently "unassimilable." According to Brimelow:

> For the first time, virtually all immigrants are racially distinct "visible minorities." They come not from Europe, previously the common homeland even for the 1890–1920 immigrants about which Americans were so nervous. Instead, these new immigrants are from completely different, and arguably incompatible, cultural traditions. And, as we have seen, they are coming in such numbers that their impact on America is enormous—inevitably within the foreseeable future, they will transform it.[5]

This view is derived from a profound misunderstanding of American history and of the true dynamics of assimilation. An accurate understanding would clarify three things: First, the new immigrants are not only no more "alien" than their nineteenth- and early-twentieth-century immigrant predecessors in forming new ethnic communities, they are behaving *exactly* like them. Second, even the descendants of old immigrants maintain much more of their ethnic identities than may be readily apparent on the surface. Finally—and most important—this is all to the good. In and of itself, the maintenance of ethnic communities in no way impairs immigrants' assimilation into American life or American national unity. Rather, it advances it.

Let me make absolutely clear, however, that this is not an endorsement or validation of multiculturalist or cultural pluralist orthodoxy; it's just the opposite. The die-hard multiculturalists—the adherents to what I call ethnic federalism—are actually in total agreement with die-hard nativists on two points: that some ethnic groups simply can't assimilate and that these groups' long-term attachment to ethnic communities proves it. They only disagree on whether this situation is good or bad. The multiculturalists say "bravo." Ethnic Americans (including African Americans) must maintain their ethnic identities at all costs and for all time, and all American institutions must recognize this fact as they allocate power, privilege, and territory in proportion to each ethnic group's relative strength. The nativists, using the same nonassimilationist assumptions, say (correctly) that the United States cannot and should not tolerate ethnic federalism and conclude (incorrectly) that if ethnic federalism is the price of continued immigration, better to do away with immigration.

Both sides, however, are mistaken in their fundamental assumption. The history of the United States has demonstrated that it is the easiest thing in the world to reconcile ethnic diversity—including the maintenance of distinctive ethnic cultures—with an unshakable commitment to American unity. That is what assimilation, American style is all about. This interpretation of the function of ethnic communities was instinctively understood and institutionally supported during most of America's immigration experiment. Only in the past few decades have Americans been distracted from this understanding by a multicultural theory and ideology that takes the very adaptability and malleability of American social life—one of this country's great and unique strengths—and gives it a sinister and dysfunctional interpretation.

There are mountains of proof—historical, sociological, and empirical evidence—that the ethnic networks, ethnic organizations (including religious ones), and ethnic neighborhoods of the United States have facilitated assimilation. These networks, organizations, and neighborhoods have provided the pathways for immigrants to make an orderly and successful adjustment to American life. In addition, they have enriched American society in general by adding to the United States' dense matrix of organizations that mediate between the individual and mass society, the individual and the state. When Alexis de Toqueville wrote about the United States in the early nineteenth century, a matrix of nongovernmental associations was already flourishing, and he marveled at it, giving it much of the credit for the energy and harmony that characterized the new republic. Thus, the layer of ethnic associations added by the immigrants was built on an established American tradition and went a long way toward Americanizing the immigrants. However exotic the immigrants' burial societies, fraternal orders, churches and temples, recreational leagues, holiday observances, and political clubs may have seemed to other Americans, they have been a uniquely American affair. Such organizations simply did not exist in the immigrants' homelands; they represent a typically American response to a typically American social circumstance. The historian Roger Daniels wrote:

> The ethnic enclave, a place where the language and customs of the old country were transplanted, however inexpertly, was a typical development of most American ethnic groups wherever their numbers reached a critical mass. Though today, ahistorically, they are called ghettos and are often viewed as a bad thing, in the past these enclaves provided an important transitory phase for millions of urban immigrants. If in some instances, these enclaves survived long enough to serve as a brake on the pace of acculturation, they nevertheless provided an important way station for immigrants on the road to fuller integration into the larger streams of American life.[6]

At the heart of the ethnic community lies the ethnic urban neighborhood. The ethnic neighborhood is the place where the newest immigrants settle as soon as they arrive in the United States. It is the place where the ethnic churches, clubs, newspapers, and restaurants exist. It is the place where the immigrants' native language is spoken. It is the place where most residents are members of a dense social web of family members, friends, and acquaintances who share the same national—perhaps even village—origin, the same language, and the same religion. They are, indeed, ethnic islands in the cosmopolitan seas of American metropolitan areas, islands as often as not cheek by jowl with the ethnic islands of other groups. As a federal commission observed in 1937:

> Never before in the history of the world have great groups of people so diverse in social background been thrown together in such close contacts as in the cities of America. The typical American city, therefore does not consist of a homogeneous body of citizens, but of human beings with the most diverse cultural backgrounds, often speaking different languages, following a great variety of customs, habituated to different modes and standards of living, and sharing only in varying degrees the tastes, the beliefs, and the ideals of their native fellow city dwellers.[7]

Ethnic and immigrant communities in the United States have never been randomly or uniformly distributed across the country. At all times, immigrants clustered in only a handful of American states and particularly in certain cities of those states. In 1910 nearly half America's foreign born lived in only eight states and one-third of that cohort lived in just three: New York, New Jersey, and Pennsylvania.[8] One hundred years later the foreign born are even more concentrated. Nearly two-thirds live in just eight metropolitan areas, and the top three areas (New York, Los Angeles, and San Francisco) account for 44 percent.[9] In fact, immigration and the ethnic vestiges of immigration have always been a distinctly urban phenomenon. Immigration's paramount role in populating the United States made it the world's first predominantly urban nation, and even in a rapidly urbanizing world, America remains the most urban nation. The fate of American immigrants and the fate of American cities have always been intimately and positively related. Immigrants caused the cities of the nineteenth century to grow and prosper, and the prosperity of the cities launched the immigrants on their trajectories of upward mobility. After immigration ceased abruptly in the late 1920s, many cities began to wither and die.[10] After immigration resumed in the late 1960s, those cities that hosted the new wave of immigrants, and only those cities, revived.[11]

*　　　*　　　*

The way to understand the pattern of ethnic settlement in American cities and towns (which is where most immigrants and their descendants have always lived) is to envision a process of "diffusion." Immigrants arrive in the United States in only a few places and gradually—sometimes over generations—spread out from their ports of entry. Pour a can of red latex-based paint into a tub of blue oil-based paint (meaning that the two colors cannot blend to create a purple mix) and, at the point of contact, you will immediately see a big solid red patch surrounded by blue. After a while more and more of the red paint will break up into smaller patches that drift outward, creating islands of red in the field of blue paint. Wait even longer and the red blotches will get ever smaller and roam ever farther from their epicenter. Eventually, if someone pours a can of yellow paint (of a different, nonblendable base) into the tub, a large yellow patch will push aside the blue and the red. The yellow patch will also break up into smaller patches, just as the red paint did, that drift among the remaining patches of blue and red. But no matter how long you wait, you will see distinctive patches of color, however small. This is diffusion. As applied to immigrants and their ethnic communities, the cans of red and yellow paint are analogous to new influxes of immigrants, and the breakaway patches are analogous to breakaway colonies of immigrants and their descendants who settle ever farther from their geographic roots.

The process of diffusion begins in what many writers on immigration have called "gateway" cities. Gateway cities are the ports of entry for immigrants to the United States. Throughout American history, the gateway city *par excellence* has been New York. In the 1890s, New York (with a population of 1.9 million) admitted 37,000 immigrants a year. In the 1920s, New York (with a population of 5.8 million) took in 67,000. And in the 1980s, New York (with a population of 7.3 million) received 100,000 annually.[12] Only the national origins of the immigrants changed over the years. In the 1840s, the immigrants were mainly Irish and German, and from 1890 to 1920 they were mainly Italian and Jewish. By 1990, many were still Jewish (from the former Soviet Union), but they were joined by Dominicans, West Indians, and Chinese. Throughout its history as a gateway city, however, New York also received hundreds of thousands of immigrants from other countries throughout the world, so that the ethnic spectrum of its people is the most diverse in the world. Today, more than 28 percent of New York's population is foreign born, and a good share of the rest have foreign-born parents and grandparents.[13]

But New York is only one of America's prominent gateway cities, and it is no longer the most important one. In the nineteenth century, it shared this role with Boston, Philadelphia, Chicago, and San Francisco; in the twentieth century, it shared this role with Los Angeles, San Francisco, Miami, Chicago, Houston, Dallas, and Washington, D.C. Sixty percent of all immigrants who arrived in the United States in 1991 initially settled in the metropolitan areas of one of these cities. Metropolitan Los Angeles led the pack, its 316,000 immigrants accounting for 17 percent of all immigrants to the United States that year. Altogether, coastal southern California, from San Diego to San Francisco, received one-third of all American immigrants, and metropolitan New York by itself accounted for over 12 percent. Since the gateway cities are in gateway states and many gateway states have more than one gateway city, a handful of states receive the lion's share of all immigrants. In 1991, only six states—California, New York, Texas. Florida, Illinois, and New Jersey—accounted for *nearly 80 percent* of all new immigrants. California alone received 40 percent. Of course, the gateway states together include a substantial portion of the entire American population (40 percent), and California itself is home to 13 percent of all Americans. Nevertheless, at twice their share of the national population, the gateway states' share of all immigrants remains disproportionate.[14]

The importance of the gateway cities and states lies in the fact that their ethnic settlements survive long after the original influx of immigrants. San Francisco's Chinatown, New York's Lower East Side, Chicago's Polonia, and Boston's North End are gateway ethnic enclaves that are more than a century old and retain as much of their ethnic flavor today as when they were first settled. Some of these neighborhoods have accommodated more than one ethnic group, either simultaneously or in succession. The Lower East Side is typical. Originally settled by German and Irish immigrants, it was legendary as the home of Jews and Italians for much of its history, and today houses Puerto Ricans, Chinese who have moved in from

an overflowing Chinatown next door, and the last vestiges of its
Italian community. But for over a century and a half, it has been an
ethnic bastion and may continue in that status indefinitely. Some of
these enclaves, such as Chicago's Polonia, remain frozen in their
original ethnic cast even when their foreign-born stock is not
replenished by new immigrants.

Nor has the establishment of such tight ethnic enclaves been
limited to the familiar ethnic groups of the third wave—the Italians,
Jews, and eastern Europeans. In 1900, Chicago, with 150,000
Swedish Americans (9 percent of the city's population), had the
second largest Swedish community in the world—nearly rivaling
Stockholm.[15] The Swedes are in no way exceptional. Every second-
wave ethnic group (the Irish, Germans, and Scandinavians), as well
as French Canadians (who have immigrated to the United States in
such a continuous and imperceptible flow that they have not been
assigned by demographers to any "wave"), has clustered in ethnic
communities exactly comparable to those of later immigrant
groups.

As their populations grow, either by natural increase or new
immigration, ethnic communities spread outward from their bases
in the gateway cities in three different patterns of diffusion.
Initially, they spill over into adjacent neighborhoods whose indigenous residents they displace, in whole or in part. The Hasidic Jews
of Brooklyn's Borough Park are typical. A notably fertile group,
they have for decades been moving into adjacent Bensonhurst, displacing many of that neighborhood's deeply rooted but numerical-
ly dwindling Italian Americans. In Manhattan's Washington
Heights and the adjacent South Bronx, the Dominican community, as it expands, is displacing the Puerto Ricans, who only a few
generations ago displaced the Jewish refugees from Nazi Germany
who settled there in the 1930s and 1940s.[16]

All over New York City, as well as other American gateway
cities, the spillover diffusion of immigrant ethnic groups continually changes the spatial ecology of ethnicity. In a striking testimony
to the social resilience of American cities, most of this ethnic shifting and ethnic succession occurs naturally, voluntarily, and without
any substantial interethnic conflict. The Brooklyn Italians welcome
and make way for the religious Jews. The Puerto Ricans coexist,

more or less amiably, with new Dominicans. This generally harmonious pattern is notably contradicted only when immigrant ethnic communities—like the Koreans in South Central Los Angeles—spill over into formerly black neighborhoods, one of many instances in which African Americans remain the sad exception to America's assimilation paradigm, a subject taken up in Chapter 9.

In another pattern of diffusion, immigrants and their descendants establish new colonies in the outer neighborhoods of their cities and in the suburbs. As America's oldest immigrant gateway and the country's most ethnically diverse metropolitan area, New York offers many illustrations of this pattern. For example, New York's Chinese community, with its roots in Manhattan's Chinatown, has established a large secondary beachhead in the Queens neighborhood of Flushing. In their new location, the Chinese join the primary and secondary ethnic enclaves of many other immigrant nationalities. In fact, northern Queens, which includes the neighborhoods of Astoria, Jackson Heights, Elmhurst, Corona, Flushing, and Bayside, has now surpassed Manhattan's Lower East Side as one of the most extensive urban ethnic arenas in the United States, housing large colonies of Koreans, Indians, Pakistanis, Greeks, and Latin Americans alongside its Chinese. So many Asians now live in northern Queens that the subway line that traverses the area has been dubbed "the Orient Express."

The ethnic ecology of northern Queens is exquisitely complex and richly illustrative. At the western end is a large first-settlement enclave of Greeks, interspersed with small colonies of recent French immigrants, that has displaced the indigenous Italian community. East of there, in Jackson Heights, once a predominantly Jewish neighborhood, there are now large enclaves of South Americans and recent immigrants from the Indian subcontinent, including one of the most intensively ethnic Indian shopping streets in the United States. To the south, in Elmhurst, and the southeast, in Corona, New York's largest immigrant communities of South Americans—mainly from Colombia and Ecuador—have settled, some displacing older enclaves of Puerto Ricans and blacks. Across Flushing Meadow Park, site of the 1939 and 1964 World's Fairs, in Flushing and Bayside lies a string of neighborhoods populated increasingly by East Asians. In the western zone of this belt are first-settlement Korean neighborhoods and, as was indicated, secondary Chinese ones. To the east, near the border with suburban Long Island, are secondary enclaves of Indians, Koreans, and Chinese. Throughout this ethnic band, the new Asian settlers are displacing, as well as living side-by-side with, the Irish, Jewish, and Italian descendants of earlier immigrants.[17]

Ethnic diffusion by satellite colonization is not limited to city districts. Every metropolitan area boasts suburban neighborhoods, both among post–World War II subdivisions and in older established towns, where new ethnic colonies have taken root. Again, the ethnically rich and diverse New York region offers ample illustrations. Its balkanized map of suburban jurisdictions corresponds to an equally balkanized map of ethnic jurisdictions. Around the tristate suburban ring, each suburb has a distinctive ethnic cast, or in the case of the larger suburbs, several distinctive ethnic casts. Northwestern Nassau County on Long Island is typical. Great Neck, right across the New York City line, is predominantly Jewish, and recognizably so. Replete with a large and diverse array of synagogues, Kosher food markets, and other markers of its ethnic identity, Great Neck is home to a number of Jewish subcommunities, ranging from older settlements of highly acculturated American-born Jews to newly established colonies of recent Iranian, South African, and Israeli immigrants (it also has a growing population of Koreans and Chinese, extensions of their settlements in eastern Queens). Manhasset, right next door, is a community dominated by second- and third-generation Irish Catholics. South of Manhasset is a large enclave of second-settlement Koreans and other Asians. Farther to the south, in Mineola, there is a large community of recent Portuguese immigrants. Port Washington, just north of Manhasset, boasts a variety of ethnic subcommunities: Italian, Jewish, Central American, Polish, Irish, and WASP. And so it goes: Not only throughout Long Island, but also in Westchester County to the north and suburban New Jersey to the west, hardly a suburban community is free of one or several readily discernible ethnic identities.[18]

Suburban ethnic enclaves are not just a New York regional phenomenon. My doctoral research on metropolitan residential patterns, completed in 1968, looked at ethnic settlement patterns in five midsize American metropolitan regions: Buffalo, Indianapolis, Milwaukee, Kansas City, and Spokane. Tracking the residential settlements of blacks, Jews, Italians, Germans, and Swedes in each region over three decennial census periods, I found not only, as expected, that every one of these groups maintained ethnic enclaves in the inner city, but that each had also established new ethnic colonies in the suburbs. With each passing decade, these suburban ethnic enclaves drifted farther out. But the most interesting finding was that even the most acculturated groups, the old-line ethnics, such as the Swedes and the Germans, maintained distinctive ethnic communities—in the suburbs and the cities—generations after their ancestors had come to the United States. And they maintained them, according to this study, not just in highly ethnicized gateway regions, but in the heart of middle America.[19]

Nevertheless, not all ethnic enclaves are alike. Two major factors differentiate the ethnic ecology of New York's suburbs (and those of other cities) from the older ethnic bastions of the cities. First, most residents in these places are second- and later-generation descendants of immigrants who speak accent-free English and therefore mask the underlying ethnic character of their communities. Second, in the suburbs they live at a lower "ethnic density." Ethnic density refers to the neighborhood's degree of internal ethnic homogeneity. The inner-city ethnic enclaves are typically characterized by high levels of ethnic density, meaning that on a typical street, all homes are occupied by members of the same ethnic group. In a suburb of low ethnic density, on the other hand, the subject ethnic group typically lives interspersed among members of other ethnic groups or among Americans who are so acculturated that they claim no ready ethnic identity.[20] Massapequa, Long Island, is not only a typical example of suburban ethnic diffusion, dominated by large colonies of second- and third-generation Jewish Americans and Italian Americans, but its low-level ethnic density has resulted in a random mix of the two dominant groups' households throughout the community. In recognition of its dual ethnicity, Massapequa's residents jokingly refer to their town as "Matzoh-Pizza."[21] Over time, the dynamics of diffusion reduce the ethnic density of all ethnic groups unless they are replenished by a large stock of new immigrants. Eventually, the ethnic density of some groups may fall to the point of near invisibility. Yet, the persistence of identifiable Irish, German, and Scandinavian American suburbs a century and a half after their residents' ancestors came to the United States testifies to the durability of ethnic residential communities, however much they are diluted.

Ethnic diffusion is not limited to the spread of immigrants within metropolitan areas. Sooner or later, mainly in response to diverse and scattered economic opportunities, immigrants or their descendants move to other cities and metropolitan areas. Sometimes they do so shortly after they settle in the United States, as is evident in small colonies of newly arrived immigrants that establish enclaves in small cities and towns some distance from the gateway cities. More typically, this type of diffusion occurs when second- and later-generation descendants of immigrants leave their gateway metropolitan homes, setting out after jobs, schools, or more congenial life-styles wherever in the United States they are to be found. Even under this pattern of ethnic diffusion, people will often seek out ethnic enclaves in their new cities or metropolitan areas that correspond to the ones they left behind.

Living apart in distinct ethnic enclaves is not the only way in which Americans demonstrate that they can maintain some measure of their original ethnic identities while they assimilate to a common American one. Although the United States has, since independence, offered its people, both native and immigrant, greater educational and economic opportunities than any other country in the world—even compared to its economically advanced peers in Europe and Asia—this opportunity has not precluded the persistence of ethnic specialization by industry and occupation. Regardless of their educational attainment and their economic milieu, neither recent nor old-line ethnics are randomly represented in the American array of jobs or enterprises. As economists put it, there are clearly discernible "ethnic niches" in the workplace.[22]

Among recent immigrants, patterns of occupational and industrial specialization are readily apparent and fairly clear-cut: Korean greengrocers and dry cleaners, East Indian newsstand vendors and gas station operators, Hasidic Jewish jewelers, Greek proprietors of luncheonettes and diners, Italian barbers and hair dressers, Chinese restaurant and laundry workers, Portuguese painters, West Indian nurses, and so forth.

But even generations after their immigrant ancestors came to the United States, many ethnic Americans continue to specialize in certain kinds of work. With full awareness of the pitfalls of over-generalization and ethnic stereotyping, it can be documented that members of many ethnic groups are overrepresented in certain fields. The widespread impression that disproportionate numbers of Jewish Americans are leaders of the entertainment and garment industries, members of college faculties, and professionals in medicine and law is grounded in reality. So is the widespread impression that disproportionate numbers of Italian Americans are construction, landscape, and sanitation contractors; that disproportionate numbers of Irish Americans can be found in politics, banking, and some branches of law; or that disproportionate numbers of German Americans dominate some skilled trades. These generalizations usually apply in only one direction; most Jewish, Italian, Irish, and German Americans are *not* working in their ethnically stereotyped occupations, but these occupations *are* dominated by members of the ethnically stereotyped groups. In any case, as in the matter of ethnic residential clustering, ethnic occupational clustering is natural, voluntary, and generally free of interethnic conflict.

One of the inevitable consequences of living in ethnic enclaves and maintaining ethnic identities is that immigrants continue to speak their native languages. If one of the three clauses in the assimilation contract demands acceptance of the public supremacy of English, should this concern other Americans? The simple answer is "No, but." At all times in America's evolution, a significant proportion of Americans spoke a language other than English at home and among their linguistic peers. Today, 14 percent of all Americans speak a foreign language in their own communities. One hundred years ago, the proportion of Americans who were not able to speak English *at all* was 25 percent and the proportion who spoke a foreign language among themselves was surely much larger.[23] That immigrants would want to continue speaking a familiar language to their spouses, parents, and children, as well as to others from their homeland with whom they interact continually, is perfectly natural, understandable, and acceptable. To the extent that speaking their native language eases immigrants' transition to life in the United States, it is even desirable.

What is unacceptable—and violates the American assimilation contract—is giving in to the demands of immigrant Americans of any linguistic heritage that their language must be adopted in the public domain. Such demands are not new. German (as indicated in Chapter 2) and Scandinavian immigrants of the nineteenth century aggressively pressed to have their children taught in German, Swedish, or Norwegian and demanded official recognition of their native languages in other contexts. But in a clear comprehension of how concessions to multilingualism might undermine the public objectives of assimilation and national unity, such demands were generally resisted, and the public supremacy of English was upheld in all official policies.[24]

During the past two decades, the United States has had to confront similar demands by its newest immigrants that Spanish and other immigrant languages be recognized and adopted for use in public schools, as well as in many other public settings. This time, both officially and unofficially, the country has substantially acquiesced to these demands. For the same reason that their nineteenth-century predecessors never entertained such a linguistic capitulation for a moment—multilingualism's corrosive impact on national unity—Americans may now wish to reconsider this recent and unprecedented accommodation. Canada, which narrowly escaped dismemberment in Quebec's secessionist referendum in 1995, is an object lesson of where official multilingual policies can lead. Assimilation, American style has, for two centuries, completely accommodated to a veritable Babel of multilingualism in private while maintaining, until a few decades ago, a solid front of English monolingualism in public.

There are many other examples of assimilation in the fabric of everyday American life—the coexistence of strong ethnic identities and communities in what nevertheless remains the most culturally unified nation on earth. One of the most widely appreciated is the maintenance of ethnic cuisines. Not only do ethnic cuisines retain their appeal to generations of descendants of the immigrants who imported them, but their popularity has spread into the rest of the American community. Nor are cosmopolitan foods available only in ethnic urban neighborhoods or the centers of large cities. In my fairly typical suburban community of only thirty-two thousand people, the repertoire of ethnic restaurants includes four Chinese, eight Italian, three Japanese, one Indian, one Mexican, one Thai, one French, three Irish, and two Turkish-Cypriot. In addition, there are three Chinese take-out restaurants, five pizzerias, and four Jewish delicatessens and food stores specializing in Central American, Japanese, Italian, and French delicacies.[25] This array of ethnic cuisines may be unusually diverse, but throughout the United States, there is hardly an urban or suburban community that does not have some ethnic culinary variety. In fact, the most underrepresented cuisine in most places is undifferentiated "American."

On a more serious note, one of the most striking examples of American assimilation is the United States' high rate of ethnic intermarriage. According to the sociologist Milton Gordon, intermarriage marks the highest level of societal integration.[26] High rates of intermarriage signify the permeability of ethnic classifications, very much the way upward economic mobility signifies the permeability of class barriers. The fact that a large number of people feel free to marry others outside their own ethnic communities—without provoking a *Romeo and Juliet*-style crisis in their families—demonstrates the malleability of Americans' ethnic identities. At the same time, entirely consistent with the premises of America's unique brand of assimilation, intermarriage does not eradicate ethnic identities. People proudly rattle off the ethnic components of their genetic heritage. A typical assimilated American may reveal: "My maternal grandmother was Jewish and my grandfather was Irish; on my father's side, both grandparents were Polish, and my father spoke Polish with his parents (I used to speak Polish as a kid); my mother was brought up Jewish, and so was I, but sometimes I went to Catholic church; my husband is mainly of German and Lutheran stock; we celebrate both Christmas and Hanukkah; my son was Bar-Mitzvahed, my unmarried daughter goes to Lutheran services, my other daughter married an Italian boy, and my grandchildren are being raised Catholic." This may be a profile of an unusually eclectic ethnic family, but it is not that far-fetched. The example illustrates two salient facts regarding intermarriage and assimilation:

the ease with which intermarriage occurs and the survival of ethnic and religious attachments and identities despite the prevalence of intermarriage. There is hardly a better example of assimilation, American style: a high degree of social and cultural integration across ethnic lines coexisting comfortably with the maintenance of strong ethnic identities and traditions.

All American ethnic groups, whether classified by religion, national origin, or race, have experienced high—and increasing— rates of intermarriage. Data on intermarriage is fragmentary because the census and other governmental surveys rarely seek respondents' religious affiliations. But such data as are available are compelling. Looking at intermarriage across religious lines, a recent survey revealed that today, more than 57 percent of all Jews marry Christians,[27] with the intermarried couples choosing a variety of religious options after marriage: one partner converting to the religion of the other, parents maintaining their native religions while raising their children in one or the other faith, or parents and/or children joining ecumenical congregations such as Unitarian or Quaker. Consistent with the rising rate of interreligious marriage, there is greater acceptance from within the affected religions. According to polls, whereas a majority of Jews disapproved of marriage between Christians and Jews in 1940, fewer than 10 percent did so by 1983.[28]

In addition to those Christians who marry Jews, there is a great deal of interreligious marriage between Catholics and Protestants. The rate of Protestant outmarriage is significantly lower than that of Catholics and Jews because the logistical possibility of members of a group marrying outside their community declines with the group's size, and Protestants constitute a majority of the American population. Even so, Protestants span many theologically distinctive denominations, from high church Episcopalians to Jehovah's Witnesses, so that if *interdenominational* unions were classified as a species of religious intermarriage, most Protestants—like Bill Clinton, who is a Baptist, and Hillary Clinton, who is Methodist— could be seen as intermarrying. Analyses of the outcomes of interfaith marriages show they are somewhat more likely to end in divorce than are religiously homogeneous ones, but this likelihood is considerably diminished by the fact that in a majority of interfaith marriages, one of the partners undergoes religious conversion.[29]

160   assimilation, american style

There is obviously an enormous amount of intermarriage between people of diverse national origins, most of it undocumented. Sociologist Richard Alba estimated that 84 percent of all third-generation Polish Americans married outside their ethnic group, as did 73 percent of all Americans of Italian ancestry.[30] There is a somewhat clearer picture of intermarriage across the official "minority" ethnic categories on which more official data are collected. According to a recent survey, 30 percent of Latinos marry non-Latinos, and the proportion of Latino outmarriage has been rising.[31] Studies show that an even larger fraction of Asians, 33 percent, marry non-Asians, and among Japanese, 65 percent marry non-Japanese. As with Latinos and Jews, the rate of Asian outmarriage has also been steadily growing. Even black-white intermarriage has increased dramatically in the past two decades, with the number of interracial marriages rising from 310,000 to 1.1 million.[32] The 1990 census registered 2 million children under the age of eighteen whose parents were of different races.[33]

Intermarriage is not limited to the masses; it pervades all socioeconomic strata of American society. Many of the most illustrious members of America's so-called WASP aristocracy have been products of interethnic marriages—it just has not been widely known. Philadelphia-born "blue-blood" William Bullitt, America's first ambassador to the Soviet Union, was descended not only from old-stock English Bullitts, but also from the Jewish financier Haym Solomon. The ancestors of the Protestant "Yankee patrician" Leverett Saltonstall included some Irish Catholic Sullivans. Celebrated products of New England WASPdom like New York congressman Jonathan Bingham and Massachusetts governor John Davis Lodge had Jewish wives. In John F. Kennedy's cabinet, no member was seen as more of a WASP than C. Douglas Dillon, yet his paternal grandfather was a Jewish immigrant named Sam Lupowski, who changed his name to Dillon. New York lawyer Oren Root numbers among his ancestors not only the English Roots, but an Italian grandmother and the Greek American theater entrepreneur Spyros Skouras.[34] More recent examples include former president George Bush's son Jeb, whose wife is Mexican American, and former New York governor Mario Cuomo's son Andrew, who married Robert Kennedy's daughter Kerry. The latter union attracted attention only because it united two political dynasties; the ethnic dimension—an Italian American marrying an Irish American—was simply a footnote.

There are some important lessons to be drawn from an accurate understanding of how ethnicity has suffused American social life. The most important is that there is nothing sinister in the maintenance of ethnic identity or living in distinct ethnic communities. Thomas Sowell, one of the most perceptive scholars of ethnicity in the United States, observed:

> The assimilation of American ethnic groups has not been a one-way process. Much of the vernacular, food, music, and other cultural characteristics of American society today were once ethnic peculiarities but are now part of the common heritage. Gershwin, the Kennedys, Andrew Carnegie, Joe DiMaggio, and O. J. Simpson are American phenomena rather than ethnic figures. Groups have not vanished in a melting pot, but neither they nor the country are the same as they were.[35]

The fact that tens of millions of assimilated, patriotic Americans maintain some measure of ethnic identity, some for many generations after their immigrant ancestors reached America's shores, forms the undeniable basis of assimilation, American style. It does not prevent them from participating fully in the United States' social and economic life. It does not even keep them from having the most intimate relations with members of other ethnic groups. And if millions of descendants of Irish, German, Scandinavian, Italian, Polish, Greek, and Jewish immigrants can hold on to their ethnic identities while feeling—and being—resolutely "American," so can millions of more recently arrived Mexicans, Koreans, Haitians, Filipinos, and Dominicans.

The second lesson is that although we need not be concerned about the ethnic predilections of immigrants and their descendants, we should be very much concerned about the way American society as a whole views ethnicity and the messages it sends to immigrants and their descendants. The attitudes of "native" Americans toward immigrants and their assimilation took several

different turns in the two centuries following American independence.

The historically dominant attitude, which prevailed from the presidency of George Washington to that of Grover Cleveland near the end of the nineteenth century, was one of passive assimilation. Immigrants were welcomed. They were free to act and dress and speak in any way that their original national or religious cultures disposed them. But they were expected to obey the canons of America's assimilation contract: work hard; learn English (or least allow their children to learn English); and, most important, believe in the American Idea. Americans were supremely tolerant of immigrants' exotic ways but made absolutely no concessions to them. Immigrants had to accept America on its own terms. This represented assimilation, American style at its purest.

With the arrival of an arguably more "alien" set of immigrants after the 1890s (the Italians, Jews, and Slavic eastern Europeans), the education and opinion elites favored a program of aggressive assimilation, an attitude that prevailed through the 1950s. In this period, immigrants were still welcome, but selectively. Their ethnic folkways were still viewed benignly, but only up to a point. Immigrants—and what is critical, their children—were to be weaned from them as quickly as possible through a campaign of Americanization conducted in the country's schools, workplaces, and other public settings. In theory, this approach stretched the rules of America's assimilation paradigm considerably, bringing it perilously close to the kind of assimilation cum acculturation demanded in countries like France. In practice, ethnicity flourished throughout this period (as amply documented by Glazer and Moynihan and others), but Americanization measures did probably speed up the acculturation of immigrant children somewhat, especially in the case of Jewish Americans who were, for the most part, happy to see their children Americanize.

It was only in the wake of the cultural upheavals of the 1960s that the attitude of America's education and opinion elite toward ethnicity turned 180 degrees to one of antiassimilation (for all the reasons laid out in Chapters 1, 3, and 9). The opinion-making groups—public school educators, university faculty, program officers of foundations, media leaders in New York and Los Angeles, and top federal government officials—now see the survival of ethnic cultures in America's midst as prima facie evidence that assimilation is a myth and are engaged in constructing a pervasive institutional enterprise that subsidizes and mandates ethnic consciousness—and what is worse, ethnic grievances—to take assimilation's place. Latino and other immigrant children are made to continue using their native languages as they go through the public schools. Elementary and secondary schools seek to bolster ethnic pride while slighting America's integrationist traditions and myths. America's main foundations cultivate ethnic consciousness in countless projects that they underwrite. Universities have set up African American, Latino American, Asian American, and other species of ethnic studies departments and curricula, which serve up dubious ethnic scholarship while stoking ethnic injuries. Ethnic "political correctness" pervades popular movies and television shows.

This move away from America's traditional assimilationist perspective has increasingly divided the American people, not only on the question of assimilation itself, but in their view of ethnic cultures and their support for further immigration. Thus, antiassimilationism has provoked a backlash with unfortunate repercussions. Because the opinion leadership has planted the notion in the public mind that the maintenance of ethnicity and cultural distinctiveness signifies the failure or, at best, irrelevance of assimilation, more and more Americans have come to view ethnic communities and the survival of ethnic cultural traits with suspicion.

Ethnic neighborhoods, foreign languages, shops, and customs that were easily tolerated, even celebrated only a decade ago, now seem sinister and threatening to many. Considering Latinos and Asians ethnic "minorities," a growing number of Americans are easily frightened by the alarms sounded by groups, such as the Federation for American Immigration Reform and journalists like Brimelow, that America's expanding islands of ethnicity will make it a "nonwhite" country by the middle of the twenty-first century.[36] Believing that bilingual curricula keep immigrant and second-generation schoolchildren from becoming rapidly proficient in English, many now heed the calls of organizations like U.S. English that want English to be designated the United States' official lan-

guage,[37] risking a level of governmental intrusiveness of unprecedented (and previously unnecessary) proportions. Worst of all, feeling threatened by ethnicity, more and more Americans feel threatened by the wellspring of ethnicity: further immigration. Evidence
of the declining support for immigration is evident in a review of
periodic Roper surveys on national attitudes toward immigrants
since 1946, in response to the question: "Should immigration be
kept at its present level, increased or decreased?" In 1953, 50 percent of the respondents thought immigration should increase or be
maintained at its present levels. By 1977, only 44 percent thought
so, and by 1990 the proportion who had a positive view of immigration had declined to 36 percent.[38]

To repair the damage that decades of antiassimilation policies
have wrought on America's hugely successful model of ethnic cultural diversity amid national cultural unity, political scientist
Lawrence Fuchs, of Brandeis University, suggested going right to
the top and asking the president of the United States to lead the
American people back on the path of assimilation:

> There is considerable evidence that recent immigrants, and espe-
> cially their children, are adapting to the American civic culture.
> . . . But civic unity and ethnic peace cannot be taken for granted,
> and [President Clinton] should begin a careful analysis of which
> . . . ethnic policies contribute to civic unity and which do not.
> . . . It would be desirable if the President could persuade the
> country and Congress to reexamine policies that now promote
> ethnic division.[39]

This chapter has attempted to put ethnicity in its correct
American historical perspective by showing that contrary to the tide
of current thinking, the survival of ethnic communities and ethnic
cultures is very much consistent with national cultural unity and
assimilation. But this proposition is only valid in the context of this
country's unique interpretation of assimilation. America's institutional and opinion leaders will never, and need not, endorse a
return to the kind of aggressive assimilation embodied in early-
twentieth-century Americanization campaigns. Yet, unless they
acknowledge that the survival of ethnicity is entirely compatible

with assimilation and rehabilitate assimilation, American style as the nation's only viable way of integrating an ethnically diverse population, they will risk ever greater ethnic and racial conflict. What is worse, they will feed an alarming rise in xenophobic and ethnocentric sentiments in the general population that will threaten the very foundations of America's civic culture. Three cheers for ethnicity, but no concessions to ethnocentricity or ethnic federalism.

9

Black Americans
and Assimilation

The strong insistence of ethnicity for black Americans came in the late 1960s as the "Black Power" or "Black is Beautiful" movement. The important point to note is the melting pot or central tendency approach presents a central option, apparently adopted by both sides. As Cleaver noted in 1968, you were part of the problem or part of the solution! Thus ethnicity was opposed to the melting pot. Black pride was opposed to assimilation. Integration was equated with assimilation and the loss of ethnic identity.

James Jones, 1991[1]

Nothing has so compromised America's assimilation project over the years as the status of its black citizens. Since the birth of the republic, black Americans have been the great exception to its assimilation paradigm. And from the birth of the republic until only a few decades ago, the nation's treatment of black Americans had been the single greatest betrayal of the American Idea. These two facts are intimately related. Most obviously, the denial of America's universal civil rights to black Americans during most of U.S. history mocked the nation's assimilationist ethos, a mockery made all the more painful by the fact that throughout the period when native-born blacks—residents of America for centuries—were kept from assimilating into American society, the country was willing and able to assimilate tens of millions of immigrants. As Nathan Glazer, America's leading scholar of ethnicity, wrote:

> In almost all the discussion of assimilation or Americanization until about World War II, the discussants had only Europeans in mind. This is true whether they favored or opposed assimilation and Americanization efforts. A reader today of the documents of the great Americanization drive of the second decade of this century will find no reference to blacks, then as now our largest minority. It is as if the turmoil of abolitionism, slavery, the Civil War, Reconstruction did not exist.[2]

Americans have paid a fearsome price for this huge lapse in the implementation of their civic ideals. The weakening of the assimilation ethos today may be another large part of this bill. America's assimilationist aspirations have been caught in a vicious—and paradoxical—historical cycle of events, policies, and popular attitudes. The United States was founded on principles that reject ethnic particularism and promise to make it the world's first nation to foster the assimilation—American style—of all ethnic groups. But from the outset, the country, although integrating an ever more diverse assortment of ethnic "races" from abroad, exempted its oldest race—black Americans—from its assimilation paradigm, first, by condoning slavery for three-quarters of a century and then by condoning institutionalized racial discrimination for another century after that. Just when the country finally made good on its universalist promises by formally embracing blacks within the parameters of the American Idea—allowing them, at long last, to assimilate— many blacks, after a brief moment of celebration, rejected essential features of the paradigm. Seeing blacks reject assimilation, other ethnic groups—native and immigrant—followed suit, and now America risks forsaking its historic assimilationist mission to embrace the kind of ethnocentrism whose eradication its founders made a keystone of the new republic's principles.

*   *   *

Americans have struggled with the status of blacks from the very beginning, in a two-century-long journey marked by missed opportunities, compromised ideals, and intervals of progress alternating with ones of retrogression, but, through it all, they have made a slow and painful march toward racial equality. Jefferson's first draft of the Declaration of Independence disavowed slavery, but Georgia and South Carolina vetoed it. Northern states ended slavery in the first decades of the nineteenth century, but southern states were determined to maintain it. In 1861 Americans went to war over the issue, and by the war's end in 1865, slavery was finally abolished, but southern Jim Crow laws and northern racism and indifference in the decades afterward made this a hollow victory for blacks. A century after the Civil War, Americans finally took a series of historic steps—bracketed by President Harry S Truman's integration of the armed forces by executive order in 1948 and passage of the Voting Rights Act in 1965—to end institutionalized racial discrimination once and for all.

Paradoxically, by the time Americans finally resolved to right their nation's historic moral and political wrong, a century and a half of moral dereliction may have irreparably undermined America's assimilation paradigm. When the hand of assimilation was finally extended to blacks, many black Americans were no longer sure they wished to grasp it. This paradox can be partially explained by the historic ambivalence of the black community. For the hundred years between the end of slavery and the final nullification of governmentally sanctioned segregation and institutional racism, the ideology of the prevailing black leadership—from Frederick Douglass and Booker T. Washington in the nineteenth century to Martin Luther King, Jr., and Thurgood Marshall in the twentieth—was integrationist and assimilationist. It was this ideology and the perseverance of blacks and whites who espoused it that ultimately secured the gains of the civil rights revolution. Nevertheless, a virulent strain of black nationalism always competed with integrationism for the allegiance of rank-and-file black Americans. Appealing to widespread despair over the prospects of ever achieving fair treatment from whites or a resentful unwillingness to beg for admission to a society so determined to exclude them, a succession of black leaders from emancipation on, including such prominent figures as Marcus Garvey in the 1920s and Louis Farrakhan today, encouraged black Americans to pursue an existence and an identity apart from whites (in the case of Garvey, even apart from the United States altogether). For black nationalists, black assimilation to a white society was fanciful and black accommodation to white racism was demeaning, which left an alienated black separatism as the only means to recover dignity and self-respect. In Garvey's words:

> We are the descendants of a suffering people; we are the descendants of a people determined to suffer no more. . . . If Europe is for the Europeans, then Africa shall be for the black peoples of the world. We say it; we mean it. . . . The other races have countries of their own and it is time for the 400,000,000 Negroes to claim Africa for themselves.[3]

The perverse tragedy of contemporary American racial relations is that just when American laws and behavior were finally moving the nation toward the kind of society the once-dominant integrationist leaders had fought for, the recessive black nationalist impulse suddenly became ascendant. The political and ideological leadership of the black community passed from an old generation of integrationists to a new generation that disdained the long-term gains of integration and assimilation in favor of the short-term and pyrrhic benefits of ethnic federalism.

This change in leadership may, to some extent, be the unhappy by-product, as political scientists Paul Sniderman and Thomas Piazza suggested, of the integrationists' victories.[4] Old-line civil rights organizations like the NAACP and the Urban League were set up to challenge segregation and discrimination on the battlefield of the American Idea. They shamed their countrymen into finally ceding to blacks the civil rights that are the birthright of all Americans. Unfortunately, like the March of Dimes in its successful fight against infantile paralysis, with each strategic victory, their importance and relevance faded. In a recent *New York Times* article on the decline of the NAACP, Steven Holmes observed: "In interviews [with NAACP members] person after person expressed an unease that, without the stark and tangible racism embodied in legalized segregation, the black community was fracturing," leaving the NAACP without a clear-cut role.[5]

Once the edifice of legal and institutional discrimination in the United States was dismantled, the black community and its leadership had two options. They could engage in the unexciting work of consolidating the victories of the civil rights revolution—in other words, help blacks to assimilate—or they could find a new basis for grievance and alienation from mainstream American society.

The majority of blacks, from the lowest-paid menial workers to members of the rapidly growing professional and managerial class, have chosen, in their everyday lives, to profit from America's liberalized racial environment and to participate—perhaps warily—in mainstream American communal life. In this, they have been aided by the efforts of the NAACP and the Urban League to continue to dismantle racial obstacles as these old-line integrationist organizations have struggled to retain their allegiance.

Unfortunately, a large minority of blacks—not necessarily the poorest—have chosen to nurture and dramatize their grievances with the rest of American society, hunkering down in an attitude of defiance and alienation. It is these members of the black community who rally behind Louis Farrakhan, Al Sharpton, or Leonard Jeffries. Remarkably, the message of alienation and antiassimilation often resonates most powerfully not with members of the impoverished black underclass, who at least have a reason to be alienated, but with black college students and others who can look forward to lives of conventional American prosperity. The minions of Jeffries and Farrakhan draw their biggest audiences on the campus circuit, not in rock concert halls or other popular arenas. Opinion surveys have also found that poor blacks often display less hostility to American society and so-called middle-class American values than do blacks who have had or are in the process of getting a college education. It is the cadre of alienated successful blacks who have spearheaded the campaign against assimilation and persuaded many whites that the assimilation of blacks, on the same terms as other Americans, is a futile undertaking. Moreover, what may increasingly be tipping the scales in favor of black nationalism among the most educated blacks is decades of an official national policy that has not merely disparaged assimilationism, but has rewarded anti-assimilationism and color consciousness.

Black antiassimilationism rests on two beliefs. The most frequently cited is the unshakable conviction of blacks, of all social classes and all ideological persuasions, that most white Americans can never be weaned from their irrevocable racist attitudes and behavior. The other is the belief that the American societal playing field has been made so unlevel by centuries of racial discrimination that blacks cannot compete with other Americans economically in a purely assimilationist, "color-blind" society.

The endemic persistence of racism is confirmed for black Americans by their day-to-day experiences and by vivid journalistic accounts of the frequent indignities—or worse—being visited upon other blacks. The beating of Rodney King by a group of white Los Angeles policemen and Los Angeles detective Mark Fuhrman's accounts of police racism during the O. J. Simpson trial may have captured national attention as particularly egregious examples of the persistence of racism, but local newspapers throughout the country carry, at least weekly, stories of white-on-black police brutality or other examples of white-on-black discrimination. What is more persuasive as evidence of racism are the personal encounters of blacks, including prominent ones, what the social commentator Arch Puddington called "the instances of petty and not-so-petty harassment and insult which black men suffer daily at the hands of policemen, cab drivers, and shop owners."[6] Even the distinguished black scholar Cornel West wrote of a recent experience hailing a cab in the heart of cosmopolitan Manhattan:

> I . . . stood on the corner of 60th Street and Park Avenue to catch a taxi. I had to meet a photographer who would take the picture for the cover of this book on the roof of an apartment building in East Harlem. . . . I waited and waited and waited. After the ninth taxi refused me, my blood began to boil. The tenth refused me and stopped for a kind, well-dressed, smiling female fellow citizen of European descent. . . .
>
> Ugly racial memories of the past flashed through my mind. Years ago, while driving from New York to teach at Williams

College, I was stopped on fake charges of trafficking cocaine. When I told the police officer I was a professor of religion, he replied "Yeh, and I'm the Flying Nun. Let's go, nigger!" ... Needless to say, these incidents are dwarfed by those like Rodney King's beating or the abuse of black targets [by] the FBI. ... Yet the memories cut like a merciless knife at my soul as I waited on that godforsaken corner.[7]

West is an outspoken integrationist and critic of black nationalism, a proponent of black assimilation. Yet his contemplation of the durability of racism in America led him to observe disparagingly: "For liberals, black people are to be 'included' and 'integrated' into 'our' society and culture."[8] It is ironic, though of small comfort to blacks, that the cabdrivers who perpetrated the racist insult against West were not whites, but "people of color," probably immigrants.

Nevertheless, there is a growing body of evidence that, notwithstanding the theory of sociologists and all the personal and publicized anecdotes, explicit racism is sharply declining. Opinion surveys and research on blacks' participation in a broad array of economic and social institutions have found that whites are displaying increasingly favorable attitudes toward blacks and that traditional racial barriers are falling. Furthermore, the United States now has so many people "of color" besides the descendants of American slaves—blacks from the Caribbean and Africa, East Indians, dark-skinned Asians, and Hispanics—that the connection between skin color or other distinctive physical traits and slave ancestry is becoming increasingly attenuated. As more blacks and whites intermarry, there is also the possibility that the entire black-white racial dichotomy itself will be obsolete, that some day Americans—both black and white—will come to view mixed racial ancestry in exactly the same terms as mixed national and religious ancestry and cease to assign all individuals who share black and white forebears (the majority of American blacks) exclusively to membership in a black "race." In a recent *New York Times* article, Michel Marriott reported:

For Alison Perry ... [a] slender almond-colored woman with delicate features drawn from both her black-American father and her Italian-American mother, race is not what defines her. "I definitely say that I'm interracial," Ms. Perry said. "I do not identify myself as a black woman. I definitely don't identify myself as a white woman, either."

The very existence of multiracial people like Ms. Perry challenges this nation's traditionally rigid notions of race.[9]

All these factors allow us to hope that the color line may become an increasingly irrelevant factor in American social relations and that white racism may not be as endemic as most blacks believe. Without downplaying the residue of racist thinking and behavior that blacks may still encounter, it is important to be honest about the real progress being made. Blacks can gain little either in sympathy or concrete assistance by exaggerating the persistence of racism or failing to acknowledge the majority of Americans' goodwill and commitment to end what Swedish sociologist Gunnar Myrdal called, in his landmark 1944 book, the American Dilemma. (See Table 1.)

TABLE 1. WHITES' CHANGING ATTITUDES TOWARD RACE: 1963–82 (PERCENTAGE AGREEING WITH STATEMENTS)

	1963–64	1972	latest (1976–82)
Black children should attend the same schools as whites	65	84	90
Blacks should have the same job opportunities as whites	85	97	NA
Blacks should be able to live in the same neighborhoods as whites	65	80	88
Would vote for a black presidential candidate	45	73	86

Source: Howard Schuman, Charlotte Steeh, and Lawrence Bobo, *Racial Attitudes in America* (Cambridge, England: Cambridge University Press, 1985), Table 3.1.

Whatever the facts, the leadership of the black community today and a large proportion of the rank-and-file black population are unwilling to believe that whites are capable of changing their view of blacks and base much of their behavior and thinking on this premise. In response to their perception that the United States will be forever racist, antiassimilationist blacks have adopted a posture of cultural separatism. In its most benign form, their cultural separatism is not so different from the cultural distinctiveness of other ethnic groups that characterizes assimilation, American style and has resulted in blacks celebrating African and African American traditions like Kwanzaa as a substitute for Christmas, a holiday that was invented in 1966 by the black activist M. Ron Karenga; giving their children African-sounding names; and, not the least, insisting on being called African American rather than black. (*Negro* and *colored*, the appellations favored by integrationist whites and blacks after the Civil War, were discarded during the civil rights revolution of the 1960s.)

In a somewhat less benign incarnation, the cultural separatist impulse has led to heightened sensitivity to "cultural diversity" in all public arenas of this country. It has resulted in ethnocentric "multicultural" curricula in the schools, designed primarily for black youngsters but, of necessity, embracing the ethnic sensibilities of Latinos and whichever other ethnic groups stand out in the local schools. It has also given us ethnically balanced television-news teams, ethnically balanced holidays, and ethnically balanced political events. In every case, these efforts to highlight and reinforce ethnicity are neither sincere celebrations of America's real ethnic diversity nor generated to satisfy the ethnocentric demands of various old and new ethnic constituencies. Rather, they are thinly veiled concessions to black cultural separatism, with other ethnicities included for camouflage.

In its most virulent and malignant form, black cultural separatism has promoted outright alienation from mainstream America. It has involved the demonization of American institutions, including those that form the core of the American Idea, and the discrediting of American political heroes (other than Lincoln); it has also demanded that schools and universities expose black children to "Afrocentric" history and other curricula. Even more disturbing, this strain of black cultural separatism has encouraged segregated housing on college campuses; "buy-black" campaigns in black neighborhood commercial areas; aggressively antiwhite and anti-American lyrics in black-oriented rock and rap music; and, what is the most shameful, the vilification of Jews, historically the blacks' most steadfast champions. A set of sentiments more antithetical to assimilation is hard to imagine. This brand of poisonous black anti-assimilationism has as its most effective spokesman and avatar Louis Farrakhan, head of the Nation of Islam, and the depth of its appeal can be gauged by the huge popularity of Farrakhan and the vast audiences he manages to attract.

The other major foundation of black antiassimilationism rests on the belief of many blacks (and whites) that after centuries of suffering, there are too many "structural" barriers in American society for blacks to overcome. Thus, simple assimilation is no longer possible, and blacks cannot be held to the assimilation contract. Expecting blacks to succeed by adhering to the terms of the Protestant ethic, the argument goes, disregards the legacy of economic and social handicaps that prevents them from seizing the opportunities open to whites or even other ethnic Americans. Aside from lingering racism itself, such structural barriers include spatial isolation, inferior education, and fragile and disorganized families and communities. Those who argue that black handicaps are too deep-seated to be erased by mere assimilation point to a variety of indicators that black Americans as a group are worse off economically than other Americans, even other nonwhites. By every measure of economic or social well-being—income levels, unemployment rates, housing conditions, life expectancy, and infant mortality, blacks fall below national norms. Furthermore, most blacks are residentially segregated from other Americans, in a pattern arguably more sinister and less voluntary than the self-segregation of other ethnic groups described in Chapter 8.

As in the case of the perception of racism, there is clear-cut evidence that, notwithstanding evidence of lingering disadvantage, blacks are nevertheless making substantial economic progress, especially if certain demographic characteristics are held constant. By any number of indicators, blacks—especially married couples and women—are catching up with whites. The high school graduation rates for black youths rose from 20 percent in 1950 to over 70 percent in 1993 and are rapidly approaching those of whites. Black college graduation rates in the same period increased fourfold, from 3 percent to over 12 percent.[10] Black educational gains have yielded solid occupational and quality-of-life benefits. In every decade since 1950, proportionately more blacks hold professional and managerial jobs, own homes, and live in suburbs; black life expectancy has risen and infant mortality fallen. Blacks have also become increasing visible in America's social and political institutions. In 1960, there were practically no elected black officials; in 1993, there were almost 8,000.[11] As Puddington pointed out:

> The principal aim of American racial policy has been to create a large class of college-educated, middle-class black professionals who would feel comfortable in an integrated setting and at home with the virtues of the American system. This ambitious agenda has, in fact, been more than partially fulfilled. Where blacks were once restricted to the lower rungs of the economy and excluded from the corporate world, today most professions and large corporations are highly integrated, and most families have joined what is roughly regarded as the middle class.[12]

At the same time, the same census data also show increasing numbers of black unwed mothers, single-parent families, and children growing up in poverty, in short, an unacceptably large black underclass that is immune to the benefits of collapsing racial barriers and ostensible increases in economic opportunity. The debate raging among sociologists and policy analysts is whether the persistence of a disadvantaged black underclass is structural or behavioral—the indirect and inadvertent product of the policies designed to fight structural handicaps.

The traditional integrationist approach to redressing black economic disadvantage has been for blacks to join forces with economically vulnerable whites and other minorities to pressure the private and public sectors to level the economic playing field. Under the auspices of racially integrated unions or the banner of liberal Democratic administrations, these efforts have resulted in a variety of governmental programs of income support or assistance with particular problems, such as job training, housing, and day care. In all these endeavors blacks have not made an issue of their uniquely dis-advantaged status. They petitioned for assistance on socioeconomic, not ethnic, grounds, and they joined interracial coalitions to do so. The resulting broad-based, means-tested programs and activities may have dented Americans' fidelity to the Protestant ethic, but they have not specifically undermined assimilation.

As prevailing sentiments in the black community have shifted from an integrationist to a black nationalist perspective, however, black leaders and their liberal white allies have increasingly discarded the integrationist approach to achieving economic gains for blacks. Instead they are seeking to remedy blacks' economic disadvantage by asserting claims for assistance based on blacks' unique status as a victimized ethnic group. Thus, the belief that immutable struc-tural barriers make it impracticable for blacks to assimilate has cre-ated a rationale for treating blacks differently from other Americans, even other poor Americans. It has led to the proposi-tion that blacks are entitled to some form of restitution, or at least the means to catch up with whites more quickly than the mere elimination of formal discriminatory barriers would permit. "You owe us" or "we owe them" is the subtext of the demands of those blacks and whites who disdain a policy of merely sweeping away racial obstacles so blacks can have a crack at the opportunities of a newly color-blind American society. Having little faith that blacks can gain much from integrationist efforts, whether government sponsored or market based, the antiassimilationists have preferred to assert blacks' discrete claims on societal resources, positions, or privileges. This rationale is inextricably intertwined with the belief in the persistence of racism because the "structural" features of American society that make it impossible for blacks to succeed on equal terms with whites or other ethnics are themselves often seen as explicit or invisible products of a racist society that is determined to discriminate against blacks.

The policies aimed at specifically compensating blacks for their structural handicaps go under the general label of affirmative action. More than anything else, affirmative action and its collateral ethnic federalist policies have solidly entrenched the antiassimilationist bias of contemporary American society. As Puddington stated:

This vast system of racial preferences, the creation of generations of liberal policy-makers and presidential administrations, both Democratic and Republican, has in fact done more to foster race consciousness in America than any single event or set of events one can possibly think of. Thanks to affirmative action, we have all been taught to count by race, and the current "crisis" in race relations is, from this perspective, but the culmination of decades of consciously implemented policy. The ultimate professed goal of that policy may have been an integrated society, but its all too predictable effects from the very beginning have been divisiveness, resentment and polarization.[13]

Americans should not be complacent about the quantum shift in blacks' attitudes toward assimilation. Assimilation, for all ethnic groups, has always been a two-way street. Although the willingness of natives to accept members of new ethnic groups into American society is an essential prerequisite for assimilation, the success of the assimilation paradigm has depended just as much on the willingness of members of ethnic groups to join American society. Therefore, when a sizable portion of the black community rejects the premises of the great American assimilation contract, the entire assimilation enterprise is challenged, and American society has to confront some highly unpalatable choices. If the society continues on its present course of acquiescing to black antiassimilationism, it will risk two dangerous developments. First, it will be establishing an unfortunate precedent for subverting the assimilation of other ethnic groups, and, second, it will be jeopardizing the hard-won gains of the civil rights revolution. Civil rights for blacks cannot, in the end, be successfully defended except by appealing to the iron logic of the American Idea and its assimilationist, universalist, antiethnocentric principles. On the other hand, as long as blacks harbor strong antiassimilationist attitudes, societal expectations and policies that depend on blacks conforming to the premises of the assimilation paradigm may founder on the rocks of racial politics.

In the end, no alternative will be better for blacks or for all Americans than fighting for an aggressively color-blind, assimilationist society and signing on to America's historic assimilation contract. Even if Americans were as racist as antiassimilationist blacks assume, it makes no sense for blacks to sidestep racism by living in an independent American subculture and trying to wrest economic and social benefits from an ostensibly antagonistic white majority by making claims to ethnic federalism. Indeed, if Americans are so racist, why should they give in to ethnic federalist demands in the first place? I suppose there are two implicit answers to this rhetorical question: blacks may believe that they need only to persuade the "enlightened" white elites of the need for ethnic federalist policies and that whites may be afraid that without ethnic federalism blacks will foment social unrest. Today, neither expectation is especially credible, and, even if it were, it would be an unworthy basis for harmonious relations between blacks and whites.

Rather than replace one kind of racism with another, Americans must banish racism altogether. To the extent that vestiges of institutional and personal racism survive in American society, they should be wiped out for the sake of both whites and blacks. If racism indeed survives, the only way blacks can challenge it and protect their interests is by appealing to traditional universal, inclusionist American values. Those who oppose relying on color-conscious remedies to overcome the legacy of racial discrimination have called this alternative to ethnic federalism "the new civil rights." According to legal scholar Peter Ferrara, this is how the new civil rights would attack racial discrimination:

> The first component of the new civil rights is to establish true equality under the law. This was the focus of the first wave of civil rights reform in the middle of this century, culminating in the landmark Civil Rights Act of 1964. The new civil rights should continue to enforce equality under the law through vigorous enforcement of existing prohibitions against discrimination. . . . This enforcement should include full compensation for actual, proven victims. Those who were denied jobs or other accommodations due to such discrimination should be granted the lost employment or other accommodation by court order. In addition they should receive full monetary damages and attorneys' fees.[14]

For American to become the kind of color-blind society envisioned by the proponents of the new civil rights, unquestionably, whites must fight lingering racist attitudes and practices more aggressively. At the same time, to bring the United States closer to the ideal of a color-blind society, the antiassimilationist premises of the current black leadership and perhaps of the majority of black citizens will have to change in three ways. For starters, a color-blind society has no tolerance for racial hatred. A solid majority of whites now disavows racism in principle, and a near majority does so in practice. In turn, blacks would do well to accept contemporary American disavowals of racism at face value; forgive American society for its legacy of injustice and discrimination; set aside any residue of anger and grievance, no matter how well justified; and let bygones be bygones. No amount of anger and grievance can repair old wrongs; only holding America to its founding ideals can do that.

Second, a color-blind society has no tolerance for ethnic federalism. Blacks should consider forgoing the hollow benefits that affirmative action and related programs confer on them as members of a "favored" group and taking their chances as individuals in a highly competitive multiethnic society. Precisely because they have been victims of color-based discrimination, blacks, more than any other American ethnic group, have the most to gain if the organizations and individuals they must relate to rigidly adhere to color-blind policies and consider only the qualifications of individuals when they award jobs, places in colleges, apartments, or bank loans. Blacks should also eschew ethnic federalism in the political arena. Racial criteria for drawing boundaries of electoral districts or making a candidate's race an issue in electoral campaigns have a way of backfiring, fueling renascent appeals to white racism, and undermining the principle that politicians must serve the interests of *all* their constituents. It is naive for blacks (and their white friends) to count indefinitely on wresting more in the way of resources and privileges from the larger society by appealing to whites' guilt and demanding ethnically based preferences, rather than by appealing to their countrymen's historic commitment to equal rights for all individuals, regardless of ethnic heritage.

Finally, a color-blind society has no room for black social and cultural alienation. Undeniably, under assimilation, American style, blacks are permitted the same measure of cultural distinctiveness available to other ethnic Americans. But assimilation, American style does not allow for the demonization of the American Idea or its authors, black anti-Semitism, demands that black children be given an "Afrocentric" education, racial segregation in college dormitories, or the boycotting of white or Asian merchants. In addition to violating American principles, all such manifestations of cultural isolation are self-defeating. Demonizing the American Idea is especially wrongheaded because the American Idea is the black community's best shield against the kind of racism and ethnocentricity that would ensure their continued victimization in a less liberal society. Black anti-Semitism alienates the most steadfast allies the blacks have had in the white community. Afrocentric scholarship denies black children a good education. Boycotts hurt black consumers and even black employees. A posture of black alienation does not avenge historic black grievances; it can only blunt American idealism and make the country meaner in ways that will inevitably harm the interests of blacks more than any other group.

Black leaders would do much better for their constituents if they would reaffirm their historic tradition of support for integration and assimilation and retreat from the netherworld of black separatism and alienation. And white liberals would be doing blacks a great favor by seconding such a reaffirmation, rather than by adding fuel to blacks' antiassimilationist bonfire. Blacks have everything to gain and virtually nothing to lose by embracing the assimilation contract and unabashedly joining the mainstream of American society.

Any plea that the black community should trade in black nationalism and ethnic federalism for the benefits of a color-blind America will most likely be countered with the argument that it cannot happen because white America is not yet—and perhaps never will be—color blind. To this I say: Let's work all the harder to make it color blind. If half the energy currently devoted to keeping America color conscious were devoted to making it color blind, such a goal might be attainable in a few decades at most. Along the way blacks would accelerate their economic advancement, repair their social relations with other Americans (especially Jews and other minorities), and once again command the moral high ground of Martin Luther King, Jr. And once blacks embraced assimilation again, America's growing population of Latinos, Asians, and other immigrants could more easily be persuaded to accept the terms of America's historic assimilation contract.

Getting It Right

part III

10

Battlegrounds of Assimilation

Ethnic ideologues . . . have set themselves against the old American ideal of assimilation. They call on the republic to think in terms not of individual but group identity and to move the polity from individual to group rights. They have made a certain progress in transforming the United States into a more segregated society. . . . They have filled the air with recrimination and rancor and have remarkably advanced the fragmentation of American life.

Arthur M. Schlesinger, Jr., 1992[1]

If Americans want to rededicate themselves to assimilation, American style where should they begin? One possibility, of course, is that nothing really needs to be done. Sociologist Nathan Glazer asserted that in spite of the political controversy, America's newest immigrants are indeed assimilating: "The concept may be disreputable, but the reality continues to flourish."[2] Immigration specialist John Miller was even more optimistic when he announced:

It's a good thing, then, that immigrants everywhere are assimilating rapidly into the American mainstream. From revitalizing central cities such as New York and Miami to stocking our graduate schools with the world's best and brightest minds, immigrants, by almost any measure, are "making it" in America. Not to say that

there aren't rough spots—the ideology of multiculturalism
threatens to retard many immigrant gains—but assimilation continues to glide over all of these arguments and maintains its irresistible lure.[3]

Other observers of immigration and American society are not
so sure. They are alarmed by the growing ethnocentricity that is
dividing Americans today and the institutions that are fueling it.
They see blacks and members of other classified minorities—or at
least their leaders—rejecting assimilation to promote minority-
group solidarity and political leverage. They see new immigrants
and their children only partially assimilating and coming increasingly into conflict with blacks. They see even white Americans
falling prey to a "cult of ethnicity." They see a divisive multiculturalism balkanizing America, an especially apt metaphor in the wake
of Bosnia's fratricide. Some are so alarmed by the rising tide of ethnocentricity and the possibility that unassimilated new immigrants
will enlarge the ethnocentric political constituency that they have
proposed that immigration should be sharply scaled back.[4] Even
Glazer qualified his belief that today's immigrants are assimilating
when he mused: "The apartness [of diverse ethnic groups] is real.
. . . The large statements of an American national ideal of inclusion,
of assimilation, understandably ring false."[5]

Those who believe that assimilation is taking place and those
who fear that it isn't are both right. On the positive side, the powerful assimilative traditions and institutions of the United States are
still at work. American mass culture is exerting an increasingly pervasive hold on the language, habits, and consumer tastes of all
Americans (not to mention millions of non-Americans). The competitive exigencies of the American labor market make it necessary
for immigrants and their children to adapt to the expectations of
their American employers and consumers. Native Americans expect
immigrants to assimilate. And increasing numbers of Americans are
intermarrying across ethnic lines. But all these forces, by themselves, will only ensure a relatively high degree of cultural conformity among immigrants and other Americans, and, as I discussed
earlier, assimilation is not so much about cultural conformity as it
is about national unity. Americans—old and new—are assimilated

when they share the same values and the same identity, not when they wear the same clothes or listen to the same music.

Americans still have a great deal to do to advance the cause of assimilation—to keep their country integrated and unified—as it enters the twenty-first century. They might begin by rehabilitating the word itself. *Assimilation,* properly understood, should once again become a *good* word—right up there with words like *liberty* and *justice*—and the process it signifies should be seen as not only reputable, but desirable. Specific American ethnic groups must be persuaded of the desirability of assimilation. Specific institutions must be enlisted in making assimilation happen. Specific antiassimilationist policies must be reversed. And specific antiassimilationist ideology must be countered.

Although all American ethnic groups have had their ethnic consciousness raised in recent years, most recent immigrants are unlikely to be deflected from the path of assimilation. Asians, especially, appear eager to assimilate and are integrating rapidly into the mainstream of American society. But two groups—segments of the Hispanic and black communities—have embraced antiassimilationism and ethnocentricity, and we must make a special effort to deal with their disaffection if the revival of assimilation is to be achieved. The concerns raised by black antiassimilationism were discussed in Chapter 9, so in this chapter, I will only address the case of Hispanics.

Why the assimilation of Hispanics should even be problematical is hard to fathom. In a lot of ways the Hispanics resemble earlier cohorts of immigrants, especially those of the "third wave," the Italians, Jews, and eastern Europeans. To begin with, Hispanics are not a single ethnic group; they span at least twenty nationalities, including large, distinctive, and regionally separated cohorts of Mexicans (centered in California and the Southwest), Cubans (based in Florida), and Puerto Ricans and Dominicans (in metropolitan New York), but also—and increasingly—migrants from every South American, Central American, and Spanish-speaking Caribbean nation. Their ethnic traditions are not "Hispanic" but are grounded in specific national or even local communities. According to the sociologists Alejandro Portes and Ruben

Rumbaut, "Colombian immigrants certainly know that they are Colombian and Mexicans that they are Mexican; what they probably do not know when they arrive in the United States is that they belong to a larger ethnic category called Hispanics."[6] Beyond nationality, Hispanics vary in countless other ways. While most Hispanics are Catholics, many are various denominations of Protestants. Their "racial" aspect can vary from white to black or Indian and any combination in between. Some "Hispanics" have lived in the United States for generations; others arrived this year.

All that Hispanics have in common is a language—Spanish—and even that commonality is illusory. In addition to the many national and regional dialects that distinguish Hispanic immigrants from different corners of the Spanish-speaking world, a growing proportion are more proficient in English than Spanish. This observation is true not only of the sizable number of American-born Hispanics who are now completely comfortable in English and rarely if ever speak their ancestral language, but also of the majority of Hispanic immigrant children who are growing up in the United States. Psycholinguists have shown that children under the age of eleven inevitably acquire the dominant language of their environment, and as they do, many stop speaking Spanish. Even Hispanic immigrant adults, like many non-English-speaking immigrants of earlier cohorts, often lose their fluency in their native language long before they master English and end up speaking that linguistic hybrid, "Spanglish."

If the linguistic and cultural glue that binds America's Hispanics to each other is relatively weak, the forces that tie them to the larger American society are compelling. Many Hispanics may be poor, but overall they have high rates of workforce participation and are making strong gains in income and education. The majority of Hispanics still live in ethnic enclaves, as did their third-wave predecessors at a comparable stage of acclimation to life in their new country, but a growing number are living among—and even marrying—non-Hispanics. According to a recent survey, an overwhelming majority of Hispanics are even eager to learn English.[7]

But working assiduously to counter the natural forces of Hispanic assimilation are a vocal and politically influential cadre of Hispanic activists who demand that American institutions treat

Hispanics differently from other Americans. Dependent primarily on funding from private foundations (Ford, Carnegie, Rockefeller, and others) and from the government, organizations like the Mexican American Legal Defense and Education Fund, the National Council of La Raza, and ASPIRA have lobbied and litigated to enshrine governmental policies of bilingual education, Hispanic job and educational preferences, gerrymandered Hispanic electoral districts, and assorted other Hispanic "rights."[8] As Linda Chavez, director of the Center for the New American Community, wrote:

> Now ethnic leaders demand that their groups remain separate, that their native culture and language be preserved intact, and that whatever accommodation takes place be on the part of the receiving society. Hispanic leaders have been among the most demanding, insisting that Hispanic children be taught in Spanish; that Hispanic adults be allowed to cast their ballots in their native language and that they have the right to vote in districts in which Hispanics make up the majority of voters; that their ethnicity entitles them to a certain percentage of jobs and college admissions; that immigrants from Latin America be granted many of these same benefits, even if they are in the country illegally.[9]

This is ethnic federalism pure and simple: group rights rather than individual rights, ethnic identity rather than national identity, and Spanish fluency rather than English fluency. However much today's Hispanics might resemble their Italian, Jewish, Polish, or Greek immigrant predecessors, a pervasive national accommodation to their leaders' ethnic federalist demands will keep them from assimilating as successfully.

What is especially frustrating is the illogic of the ethnic federalist model as applied to Hispanics. As we have seen, ethnic federalism in the United States grew out of the black campaign for civil rights. Blacks embraced it to compensate for centuries of discrimination, and whites accepted it as a way to make things up to blacks, to assuage their guilt; ethnic federalism was thus an antidote to racialist victimization. As applied to blacks, ethnic federalism may be mistaken, but it is not entirely implausible. But the status of

Hispanics in America does not resemble that of blacks in the least; it is far more comparable to that of America's other immigrants. Hispanics came to America voluntarily, they were never enslaved, and they were no more the objects of explicit segregation or discrimination than were other immigrants. Nevertheless, Hispanic activists and their non-Hispanic funders and supporters have borrowed the ideology and tactics of the black civil rights movement and have sought, successfully, to apply them to the Hispanic "cause." Some Hispanic activists base their ethnic federalist claims on the fact that Mexicans settled in Texas and California before the Anglos, who "stole" their land. But even if their complaint had any merit, it would apply only to Mexicans, not to other Hispanics—and only to the original displaced settlers or their descendants, not to recent Mexican migrants.

If ethnic federalism makes sense for Hispanics, it makes sense for all American ethnic groups—Irish, Jews, Italians, Chinese, and perhaps even the vanishing WASPs. Not only is such a scenario unthinkable to most Americans, but Hispanic activists would hardly welcome having to compete for ethnic recognition not only with blacks, but with all other American ethnic groups as well.

Not only does keeping Hispanics from assimilating not make any logical or historical sense, it runs against their individual and collective self-interest, and most rank-and-file Hispanics know it. Chavez's assertion that for most Hispanics "assimilation represents the opportunity to succeed in America" is supported by many other surveys and studies.[10] The suit against bilingual education in New York, after all, was brought by *Hispanic* parents. (A non-Hispanic judge dismissed it.) Most Hispanics want their children to learn English as quickly and proficiently as possible, have no interest in gerrymandered electoral districts, and demand no special privileges or concessions. If they possess an ethnic sensibility at all, it is centered not on a general Latino identity, but—like earlier immigrants—on their specific nationality: Cuban, Mexican, Puerto Rican, Dominican. All this would be good news except for the fact that many American institutions are supporting the demands of the Latino activists and disregarding the wishes of the usually silent Hispanic majority.[11]

Just as only a few ethnic groups disavow the American assimilation paradigm, only a few institutions are deeply involved in sabotaging it. The key culprits are public schools, colleges and universities, and mainstream foundations. To the extent that government, corporations, and the media have aided and abetted the antiassimilationist cause, they have been largely guided and informed by these institutions. Public schools offer by far the most pervasive setting for the promotion of an ideology hostile to assimilation and supportive of ethnic federalism. Through most of American history, when public education was driven by an assimilationist mission, the universality and uniformity of public education furthered assimilation. Today, however, that same universality and uniformity is harnessed to an antiassimilationist perspective. Generations of young Americans are thus exposed from an impressionable early age to currently fashionable curricula that undercut assimilation. Hispanic youngsters are imprisoned in ghettoes of bilingual instruction. Black youngsters learn bad history and alienation from mainstream American society in programs of "Afrocentricism." And everyone else learns to see their classmates as members of ethnic groups, rather than as fellow Americans, through an array of "diversity" initiatives.

But public schools are merely the instruments, not the originators, of antiassimilationism and ethnic federalism. As in all shifting intellectual fashions, the public schools are the last link in the chain of cultural diffusion. By the time ideas find their way into the schools, they have been thoroughly articulated and approved by more prestigious and rarefied layers of America's intellectual hierarchy. Most ideas and fashions originate in America's institutions of higher education. And although only 45 percent of Americans attend college or university and 22 percent graduate, higher education exerts a disproportionate influence on American life. Not only does the minority with college degrees (including, of course, public school teachers and principals) have greater authority than other Americans, the college and university faculty have enormous influence as experts and leaders of informed opinion. But the most powerful messages of ethnic federalism are transmitted on the campuses themselves. "Affinity"-based dormitories segregated by race and ethnicity send an ethnic federalist message. So does the existence of departments of African American and Latino (or Hispanic) studies and the content of "diversity" curricula. Even something as unexceptionable as the new campus codes that prohibit "hateful" speech, by focusing mainly on ethnic slurs, call attention to ethnicity, rather than promote ethnic tolerance. More insidiously, the content of many college courses in history, sociology, political science, and philosophy nurtures an ethnocentric and antiassimilationist perspective.

Institutions of higher education were not always opposed to assimilation. Through most of American history, colleges and universities were at the cutting edge of the assimilation project. University faculty wrote the history and political science texts that codified and celebrated the American Idea. The proliferation of inexpensive public colleges throughout the United States, like the City College of New York and the state land-grant universities, and the unprecedented number of college places they made available to Americans, allowed millions of immigrant youths to become upwardly mobile and integrate into mainstream American society. American colleges' and universities' broad vocational and professional curricula and emphasis on sports and social activities fostered economic and social assimilation.

Undeniably, most of higher education's historic assimilationist features are still present, but they coexist uneasily now with the antiassimilationist ideology being promoted in the classroom and the dormitory. The prevailing "political correctness" divides and confuses today's college students. As the journalist Neomi Rao put it: "Welcome to the multicultural college campus. Here you will be defined by your race, gender, ethnicity and sexual orientation even before you enroll in classes."[12] For a minority of college graduates, this experience will make them devoted disseminators of multiculturalism when they take their places in public school classrooms, corporate boardrooms, or any number of other community or workplace settings. But for the majority, it will only nurture ethnic and racial prejudice or alienate them from a common American identity. That is why, apparently inexplicably, there are so many incidents of outright racism on college campuses and why the rabidly "politically incorrect" *Dartmouth Review* attracts such a noisy following at one of the most elite bastions of the Ivy League. What colleges and universities have wrought, only colleges and universities can undo. Ethnic federalism was born in academe, and it continues to be nurtured there. Should academe come to change its mind and embrace assimilation again, the new perspective will quickly spread to the schools, the media, and the rest of American society. That academe may change its mind is not an entirely vain hope. Some of the leading promoters of an assimilationist perspective, like Lawrence Fuchs, Richard Alba, Stephen Thernstrom, Abigail Thernstrom, and Arthur M. Schlesinger, Jr., are prominent academics, and the mounting number of antiethnocentric articles and books suggests that their ranks are growing.

In *Out of the Barrio* Linda Chavez described the extensive efforts of the Ford, Carnegie, Rockefeller, and other foundations on behalf of bilingualism and other Hispanic separatist efforts.[13] But these same foundations have been committed to ethnic federalism on many other fronts. In fact, if America's colleges and universities are the incubators of ethnic federalism, foundations are its main financial backers. Indeed, foundations lie at the very heart of the ethnic federalist enterprise. They have an influence disproportionate to their very considerable pocketbooks because they are symbiotically intertwined with the universities and governmental agencies whose activities they support in a revolving-door ecology at least as integrated as that of the fabled "military-industrial complex." For starters, the leadership of foundations, universities, and "soft" state and local governmental agencies—departments of education and social services—rotate from one institutional venue to another. John Gardner, president of the Carnegie Foundation from 1955 to 1965, became Lyndon Johnson's secretary of the Department of Health, Education and Welfare (HEW) before he returned to the nonprofit sector. Donna Shalala, the current secretary of the Department of Health and Human Services (HEW's successor), was the president of two universities and is said to be seeking a foundation presidency. Beyond sending their leaders to the federal government, foundations fund governmental pilot projects, and, although they are enjoined from outright lobbying, lend critical support for or against legislation. Foundations support the creation of university departments, curricula, and research; faculty of universities become the program officers of foundations; and administrators of universities become the executives of foundations.

As journalist David Samuels pointed out in a recent *New Republic* article, whereas foundations once used their influence to promote a variety of substantive social, economic, and scientific experiments (Head Start, Model Cities, public housing, federal jobs programs, and the polio vaccine all began as foundation initiatives), they have turned their attention increasingly to the sociocultural arena, and the promotion of ethnic federalism in America is high on their sociocultural agenda.[14] As Samuels observed while attending a conference of the Council of Foundations, the foundation world's leading "industry" association:

> [The council is] influential in setting a multiculturalist agenda for foundations big and small. . . . To wander the halls of the council-sponsored conference in San Francisco is to see the cartoon pages of William Bennett and Dinesh D'Souza [two prominent opponents of multiculturalism] brought spectacularly to life. When not attending the conference sessions—which range from "Philanthropic Courage: Promoting an Agenda of Genuine Inclusion" to "The Colors of Desire: A Multimedia, Multicultural Performance"—participants can eat, drink and make new friends at receptions sponsored by any one of the council's "affinity groups": "Native Americans in Philanthropy," "Asian Americans in Philanthropy," "Hispanics in Philanthropy," . . . and the "Association of Black Foundation Executives."[15]

Whether cast in terms of the current buzzwords like *diversity* or *inclusion* or plain old generic *multiculturalism,* the goal of various foundation initiatives is to make Americans more—not less—aware of their respective ethnicities, and the aim of most such initiatives is to instill among America's ostensible ethnic "victims"—blacks, Hispanics, and Native Americans—a powerful sense of grievance and alienation. That is why activities related to the positive side of immigration and ethnicity, including the stunning success of recently arrived and initially dirt-poor Asians, are so distasteful to them and almost never get funded. Samuels reported how a delegation of foundation officers visiting San Francisco's Tenderloin, a neighborhood of poor Southeast Asians, hoping to come across tales of misery and victimization were profoundly disappointed and annoyed when an illiterate Indo-Chinese immigrant boasted of his two children in college.[16] Because Asians belie the ethnic federalist stereotype—they want to assimilate, and they are doing well—foundations have been influential in sweeping Asians (a true minority if there ever was one) off the "diversity" map, often making them ineligible for the special assistance available to other minorities, and excluding Asian studies from the pantheon of college ethnic studies programs they are apt to fund. Foundations today seem to be even more insulated from the shifting currents of public or even intellectual opinion than are colleges and universities, but if inroads against ethnocentricity take hold in academe, as I believe they will, the foundations are bound to follow suit.

Academe develops the discourse of ethnic federalism, and foundations fund its dissemination, but it is the federal government that has made ethnic federalism the law of the land. The government applies ethnic federalist policies to the classroom when it mandates bilingual, Afrocentric, and other curricula. And the government applies ethnic federalist policies to American politics when it mandates ethnically drawn electoral districts. But the most comprehensive policies of government-sponsored ethnic federalism are the repertoire of ethnic preferences imposed under the label "affirmative action."

Affirmative action policies give preferential consideration to applicants for jobs, contracts, school or college places, and other competitive positions on the basis of applicants' ethnicity or gender. The federal government originated affirmative action in the Civil Rights Act of 1964 and created the Equal Employment Opportunities Commission to enforce it, but most state and local governments now have affirmative action laws and agencies as well. The implementation of affirmative action relies on governments' ability to apply ethnic and gender criteria directly when selecting candidates for jobs or other slots in their own agencies and institutions and indirectly by threatening to enforce governmental sanctions against all noncompliant employers or institutions that receive any form of governmental assistance (including most large businesses and nonprofit agencies and all private universities). Affirmative action was originally conceived to help blacks overcome their historic legacy of racial discrimination, an undeniably worthy goal. However, since it has moved far beyond that narrow objective and now promotes a pervasive ethnic consciousness—to paraphrase the social commentator Arch Puddington, a propensity "to count by ethnicity"—affirmative action no longer does much to help members of the large black economic underclass (if it ever did), but it does make ethnic federalism pay off handsomely for other individuals, most of them nonblacks, who can successfully stake an ethnic preferential claim.

The foregoing *tour d'horizon* suggested that whether confronting the antiassimilationism of black and Hispanic activists, the antiassimilationist activities of foundations and educational institutions, or the antiassimilationist effects of governmental programs, the proponents of assimilation need to focus their attacks on one issue: ethnocentricity. The reason to oppose multiculturalism on the college campus is not mainly because it is intolerant and occasionally impales some hapless college students or faculty on the spikes of "political correctness." The reason to oppose bilingual education in the schools is not mainly because it slows down the rate at which Hispanic or other immigrant children learn English. The reason to oppose Afrocentric studies in schools and colleges is not mainly because it teaches inaccurate history. The reason to disdain foundation-sponsored programs of "diversity" is not mainly because they distract attention and resources from more urgent social causes. The reason to oppose government-sponsored affirmative action policies is not mainly because they are occasionally unfair to white men or may install unqualified applicants in jobs or colleges. These and other products of the antiassimilationist sensibility are bad because of only one overriding—and shared—reason: They make *ethnicity* a primary civic criterion in a country whose happiness depends on ethnicity being insignificant.

A number of highly respected scholars and social critics are now attacking the excesses of ethnic federalism in its various forms: Arthur M. Schlesinger, Jr., Linda Chavez, Lawrence Fuchs, Stephen and Abigail Thernstrom, William Bennett, and Arch Puddington, to name just a few members of this growing band. Their critiques are pointed and highly effective, and among their many complaints about specific aspects of muticulturalism, they all call attention to its ethnic divisiveness. My point is that multiculturalism's elevation of ethnicity and ethnic consciousness is not just one of its faults, it is its monumentally wrongheaded—and intended—principal fault. The United States is just about the only nation on earth to have premised its national identity on something other than a shared ethnic identity. For two centuries, it has maintained an extraordinary level of comity among a vast and growing population that is unmatched anywhere on earth in its ethnic diversity by deliberately disregarding ethnicity as a salient social criterion. The abiding sin of the multiculturalists, whatever their arena and however well intentioned their motives, is to subvert this centuries-old basis of national unity. It is on this singular ideological issue that the battle for the revival of assimilation, American style must be fought.

11

An Assimilationist Immigration Policy

It is simplistic to say that because we have always been a nation of immigrants, we must and should remain a country that welcomes immigrants. . . . We now admit more than 800,000 legal immigrants each year. Since it has happened before, it is likely that a sentiment to restrict growth will emerge again.

Nathan Glazer, 1994[1]

The United States Congress has, since 1995, been debating radical changes in the immigration law. The changes being considered are linked to assimilation in two ways. First, assumptions about the nature and extent of assimilation influence the kinds of policies being contemplated. Second, the contour of immigration policy is itself an important factor in facilitating or retarding the assimilation of the next generation of immigrants.

Four issues are embedded in national immigration policy: how many immigrants to admit each year, the basis for deciding whom to admit, how the government deals with those who come without permission (illegal immigrants), and how the government treats immigrants once they are here. In each of these respects, the congressional proposals that are being considered would make immigration policies more stringent: The ceiling on legal immigration would be reduced by 30 percent or more; preference would be given to applicants with the highest skills or education; sterner measures would be taken to bar or punish illegal immigrants; and nonnaturalized immigrants would be denied a variety of benefits.

The campaign to change immigration law is being driven by politicians' belief that a growing number of Americans are now alarmed at the consequences of decades of liberalized immigration policy. Since the forty-year era of restricted immigration officially ended with the passage of the Immigration and Nationality Act amendments of 1965, nearly 20 million immigrants have legally entered the United States,[2] and another 3 million to 5 million immigrants have entered the country illegally or overstayed their visitor status.[3] Until about 1992, all public discussions of immigration were overwhelmingly positive: Immigrants were praised for their initiative; immigration was celebrated for its economic and cultural benefits; and America, nation of immigrants, was considered to be alive and well. But since 1993, an increasingly noisy chorus of complaints about immigrants and immigration has dominated the public discourse, resulting finally in a clamor for more restrictionist immigration policies.

Like many sudden shifts in public opinion, changing attitudes toward immigration are difficult to interpret. Most respondents to recent opinion polls have wanted less immigration than they did just a few years earlier, but such polls have never registered much support for greater immigration, even when people held favorable views of immigrants.[4] One also cannot be sure of the depth of public feelings about immigration. Most Americans who do not live in the immigration gateway states and regions have little contact with immigrants, and immigration is rarely cited as an urgent issue in opinion surveys. Such anti-immigrant feeling as exists may reflect a delayed response to the deep economic recession of 1989 to 1992, especially in California, a state that has been heavily affected by both economic adversity and record numbers of immigrants. It may signify a threshold effect, whereby the sheer volume of immigration has now reached a level high enough to trigger a nativist backlash.

Or it may be fueled by media commentators and politicians who have been influenced by a spate of recent anti-immigrant articles and books by writers like George Borjas, Peter Brimelow, Leon Bouvier, Vernon Briggs, and Donald Huddle.[5]

But whatever the origin of the new nativism, it would be a colossal mistake for Congress to return the United States to a restrictionist immigration policy. Even on the narrowest economic grounds, it is evident that the recent immigration has been good for America, especially for those places most affected by it. The most persuasive restrictionists—Borjas, Briggs, and Brimelow—justify their hostility to immigration primarily on economic grounds, arguing that the net economic contributions of immigrants, especially the most recently arrived, have been negative, that immigrants cost gateway states and cities more in governmental services than they contribute in taxes, and that immigrants take jobs away from the native-born poor. However, their case rests primarily on tortured short-term microeconomic analyses, and even these analyses are subject to different interpretations. A better way to gauge the effects of immigration on the United states is to compare the fortunes of places that have taken in large numbers of immigrants with those that have not.

California, the largest immigrant gateway state and the epicenter of the new nativism, is perhaps the best case in point. Until it was devastated by the recent national recession (whose impact on California was greatly exacerbated by the post–cold war military demobilization), California's economy was one of the most vital in the United States. Between 1970 and 1989, its economy grew at the rate of 5 percent a year, twice the rate of the rest of the nation. Its population rose correspondingly: In 1970 California, with 20 million people, contained under 10 percent of the U.S. population; today, with 31 million residents, it accounts for over 12 percent. A large share of California's recent prosperity can be directly attributed to the state's absorption of millions of immigrants in this period. Edward J. W. Park, a University of Southern California sociologist, documented that about a quarter of California's two thousand high-technology companies in Silicon Valley, including the fifteen most successful ones, are run by immigrants.[6] The journalist Joel Kotkin concurred:

Immigrants are . . . playing a critical role in [California] as owners of technology businesses. In fact, six of the fourteen CEOs on
the *Orange County Business Journal*'s list of top manufacturers
were born outside the United States. ... .

Kingston Technologies, the nation's fastest-growing technology company . . . was founded in 1988 by Chinese immigrants.
Today, it creates jobs for hundreds of people in northeast Orange
County. . . . Its own 300-person work force includes immigrants
from at least 20 countries.[7]

Within California, there are few better advertisements for the
benefits of immigration than San Diego, where over 20 percent of
the population is foreign born and 30 percent speak a foreign language at home. San Diego's unemployment rate is nearly two
points below the statewide average; its crime rate has fallen 24 percent in recent years; and the local government's expenditures are
enviably low, even by national standards. Yet, ironically, San Diego
is one of the most fervent strongholds of Californian nativism.[8]

As dramatic as the meteoric, immigration-driven, economic and
demographic rise of places like San Diego since the 1960s has been
the revival of other American cities, in California and elsewhere,
that have attracted a large number of immigrants. Perhaps the best
example of a city whose fortunes revived because of immigrants is
New York. From 1970 to 1980, the city's economy lost nearly
600,000 jobs and its population fell by more than a million. Then,
beginning in the late 1970s, it began receiving hundreds of thousands of immigrants a year, more than a million by 1990. Its economy recovered spectacularly during most of this period, and its
population regained half its previous decade's loss. Since 1990,
New York's economy, like California's, has been in the doldrums,
but the stagnation has been due entirely to adverse national economic trends (the retrenchment and restructuring of financial services has been to New York what the collapse of the aerospace
industry was to California). Without its immigrants, New York
would be in much worse shape today.

But the most spectacular impacts of immigrants on cities cannot be gleaned from statistics; they can be understood only by visiting inner-city neighborhoods in the cities awash with new immi-

grants. Areas of New York, Miami, Los Angeles, San Francisco, and Chicago that were rapidly sinking into terminal deterioration have revived. Visit New York's Elmhurst, Jackson Heights, Flushing, and even its notorious South Bronx; Miami's Little Havana; or Chicago's Greektown, and you encounter flourishing shopping streets, new housing construction, active parks and playgrounds, lower crime rates, and a general atmosphere of vitality and hope in places that only a decade or so earlier were swamps of social pathology and physical decay.

It has been argued that these places revived at the expense of the native American—usually black—poor, but the evidence from America's cities appears to prove the opposite. A comparison of five cities with the largest proportion of recent immigrants with five cities that have the smallest share is revealing. The high-immigration cities have markedly lower unemployment rates, lower welfare rates, and more rapid employment growth than their low-immigration counterparts. The employment rates of blacks have also risen substantially more in high-immigration cities than in cities bypassed by immigration, and if New York is typical, the physical regeneration of immigrant enclaves inevitably spills over into the neighborhoods of the black poor. Although there is little evidence that immigrant-led revitalizations of inner cities have displaced or harmed the native poor, there is clear statistical evidence that American cities with the smallest immigrant cohorts—places like Detroit, St. Louis, Cleveland, and Buffalo—have continued to decline. (See Table 1.)

Although criticism of the high volume of recent immigrants is mistaken, the rules determining which immigrants get to come to the United States may profitably be reexamined. As it stands, American immigration policy, underneath its ever-changing surface complexity, is heavily skewed in its criteria for deciding whom, among the millions applying each year, to admit. Consistently and clearly favored are applicants in three key categories: those who are relatives of American citizens and residents, those who are fleeing political or religious persecution, and those who are in valued professions and occupations. Applicants in these generic categories are given "preference" according to several hierarchical principles.

TABLE 1. COMPARISON OF ECONOMIC INDICATORS IN HIGH-
AND LOW-IMMIGRATION CITIES

City	Percentage of Foreign Born	Median Income	Percentage on Welfare	Growth of Employment 1980–90
San Francisco	34.0	33,414	10.4	12.6
New York	28.4	29,823	13.1	13.2
San Jose	26.5	46,206	8.9	32.4
El Paso	23.4	23,460	9.7	27.5
Boston	20.0	29,180	11.9	14.7
Pittsburgh	4.6	20,747	13.7	–9.7
Buffalo	4.5	18,482	18.7	–1.9
Cleveland	4.1	17,822	21.9	–11.7
Detroit	3.4	18,742	26.1	–13.7
St. Louis	2.5	19,458	13.6	–6.9

Source: U.S. Bureau of the Census, *1993 City and County Data Book*
(Washington, D.C.: U.S. Government Printing Office, 1994).

Relatives of citizens are preferred to relatives of permanent residents. Among relatives, spouses, minor children, and parents are preferred over married children and siblings. Among occupations, highly educated professionals like physicians and engineers are preferred to those in less skilled occupations. Refugees from certain designated countries (such as those fleeing Communist dictatorships) have been preferred to people who randomly request asylum. These preferences are embedded in an aggregate annual immigration quota of about 700,000, exclusive of refugees and those seeking asylum.[9] In addition, the number of immigrants after 1988 was swollen by the amnesty of illegal immigrants who were given legal immigrant status under the Immigration Reform and Control Act of 1986 (IRCA). All told, the United States has admitted between 600,000 and 900,000 immigrants a year since 1986, not counting the illegal immigrants who received amnesty under the IRCA.[10]

By far the largest number of immigrants admitted each year fall under the general category of "family reunification," which reflects an overwhelming policy bias toward relatives of American residents over all other applicants. In 1993, nearly 500,000 of the 700,000 regular immigration places were reserved for family members.[11] When the "national origins" basis of prevailing immigration policy was overturned in 1965, the explicit justification for grounding the new system in family-based immigration preferences was that it would favor *European* immigrants. Since most Americans had European roots, it was supposed that most immigrants who would be admitted under a family-preference system would naturally be Europeans. Americans were prepared for the arrival of more Italians and Greeks and fewer English and Germans than under the old quota system, but they expected the net effect to be pro-European.

Events did not turn out that way because by the 1960s most Europeans—even Italians and Greeks—lived in countries that were enjoying newfound political stability and prosperity. So although Europeans immigrated to the United States in somewhat greater numbers after 1965 than they did before, they hardly exhausted the more generous immigration quotas of the new policy. If Europeans no longer found going to America so compelling after 1965, Latin Americans, Asians, and people from the Caribbean did. In the two decades before the new immigration policy, 55 percent of all immigrants came from Europe, 22 percent from Latin America and the Caribbean, and 5 percent from Asia. In the two decades afterward, 13 percent of all immigrants were European, 45 percent were Latin or Caribbean, and 37 percent were Asian.[12]

Initially, the new system attracted immigrants from a broad cross section of nationalities, but over time the idiosyncrasies of the preference system have skewed the nationality mix toward immigrants from just a handful of countries. In 1993, fifteen countries accounted for nearly 70 percent of all immigrants, and Mexico alone contributed 14 percent. The other countries in the top ten are China, the Philippines, Vietnam, the former Soviet Union, the Dominican Republic, India, Poland, El Salvador, and the United Kingdom.[13] The various nationalities owe their immigration quotas, however, to different features of current immigration policy. Applicants from Vietnam and the former Soviet Union are the most important beneficiaries of refugee preferences. Most immigrants from other countries come under one or another family preference. But by far the most important policy affecting the nationality mix of legal immigrants since 1988 has been the invitation extended to illegal immigrants to legalize their status under the amnesty provisions of the IRCA. Mexicans' disproportionate share of total immigration and the large number of Haitians and Salvadorans are mainly a product of amnesty. But to qualify for amnesty, immigrants had to have been in the United States since 1982, so the IRCA did not really result in the admission of new immigrants; it merely flushed out and legalized the status of millions of illegal immigrants who were already here.

The dramatic impact of the IRCA—the addition since 1988 of about 3 million legal immigrants to the number normally admitted—including over 1 million Mexicans, raises two important issues with regard to immigration policy. First, there is the issue of illegal immigration itself. The primary objective of the IRCA was to stem the tide of illegal immigration by outlawing the employment of illegal immigrants and imposing stringent economic sanctions on employers who flouted its provisions. The amnesty provision of the IRCA was adopted as the price its sponsors, Senator Alan Simpson of Wyoming and Representative Romano Mazzoli of Kentucky, had to pay to get congressional support for strong sanctions against employers. Ten years after passage of the IRCA, it appears that the IRCA's major feature, employer sanctions, has been largely unsuccessful in reducing the flow of illegal immigration, but its secondary provision, amnesty (included only to get employer sanctions) has been highly effective in legalizing the status of—some would say "rewarding"—a generation of illegal immigrants.

Illegal immigration is the hot issue of the immigration debate today and one of the principal factors inflaming the new nativism. During his unsuccessful run for the Republican presidential nomination in 1996, Patrick J. Buchanan was the most outspoken anti-immigration candidate, especially when he campaigned in California, but he reserved most of his fire for illegal immigration, as when he stood at the Mexican border next to one of the recently constructed giant border-control fences proclaiming, "We can keep them [illegal immigrants] out."[14] Proposition 187, the most aggressive public policy generated by California's current nativist climate, ostensibly directs its punitive sanctions mainly against illegal immigrants (as, for example, requiring teachers to report the presence of illegal immigrant children in their classes). When congressmen give speeches on immigration policy, they usually make sure to couple their disdain for illegal immigrants with praise for legal immigrants and their descendants, and the legislation they propose directs its harshest language and its most stringent provisions at illegal immigration.

Many supporters of immigration have responded to these attacks on illegal immigration by pointing out that illegal immigrants don't differ substantially in most respects from legal ones, that is, they possess the work ethic, family values, and other virtues common to all immigrants; that the newfound vitality of immigration-impacted cities and states owes as much to illegal as to legal immigrants; and that punishing illegal immigrants would be socially and economically counterproductive.[15] The more extreme advocates even propose that illegal immigrants be allowed to vote, that they be made eligible for welfare, and that they should not be deported even when arrested for felonies.[16] Explicitly and implicitly, the apologists for illegal immigration make the case for leaving illegal immigrants alone, treating them like legal residents, or legalizing them with occasional amnesties the way the IRCA did.

The other issue raised by the IRCA is that with 87 percent of all IRCA-amnestied immigrants coming from four countries— Mexico (accounting for 80 percent), Haiti, El Salvador, and Guatemala—the interaction of IRCA amnesty and family-based preferences will result in a disproportionate number of future immigration places being taken by immigrants from these countries.[17] As long as applicants for immigration who have legally resident relatives in the United States are favored over all others, and IRCA-amnestied recent immigrants represent the largest bloc of Americans eager to have their relatives join them here, the combination will impart a distinct regional bias to the nationality mix, a bias that will only be exacerbated if total immigration quotas are reduced.

Why should we care? Simple fairness is one reason, but I also believe that assimilation suffers if the nationality mix becomes too skewed. An immigration dynamic dominated by a few nationalities and concentrated in only a few places is apt to intensify the anti-immigrant sentiments of natives and contribute to the social isolation of immigrants. Perhaps California is the epicenter of current nativism not just because it is most heavily affected by immigration per se or has the largest number of illegal immigrants, but because it has the largest number of amnestied former illegal immigrants and is the state that is the most dominated by a single immigrant nationality, Mexican. Perhaps California is also fertile territory for the antiassimilationism of Latino activists for the same reasons; a rapidly growing Mexican American population, living geographically isolated in vast barrios, offers Latino advocates a growing constituency for policies of Latino-based ethnic federalism. And Californians' attitudes toward immigration and assimilation matter because their distress has infected the national debate on immigration policy.

Turning a blind eye to illegal immigration may harm the prospects for assimilation and future immigrants, but America's legal immigration system is also far from ideal. Indeed, there is probably no desirable paradigm or formula for "designing" the mix of immigrants. Every attempt to find one since the United States first developed a comprehensive immigration policy in the 1920s has been unsatisfactory. The national-origins concept, which was introduced in the Immigration Act of 1924 and sustained though the McCarran-Walter Act of 1952, was explicitly—and shamefully—discriminatory toward particular nationalities and racist to the core. The family-preference system, which has been the foundation of American immigration policy since 1965, while superficially attractive (who wants to argue against reuniting families?) has been degenerating into a latter-day version of the national-origins system by increasingly skewing immigration toward the nationalities of recent immigrants. Although this system is not generating the nationality mix that was originally envisioned, it is having precisely the effect that the architects of the 1965 immigration reforms anticipated: biasing the immigrant mix toward those nationalities that are already heavily represented.

Many proponents of immigration reforms advocate instead a "designer" immigration policy that would favor skilled and professional workers, a bias that dominates Canada's immigration policy (which also favors applicants with substantial financial resources), and is found in the lower tiers of the current American preference system. Although such a policy may guarantee a more affluent immigrant population and minimize the likelihood of immigrants being a "burden" to this country, it completely undercuts America's historic role as "the land of the new beginning," the philosophical foundation for allowing immigration in the first place. A skills-based policy would perversely vest the privilege of American immigration in those who have been the most privileged in their homelands, those with the least need to emigrate. Such a policy may not even be beneficial to the American economy because there is probably a greater need for immigrant workers at the bottom of the labor market than for immigrant professionals at the top.

Another long-standing feature of American immigration policy has granted a certain number of places to refugees—persons who are seeking to flee their countries because of "a well-founded fear of being persecuted for reasons of race, religion, nationality, membership of a particular social group or political opinion"[18]—and "asylees," refugees who have succeeded in escaping. In other words, you are a refugee if the United States grants you permission to immigrate before you leave your country and an asylee if you apply for legal immigrant status after you get here. As the policies on refugees and asylees have actually been applied by the United States, you are a refugee if you seek to leave a Communist dictatorship and an asylee if you have fled some other kind of authoritarian regime. This aspect of America's immigration-preference system is particularly subject to misapplication because it depends heavily on changing and arbitrary standards of political and personal discretion and, for most of the post–World War II period, has been merely an instrument of cold war politics. Millions of Europeans who needed a haven from German genocide in the early 1940s were turned away (and subsequently slaughtered), but those who applied from selected nations of the Communist bloc in subsequent decades—Hungarians in the 1950s, Cubans in the 1960s, Vietnamese in the 1970s, and Russians in the 1980s—were admitted with alacrity whether they were in any immediate danger or not. The political bias of the policy of giving preference to refugees and asylees continues to this day: No regime in Haiti is ever murderous enough to make more Haitians eligible as refugees, and no African country's policies of persecution or mutilation are ever cruel enough to make Africans eligible as asylees, but as long as Fidel Castro is in power, Cubans will continue to be welcome.

What, then, are the proper building blocks of an assimilationist immigration policy? There are four: First, the United States should admit a large but stable number of immigrants each year; second, the door must be closed to illegal immigrants; third, most immigration places should be awarded to applicants from all countries on a first-come, first-served basis; and fourth, immigrants should be encouraged to become citizens.

The average number of immigrants who have entered the United States annually in recent years, around 1.2 million including illegal immigrants, is actually a reasonable figure. Expressed as a ratio of the American population, it amounts to about 4.5 immigrants per thousand U.S. residents annually. To put this number in perspective, at the high point of immigration in the first decade of this century, the country was absorbing over 10 immigrants per thousand residents. But the volume of immigration has been unstable, swinging widely with changes in legal immigration policy and the zeal with which illegal immigration is tackled. For example, the IRCA amnesty dramatically swelled the number of immigrants from 1988 to 1991, raising the total to 1.8 million immigrants in the peak year of 1991, and illegal immigration can vary between 150,000 to 300,000 a year.[19] Adding to the prospective volatility in the near term, Congress is contemplating a sharp reduction in the quota of legal immigrants.

Instead of letting immigration continue to be such a wild card in America's demographic deck, the United States needs to set a single—and sustainable—aggregate annual quota of immigrants based on a percentage of the population and covering all preference categories (rather than have fixed quotas set by category), with an allowance for anticipated illegal immigration. The annual cap might be set at four immigrants per thousand U.S. residents (which would permit slightly over 1 million immigrants in 1997), and each year's population-based quota could be reduced by the estimated volume of the previous year's illegal immigration. Such a policy would maintain a reasonable relationship between immigration and the total population and would give advocacy groups for immigrants a strong incentive to cooperate in stemming illegal immigration. A policy that would provide more places for legal immigrants as it set about reducing the volume of illegal immigrants would be fairer all around and should be popular with advocates of immigrants as well as natives. A policy that would aim for a stable and predictable volume of immigrants, set at levels well within America's absorptive capacity but high enough to offer immigration seekers some hope of success, could keep the United States true to its immigration heritage, but assuage nativist fears that immigration may be getting out of control.

Even if they are right about the benign characteristics of illegal immigrants, those who argue for complacency about illegal immigration are making a big mistake. They are undermining the case for a liberal immigration policy in general and, more to the issues raised in this book, are undermining support for assimilation. As many commentators on both sides of the immigration issue have been quick to point out, if a nation cannot control its borders, it severely compromises its sovereignty.[20] But illegal immigration also hurts other immigrants. The essence of immigration policy is to establish reasonable criteria for selecting, among countless millions who wish to emigrate to America, the limited number who will be permitted to come. Even if advocates of immigration are indifferent to whether the ceiling on immigration is breached, they shouldn't be indifferent to the fact that illegal immigrants also violate the selection criteria. If the right to immigrate to the United States is a kind of "property right," illegal immigration represents a form of theft. But from whom is the "property" being taken? First, it is being taken from the native Americans who have the power to grant it, but ultimately—and perhaps more significantly—it is being seized from those who are waiting to enter the United States lawfully.

Then there is the issue of whether the United States should ever be indifferent to illegal behavior of any kind. At all times, the failure to enforce laws undermines respect for the law among the citizenry, but when immigration laws are allowed to be flouted, disrespect for American law is being communicated to the very people, immigrants, whom we should be most concerned about being socialized properly into American society. The lawbreaking doesn't even end with illegal immigration itself. The immigrants' undocumented status leads to the breaking of countless other laws, from evasion of the IRCA's employment prohibitions to minimum-wage and other labor laws to the evasion of taxes by both immigrants and their employers. The presence of illegal immigrants tempts even the most respectable Americans (such as Zoe Baird, President Clinton's first nominee for attorney general) to break the law. But another unfortunate message is also being sent: Both illegal and legal immigrants are being told that de facto immigration policy unfairly favors immigration queue jumpers over those who wait patiently for years to enter legally. An immigration law like the IRCA only reinforces both these messages. The amnesty rewards the initial lawbreaking, and the family-preference criteria of the rest of the immigration law compound the unfairness by favoring the relatives of queue jumpers over other potential immigrants.

Assimilation suffers on several counts. To begin with, the lawless climate in which illegal immigration thrives—the cottage industry of bootlegging immigrants, the immigrants' indentured servitude, the forged documents, the unsafe and overcrowded housing in violation of local building codes, the untaxed and below-minimum-wage income, and the children kept from schools and doctors—turns both natives and immigrants against assimilation. Assimilation depends on natives embracing immigrants as fellow Americans, but illegal immigration makes natives contemptuous and fearful of immigrants. Assimilation also depends on immigrants quickly integrating themselves into the civic matrix of American society—even if that matrix is initially immigrant based—but illegal immigration keeps immigrants isolated and alienated, not only from native Americans, but from civic institutions in general.

With the exception of the most die-hard advocates of immigrant rights, almost all Americans today favor stemming the tide of illegal immigration. Unfortunately, no one knows how to go about it. The IRCA policy of imposing sanctions on employers of illegal immigrants has not worked. The proposal that all American citizens and legal residents should carry forgery-resistant identification cards, advocated by California Senator Dianne Feinstein and others, is vehemently opposed by most Americans, who consider it an alien and unprecedented intrusion by the government on their personal freedoms. On the other hand, the proposals currently being considered by Congress and some state legislatures—and embedded in Proposition 187—to penalize illegal immigrants already here by denying their children an education are just as wrongheaded. In the unlikely event that it could pass judicial scrutiny or be locally implemented, such a policy would not deter new illegal immigrants from coming or make those already here go back to their homelands.

The only policy for reducing the flow of illegal immigrants that is consistent with American civic values and common sense is to keep illegal immigrants from entering the United States in the first place. With the application of sufficient resources—in money, equipment, personnel, and management strategies—it should be possible to keep most illegal immigrants from crossing the border with Mexico or coming into the country by air or by sea. And, in this computerized era, the Immigration and Naturalization Service should be able to keep track of visitors and students, to make sure they leave when their visas have expired. Clearly, the United States should be just as able to control its borders as any other country, but to do so it will have to spend a great deal more on this effort than it has until now.

Perhaps the most important change that an assimilationist immigration policy might include is to make the criteria for admitting immigrants fairer and more random. This change would allow more people without family connections to come to the United States and, in the process, would draw immigrants from a much broader array of countries. The precedent for doing so is already established because the present law has a small allotment of immigration places, awarded by lottery, specifically geared to promoting geographic diversity. The United States ought to revise the criteria for admission to enlarge this category substantially while it scales back family and refugee preferences, dispenses with skills-based allotments, and allows most immigrants to come pretty much on a first-come, first-served basis. The historic mission of American immigration would be better served by allowing more of the world's most motivated immigrants—not just those who are lucky enough to have American relatives or to have received a good education—to realize the American Dream, and the prospects for assimilation would be enhanced in the bargain.

How might such a policy work? In 1993, about 200,000 of the 500,000 immigrants admitted under family sponsorship were spouses or children of Americans, in other words, immediate relatives with the most compelling claim to family reunification.[21] Another 130,000 immigrants who were already in the United States had their status "adjusted" as refugees and asylees in 1993.[22] Assuming the adoption of a 1997 aggregate immigration cap of 900,000 (after 150,000 places were subtracted for illegal immigrants), one could set aside 200,000 places for immediate relatives and another 100,000 places for refugees and asylees and still leave about 600,000 places available for a dramatically enlarged allotment of immigrants based on geographic diversity. Right now the small diversity quota of 33,000 is awarded by lottery. A fairer approach might be to put all diversity applicants on a worldwide waiting list, their status reviewed and approved at American immigration centers in each country. To avoid having the worldwide diversity quota swamped by applicants from the largest countries (China and India could preempt 40 percent of all places), perhaps no nation's quota should exceed some percentage of the total. Applicants should also be screened to determine their motivation for immigrating, their health, and any criminal or other unsavory facts in their background. However the details of a first-come, first-served admissions process were developed, the objective of such a process would be to offer the privilege of immigration to the most highly motivated candidates from the most diverse pool of applicants, selected by the fairest and most objective criteria.

The final stage of the immigration process is citizenship, or "naturalization" as it is commonly called (citizenship being the "natural" relationship of people to the country they live in). As was noted earlier, the United States has been unique among the world's nations in the liberality of its citizenship provisions. By international standards, the country has always made it extraordinarily easy for immigrants to become citizens and has conferred a citizenship more comprehensive and unconditional than that of other places. Moreover, unlike its ever-changing immigration rules, America's naturalization provisions have hardly changed over two centuries. To become a citizen, a legal immigrant must reside in the United States for five years and pass a not very challenging examination that tests his or her English proficiency and knowledge of American history and government. Immigrants' children, if born abroad, don't even have to take the test; they "derive" their citizenship from their parents. Immigrants' children who were born in the United States are automatically citizens.

Despite such liberal naturalization provisions, only about half of all immigrants availed themselves of citizenship for most of America's history. The likelihood of naturalization has always varied enormously by nationality and may be seen as a kind of measure of the assimilation-mindedness of each nationality cohort. At all times, the overwhelming majority of Irish, German, and Jewish immigrants became citizens. But among turn-of-the-century immigrants, Italians and eastern Europeans were far less likely to become naturalized than were others, and today Mexicans and other Hispanics have disappointingly low naturalization rates. Assimilation, American style has always left the decision to become citizens up to immigrants, and the United States could always be assured that at least all American-born children of immigrants would be citizens. Nevertheless, Americans have usually believed that since citizenship is such a precious gift, it should be eagerly embraced by immigrants and that citizenship hastens and solidifies assimilation.

This is the context for the renewed attention to the issue of citizenship in the current debate on immigration policy. In the days before appeals to ethnic federalism and multiculturalism cast shadows across Americans' confidence in the magic of assimilation, Americans were not overly concerned with the failure of many immigrants to take advantage of the country's uniquely liberal naturalization law. Today, with the assimilationist aspirations of both immigrants and natives in doubt, a higher incidence of naturalization looks especially attractive as a guarantor of assimilation. Some proposals for restricting immigration, in addition to lower ceilings for legal immigration and "get-tough on illegals" language, call for making citizenship—rather than mere legal residence—a condition for receiving a wide array of social welfare benefits (already a feature of the welfare reform bill enacted by Congress in 1996) and reserving family-sponsored immigration places—already greater for citizens than for residents—exclusively for citizens. Advocates of immigration have been quick to dismiss such ideas as being yet another example of the new nativism at work. But there may be a great deal of merit in encouraging immigrants to become citizens if such a provision can be adopted in the framework of a more, rather than less, liberal immigration policy. There is already evidence that the mere prospect of a link between citizenship and other benefits has motivated a record number of recent immigrants to apply for citizenship. During the 1980s, the number of annual applications for naturalization averaged slightly over 200,000.[23] By 1993 the number jumped to over 950,000. In Los Angeles alone, immigrants are rushing to become citizens at the rate of 2,200 per day.[24]

I believe that the act of becoming citizens not only seals the assimilation contract between immigrants and natives, but can be a powerful factor in defusing nativist sentiment. Also, by turning immigrants into voters, higher rates of naturalization can make the political environment much more hospitable to immigrants. However, because the mere threat of conditioning benefits on citizenship will not indefinitely move those who are less inclined to become citizens to be naturalized, at some point incentives for naturalization must be made an explicit legislative feature of immigration policy.

For a nation to have immigration, it must have an immigration policy. Most countries of the world have no immigration policy because they neither expect nor admit immigrants. In one of the more entertaining sections of *Alien Nation*, Brimelow described the incredulous reactions of the consular officials of Japan and some other nations when he asked them how one goes about immigrating to their countries. The United States has always had an immigration policy because it both expected and welcomed immigrants. During the country's first century, the immigration policy was simple: a completely open-door policy in which anyone who wanted to come was welcome. From 1882, when Congress passed the Chinese Exclusion Act, to 1924, when the national-origins system was adopted, the United States implemented in stages an ethnically discriminatory immigration policy: Only racially superior people should come. From 1924 to 1965, America went back to a simple immigration policy, but one that turned the first century's policy on its head: Almost no one should come. Since 1965, when the country threw open its doors to immigrants, Americans have struggled to find the right formula for immigration: How many relatives? How many skilled people? Who should qualify as a refugee? And, above all, what should we do about the gate crashers?

It is to Americans' great credit that the U.S. immigration policy is as generous and enlightened as it is. What other nation in the world is willing to accept a million foreigners a year, on any terms? A few countries are periodically inundated with refugees from unstable countries next door, but those refugees aren't immigrants, and the countries they flee to don't treat them like immigrants. America's liberal immigration policy is all of a piece with its liberal political traditions in general; it was born of those traditions and, in turn, reinforces them.

But even Americans can be made to doubt from time to time the wisdom or efficacy of their liberal immigration traditions. Happily, most Americans are aware enough of the economic and cultural contributions of immigrants that they will not easily be deflected from their tolerance of immigration by neonativists and restrictionists who are working to change the thrust of immigration policy. But nothing over the years—not even concrete economic benefits—has so solidified support for America's immigration experiment as the successful assimilation of its immigrants: assimilation, American style. As the country's citizens and politicians continue to debate immigration policy in the days ahead and to fine-tune the criteria regarding how many, and which, immigrants to admit, they must keep faith with America's two most powerful icons of immigration: the Statue of Liberty, which declares that immigrants are always welcome, and the melting pot, which says that immigrants must always assimilate.

12

Living Together
in Peace and Unity

> This new invention of Americans . . . in which [immigrants] were free to
> express their ancestral affections and sensibilities, to choose to be ethnic,
> however and whenever they wished or not at all by moving across group
> boundaries easily, was sanctioned and protected by a unifying civic culture
> based on the American founding myth, its institutions, heroes, rules, and
> rhetoric. . . . The new immigrants entered a process of ethnic-
> Americanization through participation in the political system, and, in so
> doing, established even more clearly the American civic culture as a basis
> of American unity.
>
> Lawrence H. Fuchs, 1990[1]

Not a day goes by without the pages of the *New York Times*
announcing another instance of ethnic strife—often bloody—in
another country. "Russians Attack Chechen Rebel Base," "Night
Brings Terror and Arson to Sarajevo Suburb," "Turkish Kurds Go
on Rampage, Battling the Police in Germany," and "Indian Forces
Destroy Kashmiri Muslim Shrine"[2] is just a limited sample of the
daily headlines chronicling the internal ethnic feuds in which
nations around the world are embroiled. Wait another week or so,
and you can look forward to reading about Irish Republican Army

bombings in Belfast or London, Armenians killing Azerbaijanis in Nagorno-Karabakh, Rwandan Hutus plotting in Zairan refugee camps to resume their war with Rwandan Tutsis, Tamils blowing up Sinhalese community centers in Sri Lanka, Hindis defiling Muslim mosques in Bombay, and French Canadians organizing their next secessionist campaign. If most of these clashes occur between ancient ethnic antagonists, another kind of ethnic conflict characterizes relations between natives and immigrants in even the most enlightened democracies of western Europe. Algerian immigrants in France, Turks in Germany, Indonesians in the Netherlands, Italians in Switzerland, Albanians in Italy, and Gypsies everywhere all live among natives who fear and despise them and who sometimes resort to vandalism and violence to show it.

Americans view all this distant mayhem with smug detachment, thinking, "Thank God that can't happen here." But Americans don't give a great deal of thought to why it can't happen here. The United States, after all, actually has far more ethnic diversity—whether calibrated by race, religion, language, national origin, or any other variable—than any of the world's ethnic trouble spots. In fact, the same ethnic blood-antagonists who hate each other overseas often live side by side in America. The United States may not have too many Rwandan Hutus and Tutsis, but it has plenty of Greeks and Turks, Protestant and Catholic Irish, Arabs and Jews, and Croatians and Serbs, not to mention millions of English and French Canadians. And the country certainly has a great deal more immigration than just about any other country.

There is a reason that the United States has been able to maintain ethnic harmony for centuries in a world in which most other nations are beset by ethnic strife: From the beginning, America has been what Richard John Neuhaus and others have called a "civic nation," unlike most other countries that have been—and continue to be—"ethnic nations."[3] In ethnic nations, the major factor that unites their citizens is their shared ethnicity. But since the citizens of most modern nations are ethnically heterogeneous—their shared ethnicity is more or less illusory—because of immigration, territorial expansion, or other historical circumstances or because no amount of ethnic homogeneity is ever enough—they need to negotiate the terms of their ethnic coexistence. They do so by sharing rights, power, and privilege along ethnic lines; they resort to what I have called ethnic federalism to mollify their constituent ethnic groups. A civic nation, on the other hand, vests rights only in individuals and goes out of its way to avoid making invidious distinctions of any kind based on a person's ethnic or other group membership.

Posing a dichotomy between ethnic nations and civic nations suggests that there really are two divergent classes of nationhood. In truth, there has only been one civic nation in the world: the United States. America's success has caused many of the world's ethnic nations to aspire to civic nationhood, with mixed results, but no other country was explicitly founded as a civic nation. And keeping the United States a civic nation has been no easy task. It has required continuous vigilance and the maintenance of powerful institutions to help Americans resist the ever-present temptation to become an ethnic nation like all the others. In this struggle, assimilation has been the United States' unique institutional invention, designed to keep the country a civic, rather than an ethnic, nation. The previous chapters have attempted to explain what assimilation, American style actually means and some of the ways it has kept Americans united for two centuries in the face of the world's largest and longest-lasting tide of immigration and the unparalleled ethnic diversity that this immigration spawned.

However, the battle between those who want America to remain a civic nation and those who want it to join the ranks of the world's ethnic nations is not over. And if the idea of civic nationhood is to prevail, it will continue to depend, as it has in the past, on the magical process of assimilation, not just to integrate the burgeoning ranks of new immigrants, but to keep integrated those Americans already here who are being asked to forsake their American identity for an ethnic one.

There is one important difference between the terms of that battle today and in the past. One hundred years ago, it was factions of "native" Americans (the children and grandchildren of immigrants) who wanted to make the United States an ethnic, rather than a civic, nation, and politically, it was "conservatives" who were less willing to embrace the universalist propositions of civic nationhood. And in those days, it was representatives of immigrants and ethnics, joined by political "liberals" (including descendants of those who came on the *Mayflower* and of those who arrived during the revolutionary era) who demanded that the United States should be true to its founding civic traditions and eschew all distinctions based on ethnicity. Today the factions are reversed. It is advocates of ethnic minorities, sometimes joined by immigrant leaders (a single faction in the case of Hispanics) and political "liberals" who want America to be more of an ethnic nation. And it is from the ranks of political "conservatives" that one hears the loudest cries that the country must remain a civic one. Jesse Jackson, the Ford Foundation, and ASPIRA on the side of ethnic nationhood versus William Bennett, Linda Chavez, and the Heritage Foundation on the side of civic nationhood.

It is attitudes toward, and definitions of, assimilation that account for this apparently paradoxical reversal of roles. The advocates of heightened ethnic consciousness are children of the civil rights revolution and disdain assimilation on both practical and philosophical grounds. Practically, they are convinced they can now turn the kind of ethnic discrimination that once harmed their constituents (and subverted America's liberal, universalist traditions) into an instrument of advantage for blacks and members of other ethnic groups who were formerly discriminated against; that America can be persuaded to practice indefinitely what Nathan Glazer called "affirmative discrimination."[4] Their tactical advocacy of affirmative discrimination—ethnic federalism, as I have named it—depends on members of ethnic groups vigorously maintaining their ethnic identities and valuing these identities more than a shared nonethnic American identity; in other words, it depends on their spurning assimilation. Looking beyond the short-term tactical advantages of ethnic federalism, its supporters have deeper philosophical objections to assimilation. Like the advocates of ethnic nationhood everywhere, American ethnic federalists resent having to participate in the kind of collective culture that civic nationhood inevitably develops. This resentment is all the more intense when the collective culture is seen as alien. That is the context in which advocates for "people of color" (including a large number of liberal whites) resist assimilation in a society grounded, by their reckoning, in an Anglocentric, or at least Eurocentric, culture. If the current practical justification for ethnic federalism leads to affirmative action, the philosophical objections to assimilation lead inexorably to multiculturalism.

But the philosophical premise behind antiassimilationism is a red herring. The efficacy of assimilation, American style is based precisely on the fact that it does *not* require ethnic Americans to give up any more of their ethnic heritage than they want to or make them conform to any collective national culture, Anglo-based or otherwise. What Americans have fought against for two centuries in building a civic nation is not ethnicity but ethnocentricity. The distinction is critical. Americans' rejection of ethnocentricity has been succinctly characterized by Glazer this way: "No separate ethnic group was to be allowed to establish an independent polity in the United States. This was to be a union of states and a nation of free individuals, not a nation of politically defined ethnic groups."[5]

On the other hand, ethnicity—the tendency of immigrants and the descendants of immigrants to hold onto aspects of their ancestral cultures—has been a natural part of America's assimilation process. The manifestation of ethnic pride, the practice of ethnic customs, and even the speaking of foreign languages are neither feared nor discouraged by the larger society. The United States' unique approach to assimilation unequivocally lets Americans identify with the cultures of their ancestral homelands to whatever degree they please. One can not only look upon the Amish riding through the Pennsylvania countryside in their horses and buggies, the Hasidim strolling through Brooklyn's Borough Park on a Saturday morning in their long black coats and distinctive headgear, the Chinese observing the Year of the Rat in New York's or San Francisco's Chinatown, the black children in Harlem celebrating Kwanzaa, and the Italian men playing bocci in Boston's North End (around the corner from Paul Revere's home) with a fascinated equanimity, but can actually rejoice in these things as emblematic *American* events. And, of course, ethnic jokes, which highlight rather than disguise America's ethnic diversity, have always been a staple of American humor, from "Abie's Irish Rose" to any night's Jewish or Italian stand-up routines on *The Tonight Show* with Jay Leno.

Assimilation, American style has inoculated the United States against the ethnocentricity that is the defining feature of an ethnic nation and promoted the tolerance of ethnic diversity that has allowed America to be a civic one. As I have discussed, many anti-assimilationist straw men had to be knocked down to make that case. Yes, American history has been shadowed with countless displays of ethnic bigotry and, in the case of blacks, a period of enslavement followed by unconscionable discrimination. When the nation's founders set America on the course of civic nationhood in the eighteenth century, they did not eradicate millenia of ethnically biased social impulses with a few strokes of the constitutional pen. But America, uniquely among nations, has always been able to find its way back to the path of universalist, liberal principles laid down by its founding civic charter. That Americans have not always been as good as their principles is no reason to discount those principles today nor to justify discarding the notion of civic, rather than ethnic, nationhood.

Yes, American culture and political institutions owe a great deal to the United States' English legacy. But, to begin with, the image of an Anglicized American society has been greatly exaggerated, as in the largely illusory notion of the hegemony of WASPs (or even the notion of WASPs altogether). And as to those aspects of English influence that have endured, even non-English-descended Americans should be grateful rather than critical. Even Hispanics would not like living in a United States that owed its political and civic institutions to Spain rather than England.

Yes, American immigrants never quite "melted" ethnically, the way they were supposed to do according to the premises of the melting-pot metaphor, but that is actually the major virtue of America's assimilation paradigm: It has not demanded literal ethnic melting. The experience of the world's ethnic nations proves that people can never melt enough ethnically for ethnic distinctions and conflicts to be overcome. The secret of a civic nation's success is a tradition of tolerance, ethnic and otherwise, and the essence of tolerance is to allow individuals to choose for themselves how they wish to be defined and which cultural traditions and habits they want to follow. Yet, for all this nonmelting, assimilation, American style has allowed Americans, despite their unmatched ethnic diversity, to have a more unified national cultural identity—even a more unified national culture in the lower-case "c" meaning of the term—than have the citizens of the world's ethnic nations, even the most ethnically homogeneous among them.

Yes, many of the ideas, symbols, and rituals that unify Americans are the products of a national mythology, but that mythology is to be applauded, not ridiculed. Myths unify a society, and a civic society that does not seek to be unified by ethnic bonds needs civic myths. The American mythology is, for the most part, grounded in universalist and idealistic notions. Therefore, an assimilationist perspective on American society should look indulgently and approvingly on the country's civic mythology, rather than cynically and iconoclastically.

Having developed and refined its institutions of civic and ethnic unity over two centuries and finally eliminated the most egregious violations of its idealistic civic principles, the United States would find it more than tragic if it discarded them at this late date—if after centuries of painfully acquired tolerance and civic wisdom, Americans snatched the defeat of ethnocentic divisiveness from the victorious jaws of national civic unity. It would be especially perverse if America did so in a fit of high-minded thoughtlessness. If Americans now give in to ethnocentricity and ethnic federalism, it will not be because they are being made to do so by the demands of long-aggrieved ethnic constituencies, as has been the case with the Francophones of Canada, the Chechens of Russia, and the Arabs of Israel, but because the mainstream institutions of the United States have almost absent-mindedly decided to promote a synthetic and forced ethnic consciousness or, what is worse, a sense of ethnic grievance among American ethnic groups.

When public schools decided to push children who might quickly and easily become fluent in English into bilingual classes to ensure the survival of their parents' ethnic identity, when every workplace and university decided to allocate places by race and ethnicity, when history teachers in high schools and colleges were pressured to make the promotion of ethnic self-esteem the primary purpose of history instruction, when the media decided that *diversity* was a good word but *assimilation* was a bad one, such decisions were not driven by the ethnic federalist demands of particular ethnic constituencies, but by a fashionable ideology. However, the raising of national ethnic consciousness, even if undertaken casually, can become self-reinforcing and impossible to reverse. If Americans persist in behaving as though America were an ethnic nation, then America will become an ethnic nation.

Now is the time to revive assimilation, American style. When nearly a million immigrants a year are entering the United States, an assimilationist perspective is needed more than ever to integrate them successfully into the mainstream of American life. When the desirability of immigration is being questioned, an assimilationist perspective is needed more than ever to convince the opponents of immigration that the newest immigrants are no less likely than their predecessors to become fully assimilated Americans. When affirmative action and multiculturalism are being heatedly attacked, an assimilationist perspective is needed more than ever to explain to its supporters that scaling back ethnic federalism does not mean turning back the clock to a more racist and intolerant phase of American history, but setting it forward to the full realization of America's civic ideals.

The revival of assimilation entails a revival of America's historic assimilation contract—not just for immigrants, but for all Americans. Most immigrants will have no problem because they are already fulfilling its terms. Immigrants have only to learn English, work hard, and embrace the American Idea. And to seal the bargain, they should become citizens. Other Americans have more work to do. First, they must once again consider assimilation an essential feature of American society; it is especially important that liberals and members of minority communities come to appreciate the value of assimilation. Second, Americans must restore public schools to their historic role as crucibles of assimilation, training grounds of national civic unity. Third, Americans must gradually dismantle the institutional architecture of ethnic federalism that has been assembled over the past twenty years. And finally, having put the United States back on a solid trajectory of civic nationhood, Americans should be ready to welcome coming generations of immigrants with open and appreciative arms.

Notes

1: We're All Americans

1. Philip Schaff, commencement address, College of St. James, Maryland, June 11, 1856.

2. A referendum in November 1995 had Quebec voters choosing to stay in Canada by the narrowest margin.

3. *Americanization* is the term used to describe the attempts employed after the cutoff of immigration in 1924 to speed up the assimilation of the last wave of eastern and southern European immigrants and their children.

4. *Grolier Electronic Encyclopedia*, 1993.

5. The term *Protestant ethic* was coined by Max Weber in *The Protestant Ethic and the Spirit of Capitalism,* trans. Talcott Parsons (New York: Charles Scribners' Sons, 1930 [German original, 1905]). For a more detailed discussion, see Chapter 7.

6. The term *American Idea* corresponds to Gunnar Myrdal's formulation of "the American Creed" in *An American Dilemma: The Negro Problem and Modern Democracy* (New York: Harper and Row, 1944).

7. Reed Ueda, "Naturalization and Citizenship," in *Harvard Encyclopedia of American Ethnic Groups,* ed. Stephen Thernstrom (Cambridge, Mass.: Harvard University Press, 1980), p. 734.

8. Craig R. Whitney, "Europeans Redefine What Makes a Citizen," *New York Times,* January 7, 1996, Week in Review, p. 6.

9. Robert L. Church, *Education in the United States: An Interpretive History* (New York: Free Press, 1976).

10. Ibid.

11. Ibid.

12. Richard Alba, "Assimilation's Quiet Tide," *The Public Interest*, no. 119 (Spring 1995), p. 31.

13. Nathan Glazer, "Is Assimilation Dead?" *Annals of the American Academy of Political and Social Science* 530 (November 1993), p. 123.

14. See Gertrude Himmelfarb, *The New History and the Old* (Cambridge, Mass.: Harvard University Press, 1987).

15. Howard Zinn, *The Politics of History* (Boston: Beacon Press, 1970).

16. Russell A. Kazal, "Revisiting Assimilation: The Rise, Fall, and Reappraisal of a Concept in American Ethnic History," *American Historical Review* 100 (1995), pp. 437–72.

17. Israel Zangwill, *The Melting-Pot* (New York: Macmillan, 1913).

18. Nathan Glazer and Daniel Patrick Moynihan, *Beyond the Melting Pot* (Cambridge, Mass.: MIT Press, 1963).

19. Michael Novak, *The Rise of the Unmeltable Ethnics* (New York: Macmillan, 1972).

20. *Multiculturalism* can be defined as a set of beliefs that stress the ethnic basis of American social relations and advocate policies that recognize, reward, and celebrate Americans' ethnic backgrounds, especially in the case of ethnic "minorities."

21. Richard Sennett, quoted in Suzanne Fields, "The Melting Pot Is Cooking a Highly Indigestible Stew," *Insight on the News* 10 (March 14, 1994), p. 40.

22. Schaff, commencement address.

23. Arthur M. Schlesinger, Jr., *The Disuniting of America* (New York: W. W. Norton, 1992).

24. Sheldon Hackney, quoted in Suzanne Fields, "The Melting Pot Is Cooking a Highly Indigestible Stew," *Insight on the News* 10 (March 14, 1994), p. 40.

25. Church, *Education in the United States.*

26. Nathan Glazer, *Ethnic Dilemmas, 1964–1982* (Cambridge, Mass.: Harvard University Press, 1983).

27. Glazer, "Is Assimilation Dead?" p. 135.

28. See Edward D. Garten's review of *Missionary Conquest: The Gospel and Native American Cultural Genocide* by George S. Tinker in *The Christian Century* 111 (July 27–August 3, 1994), p. 728. Garten discusses the argument that assimilation (in this case, religious) is cultural genocide.

29. Church, *Education in the United States.*

30. *Lau* v. *Nichols*, U.S. Supreme Court, 1974.

31. New York State Social Studies Review and Development Committee, *One Nation, Many Peoples: A Declaration of Cultural Interdependence* (Albany: New York State Education Department, June 1991).

32. Refers to policies of affirmative action, minority set-asides, and the like.

33. Refers to a host of social welfare policies, including Aid to Families with Dependent Children, Supplemental Security Income, and public housing.

34. David Reimers, "The New Nativism," unpublished manuscript, New York University, 1995.

35. John Miller, "Assimilation Enriches America's Melting Pot," *Insight on the News* 10 (October 3, 1994), p. 20.

36. John O'Sullivan, "America's Identity Crisis," *National Review* 46 (November 21, 1994), pp. 36–38; and Laurence Auster, "Avoiding the Issue: Conservatives and Immigration," *National Review* 46 (November 21, 1994), pp. 48–54.

37. U.S. Department of Justice, Immigration and Naturalization Service, *Statistical Yearbook of the Immigration and Naturalization Service, 1994* (Washington, D.C.: U.S. Government Printing Office, 1995), Table 1.

2: The More Things Change

1. Teresa O'Neill, "Immigrants Endanger America," in *Immigration: Opposing Viewpoints*, ed. Teresa O'Neill (San Diego, Calif.: Greenhaven Press, 1992), p. 61.

2. Peter Brimelow, *Alien Nation* (New York: Random House, 1995), pp. x, xiv.

3. Henry Steele Commager, *The American Mind* (New Haven, Conn.: Yale University Press, 1950), chap. 1.

4. Ibid., p. 11.

5. Thomas Paine, *The Rights of Man, Part II* (1792), chap. 5, in *The Collected Works of Thomas Paine*, ed. P. S. Foner (New York: Citadel Press, 1945), p. 414.

6. William Lloyd Garrison, *Motto of the Liberator* (1831).

7. Commager, *The American Mind*, p. 11.

8. Ibid.

9. Reed Ueda, "Naturalization and Citizenship," in *Harvard Encyclopedia of American Ethnic Groups,* ed. Stephen Thernstrom (Cambridge, Mass.: Harvard University Press, 1980), p. 734.

10. Ibid.

11. Robert H. Farrell, "Manifest Destiny," *Grolier Electronic Encyclopedia,* 1993.

12. See, among the many sources, especially Thomas Muller, *Immigrants and the American City* (New York: New York University Press, 1993); and John Bodnar, *The Transplanted* (Bloomington: Indiana University Press, 1985).

13. U.S. Bureau of the Census, *Historical Statistics of the United States* (Washington, D.C.: U.S. Government Printing Office, 1975).

14. Ueda, "Naturalization and Citizenship."

15. Ibid.

16. Bodnar, *The Transplanted,* chap. 7.

17. Jesse Chickering, "Immigration into the United States" (1848), in *Immigration: Opposing Viewpoints,* ed. Teresa O'Neill (San Diego, Calif.: Greenhaven Press, 1992), p. 63.

18. Brimelow, *Alien Nation.*

19. Benjamin Franklin (1751), cited in Robert C. Christopher, *Crashing the Gates* (New York: Simon and Schuster, 1989), p. 30.

20. U.S. Department of Justice, Immigration and Naturalization Service, *Statistical Yearbook of the Immigration and Naturalization Service, 1994* (Washington, D.C.: U.S. Government Printing Office, 1995), Table 2.

21. Charlotte Curtis, *New York Times* (1985).

22. Christopher, *Crashing the Gates,* p. 29.

23. See, for example, O'Neill, "Immigrants Endanger America," p. 59; Ellis Cose, *A Nation of Strangers* (New York: William Morrow, 1992), chap. 1; and Thomas Sowell, *Ethnic America* (New York: Basic Books, 1981), chap. 2.

24. A. Piatt Andrew, "The New Immigrants Do Not Harm Society," in *Immigration: Opposing Viewpoints,* p. 141.

25. Ibid.

26. Cose, *A Nation of Strangers,* p. 27.

27. U.S. Bureau of the Census, *1990 Census of Population, Supplementary Reports, Detailed Ancestry Groups by States.*

28. Muller, *Immigrants and the American City,* p. 229.

29. Maldwyn Allen Jones, *American Immigration* (Chicago: University of Chicago Press, 1960) p. 248.

30. Cose, *A Nation of Strangers,* pp. 32–33.

31. Ibid., chap. 3.

32. Prescott F. Hall, "The New Immigrants Threaten America's Racial Stock," reprinted from *North American Review* (January 1912) in *Immigration: Opposing Viewpoints*, pp. 107–8.

33. Ibid.

34. Ibid.

35. U.S. Department of Justice, Immigration and Naturalization Service, *Statistical Yearbook of the Immigration and Naturalization Service, 1994,* Appendix 1.

36. Muller, *Immigrants and the American City;* and Julian Simon, *The Economic Consequences of Immigration* (Cambridge, Mass.: Blackwell, 1989).

37. Louis Hacker, *The Course of Economic Growth and Development* (New York: John Wiley and Sons, 1970).

38. Muller, *Immigrants and the American City,* pp. 296–97.

39. Ibid.

40. Ibid.

41. Cose, *A Nation of Strangers,* p. 38.

42. Muller, *Immigrants and the American City.*

43. Bodnar, *The Transplanted,* chap. 4.

44. Maldwyn Allen Jones, *American Immigration* (Chicago: University of Chicago Press, 1960), pp. 308–13.

45. Muller, *Immigrants and the American City,* pp. 99–100.

46. Max Lerner, *America as a Civilization* (New York: Simon and Schuster, 1957), pp. 88–89.

47. Sowell, *Ethnic America,* chap. 2.

48. Ibid., chap. 3.

49. Ibid., p. 64.

50. Jones, *American Immigration,* p. 314.

51. Cose, *A Nation of Strangers;* and Sowell, *Ethnic America.*

52. Milton Gordon, *Assimilation in American Life* (New York: Oxford University Press, 1964).

53. Jones, *American Immigration,* pp. 317–18.

54. Arthur M. Schlesinger, Jr., *The Disuniting of America* (New York: W. W. Norton, 1992), p. 107.

55. Lerner, *America as a Civilization*, p. 29.

56. Ibid., p. 89.

3: Assimilation, American Style

1. John Steinbeck, *Travels with Charley* (New York: Viking Press, 1962), pp. 185–86.

2. Henry Fairchild, "Assimilation of Immigrants Is Almost Impossible," reprinted from *The Melting-Pot Mistake* (Boston: Little Brown, 1926) in *Immigration: Opposing Viewpoints*, ed. Teresa O'Neill (San Diego, Calif.: Greenhaven Press, 1992), p. 176.

3. Israel Zangwill, *The Melting-Pot* (New York: Macmillan, 1913).

4. Philip Gleason, "American Identity and Americanization," *Harvard Encyclopedia of American Ethnic Groups*, ed. Stephen Thernstrom (Cambridge, Mass.: Harvard University Press, 1980), p. 43.

5. Ibid. p. 45.

6. Nathan Glazer and Daniel Patrick Moynihan, *Beyond the Melting Pot* (Cambridge, Mass.: MIT Press, 1963), p. v.

7. Henry Fairchild, "Assimilation of Immigrants Is Almost Impossible," p. 184.

8. Olivier Zunz, "American History and the Changing Meaning of Assimilation," *Journal of Ethnic History* (Spring 1985), p. 55.

9. Abigail M. Thernstrom, "Language Issues and Legislation," in *Harvard Encyclopedia of American Ethnic Groups*, p. 619.

10. Barbara Jordan, "The Americanization Ideal," *New York Times*, September 11, 1995, p. A13.

11. Horace M. Kallen, *Culture and Democracy in the United States* (New York: Boni and Liveright, 1924).

12. From Richard John Neuhaus, "Alien Notion," *National Review* 47 (February 6, 1995), p. 65.

13. Cited in Milton Gordon, *Assimilation in American Life* (New York: Oxford University Press, 1964), p. 63.

14. Richard Alba, "Assimilation's Quiet Tide," *The Public Interest*, no. 119 (Spring 1995), p. 3.

15. Gordon, *Assimilation in American Life*.

16. This is a liberal reworking of Gordon's typology in which "legitimacy" corresponds to Gordon's "receptional assimilation," "competence" to his "structural assimilation," "civic responsibility" to his "civic assimilation," and "identify as Americans" to his "identificational assimilation."

17. Richmond Mayo-Smith, *Emigration and Immigration: A Study in Social Science* (1898), quoted in Grover G. Huebner, "Forces in American Society Aid Assimilation," in *Immigration: Opposing Viewpoints*, p. 173.

18. Thomas Sowell, *Markets and Minorities* (New York: Basic Books, 1981).

19. George Borjas, *Friends or Strangers* (New York: Basic Books, 1990), p. 101.

20. Francis Fukuyama, *Trust* (New York: Free Press, 1995).

21. Maldwyn Allen Jones, *American Immigration* (Chicago: University of Chicago Press, 1960), pp. 318–19.

22. Max Lerner, *America as a Civilization* (New York: Simon and Schuster, 1957), p. 30.

23. Gleason, "American Identity and Americanization," p. 33.

24. Gordon, *Assimilation in American Life,* p. 71; see also the "authoritative" definition of acculturation by the Social Science Research Council, Subcommittee on Acculturation (1936): "acculturation comprehends those phenomena which result when groups of individuals having different cultures come into continuous first-hand contact, with subsequent changes in the original cultural patterns of either or both groups."

25. Gordon, *Assimilation in American Life,* p. 81.

26. James C. McKinley, Jr., "Parents of Bomb Suspect Weep and Insist He Is No Terrorist," *New York Times*, August 17, 1995, p. A12.

27. David Willman, "McVeigh Lashed Out at Government in '92 Letters," *Los Angeles Times*, April 27, 1995, p. A1; and James Barron, "Suggestion of Violence to Change Government," *New York Times*, April 27, 1995, p. A10.

28. Gordon, *Assimilation in American Life,* p. 71.

29. Luis E. Guarnizo, *Los Dominicanyorks: The Making of a Binational Society* (Thousand Oaks, Calif.: Sage Publications, 1994).

30. Stephen Thernstrom, "Comment" (on essay by Olivier Zunz), *Journal of American Ethnic History* (Spring 1985), p. 77.

4: Crucibles of Assimilation

1. Michael R. Olneck and Marvin Lazerson, "Education," in *Harvard Encyclopedia of American Ethnic Groups,* ed. Stephen Thernstrom (Cambridge, Mass.: Harvard University Press, 1980) p. 303.

2. Alexis de Tocqueville, *Democracy in America* (New York: Alfred A. Knopf, 1945), p. x.

3. Robert L. Church, *Education in the United States: An Interpretive History* (New York: Free Press, 1976), chap. 1.

4. de Tocqueville, *Democracy in America*, p. 46.

5. Church, *Education in the United States*.

6. Ibid., p. 59.

7. Ibid., p. 61.

8. Ibid., chap. 5.

9. Ibid., pp. 57–58.

10. Ibid., chap. 3.

11. Statement of the Public School Society of the City of New York, 1830, cited in Church, *Education in the United States*, pp. 161–62.

12. Alan Jay Lerner and Frederick Loewe, *My Fair Lady* (New York: Coward McCann, 1956), p. 28.

13. Noah Webster, *Dissertations on the English Language with Notes Historical and Critical* (Boston, 1789), pp. 20–21.

14. Church, *Education in the United States*, p. 17.

15. Ibid., chap. 8.

16. Ibid., chap. 6.

17. Olneck and Lazerson, "Education," p. 307.

18. Church, *Education in the United States*, chap. 7.

19. Olneck and Lazerson, "Education," p. 313.

20. Neil G. McCluskey, *Catholic Education in America* (New York: Bureau of Publications, Teachers College, Columbia University, 1964); and Glen Graebet, Jr., *In Hoc Signo: A Brief History of Catholic Parochial Education in America* (Port Washington, N.Y.: Kennikat Press, 1973).

21. Ibid.

22. George Gonzalez, "An Examination of Transitional Bilingual Education and Latino Students in New York City," research paper for the course Introduction to Public Policy, Hunter College, Fall 1996.

23. Linda Chavez, *Out of the Barrio: Toward a New Politics of Hispanic Assimilation* (New York: Basic Books, 1991); and Rosalie Pedalino Porter, *Forked Tongue: The Politics of Bilingual Education* (New York: Basic Books, 1990).

24. Gonzalez, "An Examination of Transitional Bilingual Education."

25. Jacques Steinberg, "Parents' Suit on Classes Is Rebuffed," *New York Times*, January 18, 1996, p. B2.

26. Gonzalez, "An Examination of Transitional Bilingual Education."

27. E. H. Lenneberg, *Biological Foundations of Language* (New York: John Wiley and Sons, 1967).

28. Gonzalez, "An Examination of Transitional Bilingual Education."

29. Arthur M. Schlesinger, Jr., *The Disuniting of America* (New York: W. W. Norton, 1992), p. 108.

30. Ibid., pp. 108–9.

31. Ibid.

32. New York State Social Studies Review and Development Committee, "Multiculturalism Benefits All Students," in *Education in America: Opposing Viewpoints,* ed. Charles P. Cozic (San Diego, Calif.: Greenhaven Press, 1992), p. 149.

33. Richard Bernstein, *Dictatorship of Virtue* (New York: Alfred A. Knopf, 1994), p. 5.

34. Robert Hughes, "The Fraying of America," *Time* 139 (February 3, 1992), p. 44.

35. Bernstein, *Dictatorship of Virtue*, p. 263.

36. Ibid., pp. 6–7.

37. New York State Social Studies Review and Development Committee, "Multiculturalism Benefits All Students," p. 148.

38. Bernstein, *Dictatorship of Virtue,* pp. 280–83.

39. Ibid., p. 267.

40. Schlesinger, *The Disuniting of America,* p. 134.

41. Ibid.; Thomas Sowell, *Inside American Education* (New York: Free Press, 1993); Bernstein, *Dictatorship of Virtue;* and Charles J. Sykes, *Dumbing Down Our Kids: Why America's Children Feel Good About Themselves But Can't Read, Write or Add* (New York: St. Martin's Press, 1995).

42. Sowell, *Inside American Education,* p. 73.

5: Assimilation's Anglo Base

1. Jesse Chickering, "Immigration into the United States" (1848), in *Immigration: Opposing Viewpoints,* ed. Teresa O'Neill (San Diego, Calif.: Greenhaven Press, 1992).

2. John Keegan, "Shedding Light on Lebanon," *The Atlantic* 253 (April 1984), p. 46, quoted in Stephen Thernstrom, "Comment" (on essay by Olivier Zunz), *Journal of American Ethnic History* (Spring 1985), p. 78.

3. Arthur M. Schlesinger, Jr., *The Disuniting of America* (New York: W. W. Norton, 1992), p. 135.

4. Randolph Bourne, quoted in Benjamin Schwarz, "The Diversity Myth: America's Leading Export," *Atlantic Monthly* (May 1995), p. 62.

5. Andrew M. Greeley, *Ethnicity in the United States: A Preliminary Reconnaissance* (New York: John Wiley and Sons, 1974).

6. Norman Podhoretz, *Making It* (New York: Random House, 1967).

7. Schwarz, "The Diversity Myth," p. 62.

8. Michael Novak, *The Rise of the Unmeltable Ethnics* (New York: Macmillan, 1972), pp. 113–14.

9. Ibid., pp. 114–15.

10. Alexis de Tocqueville, *Democracy in America* (New York: Alfred A. Knopf, 1945), p. 613.

11. Schlesinger, *The Disuniting of America*, p. 54.

12. Richard Bernstein, *Dictatorship of Virtue* (New York: Alfred A. Knopf, 1994), p. 280.

13. Philip Gleason, "American Identity and Americanization," *Harvard Encyclopedia of American Ethnic Groups*, ed. Stephen Thernstrom (Cambridge, Mass.: Harvard University Press, 1980), p. 56.

14. Schlesinger, *The Disuniting of America*, p. 135.

15. Attributed to George Bernard Shaw, but not found in his published work; noted in Angela Partington, ed., *The Oxford Dictionary of Quotations*, p. 638.

16. Andrew Hacker, "Liberal Democracy and Social Control," *American Political Science Review* 51 (1957).

17. Joseph Alsop, *I've Seen the Best of It* (New York: W. W. Norton, 1992).

18. Gleason, "American Identity and Americanization," p. 31.

19. Hans Kohn, quoted in ibid., p. 32.

20. Ibid., p. 56.

21. Malcolm Jones, Jr., "The Desi Chain: The Rewriting of the American Identity," *Newsweek*, July 10, 1995; and interpretation of *Newsweek* poll taken February 1–3, 1995, in Tom Morgenthau, "What Color Is Black?" *Newsweek*, February 13, 1995, pp. 62–66.

22. Bernstein, *Dictatorship of Virtue*, p. 272, referring to Molefi Kete Asante, a prominent Afrocentric scholar.

23. Linda Chavez, *Out of the Barrio: Toward a New Politics of Hispanic Assimilation* (New York: Basic Books, 1991), p. 20.

24. Jones, "The Desi Chain," p. 34.

25. Schlesinger, *The Disuniting of America*, p. 135.

26. Ibid.

27. Peter Brimelow, *Alien Nation* (New York: Random House, 1995); John O'Sullivan, "Nationhood: An American Activity," *National Review* 46 (February 21, 1994), p. 36; and Laurence Auster, "Avoiding the Issue: Conservatives and Immigration," *National Review* 46 (November 21, 1994), pp. 48–54.

28. Gleason, "American Identity and Americanization," pp. 56–57.

6: Americans United by Myths

1. James Oliver Robertson, *American Myth, American Reality* (New York: Hill and Wang, 1980), p. 3.

2. Robert L. Church, *Education in the United States: An Interpretive History* (New York: Free Press, 1976), pp. 57–58.

3. Seymour Martin Lipset, *The First New Nation: The United States in Historical and Comparative Perspective* (New York: Basic Books, 1963).

4. Oscar Handlin, *The Americans: A New History of the People of the United States* (Boston: Little Brown, 1983), p. 161.

5. Percy Bysshe Shelley, *The Revolt of Islam*, Canto 11, "America."

6. Robertson, *American Myth, American Reality*, p. 149.

7. Woodrow Wilson, speech, Chicago, Illinois, April 6, 1912, cited in Microsoft Bookshelf, "Quotations," 1995.

8. Henry Steele Commager, *The American Mind: An Interpretation of American Thought and Character Since the 1880s* (New Haven, Conn.: Yale University Press, 1950), p. 10.

9. Robertson, *American Myth, American Reality*, p. 147.

10. Hector St. John de Crevecoer, "What Is an American?" in *Immigration: Opposing Viewpoints*, ed. Teresa O'Neill (San Diego, Calif.: Greenhaven Press, 1992), p. 27.

11. Patrick J. Buchanan, speaking on *One on One*, John McLaughlin, moderator, WNET, October 14, 1995.

12. John Gunther, *Inside U.S.A.* (New York: Harper and Row, 1951).

13. *Declaration of Independence*, July 4, 1776, ¶2 and 3.

14. *Gettysburg Address*, November 19, 1863.

15. U.S. labor leader Meyer London, speech to Congress, January 18, 1916, cited in Microsoft Bookshelf, "Quotations," 1995.

16. Commager, *The American Mind*, p. 11.

17. Walt Whitman, *Leaves of Grass*, 1855.

18. Quoted in Victor Bokris, *Warhol* (New York: Bantam, 1989).

7: Americans United by the Protestant Ethic

1. Max Lerner, *America as a Civilization* (New York: Simon and Schuster, 1957), p. 238.

2. Louis Hacker, *The Course of American Economic Growth and Development* (New York: John Wiley and Sons, 1970); Stanley Lebergott, *The Americans: An Economic Record* (New York: W. W. Norton, 1984); and Lance E. Davis et al., *American Economic Growth: An Economists History of the United States* (New York: Harper and Row, 1972).

3. Lerner, *America as a Civilization*, p. 88.

4. Francis J. Grund, *The Americans in Their Moral, Social and Political Relations* (London: Longman, 1837).

5. Daniel T. Rodgers, *The Work Ethic in Industrial America, 1850–1920* (Chicago: University of Chicago Press, 1978), p. 9.

6. Max Weber, *The Protestant Ethic and the Spirit of Capitalism,* trans. Talcott Parsons (New York: Charles Scribners' Sons, 1930 [German original, 1905]).

7. Rodgers, *The Work Ethic in Industrial America*, p. 171.

8. Oscar Handlin, *The Americans* (Boston: Little Brown, 1963), p. 274.

9. Henri Grunwald, quoted in G. Hocmard et al., *The American Dream: Advanced Readings in English* (New York: Longman, 1982), p. 17.

10. Lerner, *America as a Civilization*, p. 89.

11. Lebergott, *The Americans*.

12. Nicholas Serantis, "Distribution, Aggregate Demand, and Unemployment in OECD Countries," *The Economics Journal* 103 (March 1993), pp. 459–67.

13. Seymour Martin Lipset, *The First New Nation* (New York: Basic Books, 1963), p. 321.

14. California Proposition 187, passed November 1994.

15. Thomas Sowell, *Ethnic America* (New York: Basic Books, 1981).

16. John Bodnar, *The Transplanted* (Bloomington, Ind.: Indiana University Press, 1985), chap. 3.

17. Irving Kristol, *Two Cheers for Capitalism* (New York: Basic Books, 1978).

18. Adrian Furnham, Michael Bond, and Patrick Heaven, "A Comparison of Protestant Work Ethic Beliefs in Thirteen Nations," *Journal of Social Psychology* 133 (April 1993), pp. 185–97.

19. Abbas J. Ali, Thomas Falcone, and A. A. Azim, "Work Ethic in the U.S.A. and Canada," *Journal of Management Development* 14 (June 1995), p. 26.

20. Michael Harrington, *The New American Poverty* (New York: Holt, Rinehart and Winston, 1984), p. 29.

21. Dennis P. McCann, "Apology for the Hireling: A Work Ethic for the Global Marketplace," *The Christian Century* 112 (May 17, 1995), p. 54.

22. Thomas Muller, *Immigrants and the American City* (New York: New York University Press, 1993).

23. Edward Hamilton, "Urban Pressures and Urban Priorities," in *The American City: Realities and Possibilities* (Austin: Lyndon B. Johnson School of Public Affairs, University of Texas at Austin, 1974), pp. 87–88.

24. James L. Spates and John J. Macionis, *The Sociology of Cities* (Belmont, Calif.: Wadsworth, 1987), pp. 365–66.

25. New York City Planning Department, "Annual Report on Social Indicators, 1994," Table 1-2.

26. See George J. Borjas, "Immigrants, Minorities and Labor Market Competition," *Industrial and Labor Relations Review* 40 (April 1987), pp. 382–92; and Robert H. Topel, "Immigrants in the American Labor Market: Quality, Assimilation and Distributional Effects," *American Economic Review* 81 (May 1991), pp. 297–302.

27. Richard Freeman, "Young Blacks and Jobs—What We Know," *The Public Interest* 78 (Winter 1985), pp. 18–31.

28. Roger Waldinger, "The Jobs Immigrants Take," *New York Times*, March 11, 1996, p. A17; Saskia Sassen, *Cities in a World Economy* (Thousand Oaks, Calif.: Pine Forge Press, 1994); and Borjas, "Immigrants, Minorities and Labor Market Competition."

29. James Treires, "Dark Side of the Dream," *Newsweek* 113 (March 20, 1989), pp. 10–11.

30. Barry Chiswick, "The Effect of Americanization on the Earnings of Foreign-Born Men," *Journal of Political Economy* 86 (October 1978), Table 3.

31. Charles Baillou, "One in Three Blacks Jailed, Study Finds," *Amsterdam News*, October 14, 1995, p. 33.

8: Americans United but Living Apart

1. Sanford J. Ungar, *Fresh Blood* (New York: Simon and Schuster, 1995), p. 222.

2. Thomas J. Archdeacon, *Becoming American* (New York: Free Press, 1983), p. 231.

3. Nathan Glazer and Daniel Patrick Moynihan, *Beyond the Melting Pot* (Cambridge, Mass.: MIT Press, 1963).

4. Ungar, *Fresh Blood*.

5. Peter Brimelow, *Alien Nation* (New York: Random House, 1995), p. 56.

6. Roger Daniels, *Coming to America: A History of Immigration and Ethnicity in American Life* (New York: HarperCollins, 1990), p. 170.

7. National Resources Committee, *Our Cities: Their Role in the National Economy* (1937), quoted in John C. Bollens and Henry J. Schmandt, *The Metropolis* (New York: Harper and Row, 1965), p. 10.

8. Walter Laidlaw, *Population of the City of New York* (New York: Cities Census Committee, 1932), Table 41.

9. U.S. Department of Justice, Immigration and Naturalization Service, *Statistical Yearbook of the Immigration and Naturalization Service, 1994* (Washington, D.C.: U.S. Government Printing Office, 1995), Table 15.

10. Thomas Muller, *Immigrants and the American City* (New York: New York University Press, 1993), p. 298.

11. See Table 1, chapter 11.

12. Laidlaw, *Population of the City of New York*, Table 40.

13. U.S. Department of Justice, Immigration and Naturalization Service, *Statistical Yearbook of the Immigration and Naturalization Service, 1991* (Washington, D.C.: U.S. Government Printing Office, 1992), Table 17.

14. Ibid., Table 18.

15. Daniels, *Coming to America*, p. 169.

16. NYC Department of City Planning, "Socioeconomic Profiles," "Selected Social Characterisitics: Bronx, Manhattan, Queens, Brooklyn," March 1993.

17. Ibid.

18. This discussion is based on the author's familiarity with the area.

19. Peter Daniel Salins, *Household Location Patterns in Selected American Metropolitan Areas*, unpublished doctoral dissertation, Syracuse University, 1969.

20. Ibid.

21. The discussion of Massapequa is based on the author's familiarity with the area.

22. Roger Waldinger, *Still the Promised City* (Cambridge, Mass.: Harvard University Press, forthcoming), chap. 4.

23. U.S. Bureau of the Census, *Statistical Abstract of the United States, 1994*, Table 5; and Rena Michaels Atchison, "Retention of Immigrants' Native Language Harms America," in *Immigration: Opposing Viewpoints,* ed. Teresa O'Neill (San Diego, Calif.: Greenhaven Press, 1992), p. 95.

24. Dennis Baron, *The English Only Question* (New Haven: Yale University Press, 1990), ch. 3.

25. This discussion is based on the author's familiarity with the area.

26. Milton Gordon, *Assimilation in American Life* (New York: Oxford University Press, 1964), p. 80.

27. Richard D. Alba, "Assimilation's Quiet Tide," *The Public Interest* 119 (Spring 1995), p. 3.

28. Ibid.

29. David M. Heer, "Intermarriage," in *Harvard Encyclopedia of American Ethnic Groups,* ed. Stephen Thernstrom (Cambridge, Mass.: Harvard University Press, 1980), pp. 513–21.

30. Alba, "Assimilation's Quiet Tide."

31. Ibid.

32. Jill Smolowe, "Intermarried . . . With Children," *Time* 142 (Fall 1993), p. 64.

33. Lisa Funderburg, *New York Times,* July 10, 1996, p. A15.

34. Robert C. Christopher, *Crashing the Gates* (New York: Simon and Schuster, 1989), pp. 32–33.

35. Thomas Sowell, *Ethnic America* (New York: Basic Books, 1981), p. 14. This passage underscores the irony and significance of O. J. Simpson's prosecution for allegedly murdering his wife. He was not just another prominent black athlete; he was a legend and a symbol of successful assimilation.

36. Brimelow, *Alien Nation.*

37. Kate O'Beirne, "Bread and Circuses," *National Review* 48 (July 1, 1996), p. 21.

38. Rita Simon, "Old Minorities, New Immigrants: Aspirations, Hopes, and Fears," *Annals of the American Academy of Political and Social Science* 530 (November 1993), p. 63.

39. Lawrence H. Fuchs, "An Agenda for Tomorrow: Immigration Policy and Ethnic Policies," *Annals of the American Academy of Political and Social* Science 530 (November 1993), pp. 180–81.

9: Black Americans and Assimilation

1. James Jones, "Piercing the Veil," in *Opening Doors: Perspectives on Race Relations in Contemporary America* (Tuscaloosa, Ala.: University of Alabama Press, 1991), p. 192.

2. Nathan Glazer, "Is Assimilation Dead?" *Annals of the American Academy of Political and Social Science* 530 (November 1993), p. 126.

3. Marcus Garvey, quoted in Ronald Takaki, *A Different Mirror: A History of Multicultural America* (Boston: Little Brown, 1993), p. 356.

4. Paul M. Sniderman and Thomas Piazza, *The Scar of Race* (Cambridge, Mass.: Belknap Press, 1993), p. 178.

5. Steven A. Holmes, "As the N.A.A.C.P. Regroups, Many Blacks Doubt Its Relevance," *New York Times*, January 9, 1996, p. A6.

6. Arch Puddington, "Speaking of Race," *Commentary* 100 (December 1995), p. 22.

7. Cornel West, *Race Matters* (New York: Vintage Books, 1993), pp. x–xi.

8. Ibid., p. 3.

9. Michel Marriott, "Multiracial Americans Ready to Claim Their Own Identity," *New York Times*, July 20, 1996, p. A1.

10. U.S. Bureau of the Census, *Statistical Abstract of the United States, 1995,* 115th ed. (Washington, D.C.: U.S. Government Printing Office, 1995).

11. Ibid.

12. Puddington, "Speaking of Race."

13. Ibid., p. 23.

14. Peter J. Ferrara, review of *The Affirmative Action Fraud* by Clint Bolick, in *The Defender* 2 (May/June 1996), p. 21.

10: Battlegrounds of Assimilation

1. Arthur M. Schlesinger, Jr., *The Disuniting of America* (New York: W. W. Norton, 1992), p. 130.

2. Nathan Glazer, "Is Assimilation Dead?" *Annals of the American Academy of Political and Social Science* 530 (November 1993), p. 134.

3. John J. Miller, "Assimilation Enriches America's Melting Pot," *Insight on the News* 10 (October 3, 1994), p. 20.

4. Richard Alba, "Assimilation's Quiet Tide," *The Public Interest* 119 (Spring 1995), p. 3; Schlesinger, *The Disuniting of America;* DeRoy Murdoch, "Learn the Lessons of Balkanization," *Insight on the News* 11 (August 28, 1995), p. 22; Alejandro Portes and Min Zhou, "The New Second Generation: Segmented Assimilation and Its Variants," *Annals of the American Academy of Political and Social Science* 530 (November 1993), pp. 74–97; Peter Skerry, "The Black Alienation: African Americans vs. Immigrants," *New Republic* 212 (January 30, 1995), p. 19; and John O'Sullivan, "Nationhood: An American Activity," *National Review* 48 (February 21, 1994), p. 36.

5. Glazer, "Is Assimilation Dead?" p. 135.

6. Alejandro Portes and Ruben Rumbaut, "From Immigrants to Instant Ethnics," in *Strangers at Our Gate,* ed. John J. Miller (Washington, D.C.: Manhattan Institute, 1994), p. 49.

7. "The New Yanquis," *National Review* 45 (January 18, 1993), p. 13.

8. Linda Chavez, *Out of the Barrio: Toward a New Politics of Hispanic Assimilation* (New York: Basic Books, 1991), chap. 3.

9. Ibid., pp. 161–62.

10. Ibid.

11. "The New Yanquis."

12. Neomi M. Rao, "Multicultural Nightmare Is Antithetical to Tolerance," *Insight on the News* 10 (August 22, 1994), p. 38.

13. Chavez, *Out of the Barrio.*

14. David Samuels, "Philanthropical Correctness: The Failure of American Foundations," *New Republic* 213 (September 18, 1995), pp. 12–13.

15. Ibid., p. 28.

16. Ibid.

11: An Assimilationist Immigration Policy

1. Nathan Glazer, *Strangers at Our Gate: Immigration in the 1990s* (Washington: D.C.: Center for the New American Community, 1994), p. 18.

2. U.S. Department of Justice, Immigration and Naturalization Service, *Statistical Yearbook of the Immigration and Naturalization Service, 1993* (Washington, D.C.: U.S. Government Printing Office, 1994).

3. Estimates drawn from data in Richard Rayner, "What Immigration Crisis?" *New York Times Magazine*, January 7, 1996, p. 29.

4. Joel Kotkin, "U.S. Immigration Policy Should Be Based on Citizenship," in *Immigration Policy*, ed. Bruno Leone (San Diego, Calif.: Greenhaven Press, 1995), p. 84.

5. George J. Borjas, *Friends or Strangers: The Impact of Immigration on the U.S. Economy* (New York: Basic Books, 1990); Peter Brimelow, "Time to Rethink Immigration," *National Review* 44 (June 22, 1992), pp. 30–42, and *Alien Nation* (New York: Random House, 1994); Leon F. Bouvier, *Peaceful Invasions: Immigration and Changing America* (Lanham, Md.: University Press of America, 1992); Leon F. Bouvier and John L. Martin, "Four Hundred Million Americans! The Latest Census Bureau Projections," Center for Immigration Studies *Backgrounder* (January 1993); Vernon M. Briggs, Jr., *Mass Immigration and the National Interest* (Armonk, N.Y.: M. E. Sharpe, 1992); and Donald L. Huddle, *The Net National Costs of Immigration* (Washington, D.C.: Carrying Capacity Network, July 20, 1993).

6. Carey Goldberg, "Asian Immigrants Help Bolster U.S. Economy, New Report Says," *New York Times*, March 31, 1995, p. 32.

7. Kotkin, "U.S. Immigration Policy," p. 86.

8. James Sterngold, "Parallel Agonizing Over Immigration," *New York Times*, March 23, 1996, p. 8.

9. U.S. Department of Justice, Immigration and Naturalization Service, *Statistical Yearbook, 1993*, Table A.

10. Ibid., Table 2.

11. Ibid., Table B.

12. Ibid., Table 3.

13. Ibid., Table D.

14. Patrick J. Buchanan, quoted in Stephen Braun, "Last Mad Dash for Patrick Buchanan's Crusade," *Los Angeles Times*, March 26, 1996, p. A12.

15. Ron K. Unz, "Sinking Our State," *Reason* 26 (November 1994), p. 46.

16. Kotkin, "U.S. Immigration Policy," p. 87.

17. U.S. Department of Justice, Immigration and Naturalization Service, *Statistical Yearbook, 1993*, Table 8.

18. This definition of *refugee* originated in the *United Nations Convention Relating to Refugees* (New York: United Nations, 1951).

19. U.S. Department of Justice, Immigration and Naturalization Service, *Statistical Yearbook, 1993,* Table 4; estimates of illegal immigration are extrapolated from data cited in Richard Rayner, "What Immigration Crisis?" *New York Times Magazine*, January 7, 1996, p. 29.

20. Mortimer Zuckerman, "Beyond Proposition 187," *U.S. News and World Report* 117 (December 12, 1994), pp. 124–25, and "Tough Proposition" (editorial), *National Review* 46 (November 21, 1994), pp. 20–21.

21. U.S. Department of Justice, Immigration and Naturalization Service, *Statistical Yearbook, 1993*, Table A.

22. Ibid., Table B.

23. Ibid., Table 45.

24. Seth Mydens, "The Latest Big Boom: Citizenship," *New York Times*, August 11, 1995, p. A12.

12: Living Together in Peace and Unity

1. Lawrence H. Fuchs, *The American Kaleidoscope: Race, Ethnicity and the Civic Culture* (Middletown, Conn.: Wesleyan University Press, 1990), p. 5.

2. *New York Times*, March 14, 1996, p. A15; March 17, 1996, p. 10; March 18, 1996, p. A7; and March 31, 1996, p.15.

3. Richard John Neuhaus, "It Is Not Necessary to Reduce Immigration to Preserve the Nation," in *Immigration Policy*, ed. Bruno Leone (San Diego, Calif.: Greenhaven Press, 1995), pp. 90–94.

4. Nathan Glazer, *Affirmative Discrimination* (New York: Basic Books, 1975).

5. Ibid., p. 5.

Index

Abe Lincoln in Illinois (movie), 111

Academy Awards, 117–19

Acculturation, 55–59; as option in assimilation process, 56–57; without assimilation, 57–58

Adams, John, 110

Addams, Jane, 34

Affirmative action, 178–79, 181, 195–96

Affirmative discrimination. *See* Ethnic federalism

Africa, 5

African Americans. *See* Black Americans

Afrocentrism, 78, 96, 97–98, 175–76, 181–82, 191, 195

Alba, Richard, 7, 49, 160, 193

Alger, Horatio, 14, 103–4

Alien and Sedition Acts of 1798, 24, 29

Alien Nation (Brimelow), 25, 145, 216

Alsop, Joseph, 93

American Dilemma (Myrdal), 174

American Dream, 118, 145, 214

American Idea: as basis of assimilation, 6, 18, 38–39, 51, 192, 226; civic idealism of, 52, 220–26;

civil rights and, 179; described, 6; under ethnic federalism, 13, 15, 180–82; and ethnic quotas and preferences, 14, 203–6; historical revisionism and, 8, 80–83, 181–82; importance of, 20, 38–39, 162; in literature, 103–4, 112, 115, 116, 119–20; moral superiority and, 109–10; in movies, 111, 114, 116–19; national mythology in, 101–21; segregation and discrimination versus, 168, 170–71; in the Western genre, 112–16

Americanization: ethnic identity and, 161–64; resistance to, 145; in schools, 68–70; support for, 5–6, 46, 54

American Protective Association, 24

American Socialist Party, 133

Amnesty, for illegal aliens, 204, 206, 207, 208, 212, 214

Anglocentrism, 85–99, 224; cultural imperialism and, 87–88; cultural pluralism and, 95–99; doubts about legitimacy of, 87–89; English culture as basis of, 89–92, 94–95; English language

Anglocentrism (*cont.*)
and, 85–87; and exaggerated
WASP influence, 92–94; and
forced Anglo-conformity, 99; and
promotion of assimilation,
88–99; and unicultural bias,
95–97
Anglophobia, 90
Antiassimilationism: of black
Americans, 12, 16, 152, 167–82,
187, 191, 192; in ethnic versus
civic nation, 223–24; of Hispanic
immigrants, 187–97, 208; and
historical revisionism, 8, 73,
80–83; impact of, 14–18,
163–64; and public schools,
72–82. *See also* Bilingualism;
Ethnic federalism; Nativism
Anti-Semitism, 35, 69, 117, 141,
181–82
Argentina, 51
ASPIRA, 74, 189, 222
Assimilation, American style: acculturation versus, 55–59, 143–65;
Americanization, 5–6, 46, 54,
68–70, 145, 161–64; in
American mythology, 106–8,
116, 118; Anglocentrism and,
88–99; basic precepts of, 6–7, 18,
37–40; capitalism and, 52–53;
citizenship in, 6, 30, 40, 51, 52,
214–16; in civic versus ethnic
nation, 220–26; concept of, 5–6,
43–44, 176; cultural conformity
and, 9–10; diffusion process in,
149–55; discrediting of, 8–12;
immigration policy in, 199–217;
melting-pot metaphor for, 10,
13, 44–49, 144–45; miracle of,
4–7, 37–40; organizational life
and, 36–37, 53–54, 146–47;
political impact of, 24, 35–36,
51–52; and postassimilationist

era, 12–15; process of, 49–51;
progress and, 54–55; and public
schools, 61; as religious conver-
sion, 48–49; requirements of,
49–51. *See also* American Idea;
Antiassimilationism; English lan-
guage; Protestant ethic
Assimilation in American Life
(Gordon), 49, 59
Asylees, 204, 209–10, 214, 217
Atgeld, John Peter, 35
Auster, Laurence, 17, 98
Australia, 51

Baird, Zoe, 212
Baldwin, James, 97
Belgium, 5
Bell, Alexander Graham, 104
Bellow, Saul, 120
Bennett, William, 194, 196–97, 222
Bernstein, Richard, 77, 78, 81, 82
Best Man, The (movie), 111
Best Years of Our Lives, The (movie),
117
Beyond the Melting Pot (Glazer and
Moynihan), 10, 45, 144
Bilingual Education Act of 1968,
14, 73
Bilingualism: under ethnic federal-
ism, 14, 189–91, 193, 195,
225–26; and German immi-
grants, 27–28, 38, 157; of
Hispanic immigrants, 74–75,
163; impact of, 8, 74–75; origins
of, 15; and public schools,
73–76, 182, 189–91, 193, 195,
196
Bingham, John, 160
Black Americans, 167–82; and acculturation, 56; and Afrocentrism,
78, 96, 97–98, 175–76, 181–82,
191, 195; and antiassimilationism,
12, 16, 152, 167–82, 187, 191,

192; and civil rights revolution,
11, 12, 46, 169, 170–71, 175,
179–82, 189–90, 195, 222; in
the criminal justice system, 141;
and cultural pluralism, 96–97; and
cultural separatism, 175–76; discrimination against, 12, 109, 168,
169, 172–76, 178, 180; education of, 171–72, 176–77; ethnic
enclaves of, 154; and ethnic federalism, 180–82; ethnic identities
of, 146; impact of immigrants on,
135–42, 203; impact on
European cultures, 90; intermarriage of, 160, 173–74; and multicultural curricula, 12, 77, 78, 79,
175–76; and public schools, 63;
rights of, 21; and slavery legacy,
21–22, 36, 78, 90, 168, 169,
224; in underclass, 177–78; and
voting rights, 169
Black nationalism, 169–72, 176,
178, 182
Blaming the victim, 14
Bobo, Lawrence, 174
Bond, Michael, 134
Borjas, George, 52, 137, 201
Bosnia, 57, 82, 186
Boston, 24, 33, 150
Bourne, Randolph, 87
Bouvier, Leon, 201
Brazil, 51
Briggs, Vernon, 201
Brimelow, Peter, 19, 25, 98, 145,
163, 201, 216
Buchanan, Patrick J., 108, 206
Buffalo, New York, 63, 154, 203
Bullitt, William, 160
Bureau of the Census, U.S., 204
Bush, Jeb, 160

California: Chinese immigrants and,
28–30; as immigrant gateway,

148, 150, 152, 190, 201, 203,
216; nativism, resurgence of,
16–17, 131, 200–201, 206–7,
208, 212–13; Proposition 187
(illegal immigration), 16, 206–7,
213
Calvinism, 126
Canada, 4, 20, 22, 38, 51, 101,
134; ethnic federalism of, 11;
immigration policy of, 208–9;
multilingualism in, 157
Capitalism: assimilation and, 52–53;
and Protestant ethic, 127, 130
Capra, Frank, 117
Castro, Fidel, 210
Cather, Willa, 112
Catholicism, 27, 37, 92; and intermarriage, 159; and Protestant
ethic, 126, 127; and schools,
69–70
Central Pacific Railroad, 28
Chavez, Linda, 74, 189, 190, 193,
196–97, 222
Chesterton, G. K., 49
Chicago, 24, 33, 150, 151, 203
Chickering, Jesse, 24–25, 85
Chinese Exclusion Act of 1882, 24,
29, 30, 217
Chinese immigrants, 149, 150, 152,
153; assimilation of, 145, 190;
occupational specialization by,
155–56; percentage of, 205, 214;
and Protestant ethic, 124, 202;
and public schools, 69; resistance
to, 24, 28–30, 98, 217
Chisholm, Shirley, 47
Chiswick, Barry, 139–40
Christopher, Robert, 26
Church, Robert, 66
Citizenship: as basis of assimilation,
6, 30, 40, 51, 52, 214–16; concept of, 6; and ethnic federalism,
14; and immigration policy, 210,

Citizenship (*cont.*)
  214–16; rights of, 6, 21, 24, 30;
  voting rights and, 21, 24, 169
Civic assimilation, 58
Civic nation, ethnic nation versus,
  220–26
Civil Rights Act of 1964, 180, 195
Civil rights revolution, 11, 12, 46,
  169, 170–71, 175, 179–82,
  189–90, 195, 222
Civil War, 22, 26, 28, 33, 35, 36,
  63
Class. *See* Poverty; Social class
Cleveland, 33, 169, 203
Cleveland, Grover, 162
Clinton, Bill, 159, 212
Clinton, Hillary Rodham, 159
College education: antiassimilation-
  ist ideology in, 192–93; of black
  Americans, 171–72; and ethnic
  federalism, 191–93; ethnic stud-
  ies in, 79, 163, 192
Colombian immigrants, 152, 188
Columbus, Christopher, 80, 106
Commager, Henry Steele, 20, 106,
  110
Command Decision (movie), 111
Common schools, 63–65
Communist Party, 132, 133
Communities. *See* Ethnic communi-
  ties
Competence, in assimilation, 50
Constitution of the United States, 6,
  51, 81, 108
Cooper, James Fenimore, 103–4,
  112, 115, 119
Cortines, Ramón, 75
Cose, Ellis, 27
Crevecoeur, Hector St. John de,
  107
Cuban immigrants, 187, 190, 209
Cukor, George, 117
Cult of ethnicity, 186–91

Cultural conformity, assimilation
  equated with, 9–10
Cultural diversity, 175–76
Cultural imperialism, 87–88
Cultural pluralism, 95–99;
  Afrocentrism versus, 96;
  approaches to, 95–97; and cultur-
  al separatism, 97–99, 175–76;
  and ethnic federalism, 47; poly-
  culture approach to, 95–96
Cuomo, Andrew, 160–61
Cyprus, 5

Dallas, 150
Dances with Wolves (movie), 114,
  118–19
Daniels, Roger, 147
Danticat, Edwige, 97
Dartmouth Review, 192–93
Declaration of Independence, 108,
  169
Deer Hunter, The (movie), 118
Deerslayer, The (Cooper), 115
Democracy in America
  (Tocqueville), 89, 105
Democratic Party, 133–34
Detroit, 33, 203
Dictatorship of Virtue (Bernstein),
  78, 82
Diffusion process, 149–55; to other
  cities and metropolitan areas,
  155; satellite colonization,
  152–55; spillover, 151–52; to
  suburbs, 152–53
Dillon, C. Douglas, 160
Dinkins, David, 46–47
Discrimination, and black
  Americans, 12, 109, 168, 169,
  172–76, 178, 180
Disuniting of America, The
  (Schlesinger), 76, 82, 90
Dominican immigrants, 58, 149,
  151–52, 187, 190, 205

Douglass, Frederick, 169
Dreiser, Theodore, 119–20
D'Souza, Dinesh, 194
Dumbing Down of America's Kids
  (Sykes), 82

East Asian immigrants, 152
Eastern European immigrants, 4–5,
  144, 187
East Indian immigrants, 155
Economic growth, immigration and,
  22, 31–35, 124–25, 127–28,
  130–31, 201–3
Ecuadorian immigrants, 152
Edison, Thomas, 104
Electoral districts, ethnically drawn,
  11, 189, 195
Emerson, Ralph Waldo, 115
England, 64
English language: and
  Anglocentrism, 85–87; as basis of
  assimilation, 6, 18, 38, 154, 162,
  190; as citizenship requirement,
  30; and English as a second-lan-
  guage programs, 75; under ethnic
  federalism, 13, 15; "native" language versus, 11; as official language, 163–64; in public schools,
  7, 65–66. *See also* Bilingualism
E Pluribus Unum (from many, one),
  6, 11
Equal Employment Opportunities
  Commission, 195
Ethnic communities, 144–55; ethnic
  density of, 154–55; ethnic federalism and, 146, 188; organizations in, 36–37, 53–54, 146–47;
  in urban neighborhoods, 147–55
Ethnic density, 154–55
Ethnic federalism, 185–87, 222–26;
  affirmative action programs and,
  178–79, 181, 195–96; Afrocentrism as, 78, 96, 97–98, 175–76,

181–82, 191, 195; assimilationism versus, 47, 76–77; and black
  Americans, 180–82, 189–90; civil
  rights revolution in, 11, 12, 46,
  169, 170–71, 175, 179–82,
  189–90, 195, 222; colleges and
  universities and, 191–93; critics
  of, 193, 196–97; and cult of ethnicity, 186–91; and cultural pluralism, 47; emergence of, 11–12,
  189–90; and ethnic communities,
  146; federal government and,
  195–96; foundations and, 189,
  193–95, 196; impact on immigrants, 15–18, 141; and multicultural curricula in schools, 14, 73,
  76–83, 175–76, 191–93, 195;
  precepts of, 13–14. *See also* Antiassimilationism; Bilingualism;
  Ethnic identity
Ethnic identity, 13, 26, 144; and
  Americanization process, 161–64;
  cuisines in, 157–58; ethnic communities and, 144–55; and ethnic
  federalism, 186–91; intermarriage
  and, 51, 53, 158–61; native language in, 156–57; occupational
  and industrial specialization and,
  155–56. *See also* Ethnic federalism
Ethnic nation, civic nation versus,
  220–26
Ethnic pride, 223
Ethnocentricity, 186–91, 225
Eurocentrism, 77

Factory system, 133
Fairchild, Henry, 44, 46
Family-based immigration preferences, 203–6, 208, 212, 214,
  216
Family values, economic success and,
  140–41

Farrakhan, Louis, 141, 170, 171, 176
Farrell, John, 120
Federation for American Immigration Reform, 163
Feinstein, Dianne, 213
Ferrara, Peter, 180
Filipino immigrants, 145, 205
Firmat, Perez, 97
Fishlow, Albert, 64
Florida, 150, 203
Ford, Henry, 46
Ford Foundation, 222
Forked Tongue (Porter), 74
Foundations, and ethnic federalism, 189, 193–95, 196
France, 5, 44, 62, 64, 162
Franklin, Benjamin, 25, 110
Freedmen's Bureau, 63
French immigrants, 152
Fresh Blood (Ungar), 145
Friends or Strangers (Borjas), 52
Fuchs, Lawrence H., 164, 193, 196–97, 219
Fuhrman, Mark, 172
Fukuyama, Francis, 53
Furnham, Adrian, 134

Gadsden Purchase (1853), 22
Gardner, John, 193
Garrison, William Lloyd, 20
Garvey, Marcus, 170
Genocide, 10
Gentleman's Agreement (movie), 117
Georgia, 169
German immigrants: assimilation of, 144, 215; and bilingualism, 27–28, 38, 157; ethnic enclaves of, 149, 150, 151, 154, 155; occupational specialization by, 156; politics and, 35–36; and Protestant ethic, 124; resistance
to, 27–28, 29, 98; as WASPs, 92–94
Germany, 5, 6, 64
Gettysburg Address, 108, 109
Glazer, Nathan, 8, 10, 12, 45, 144, 162, 168, 185, 186, 199, 222, 223
Gleason, Philip, 55, 90–91, 94–95, 98
Godfather movies, 118
Gonzalez, George, 73–74
Gordon, Milton, 36, 49, 56, 58, 59, 158
Great Britain: and Anglocentrism of U.S., 85–92, 94–95; immigrants from, 26; and independence of U.S., 20, 89–90; national identity of, 102
Great Depression, 31, 34
Greek immigrants, 152, 155, 189
Greeley, Andrew, 87
Grey, Zane, 103–4, 112
Grund, Francis, 125–26
Grunwald, Henry, 129
Guarnizo, Luis, 58
Guatemalan immigrants, 207
Gunther, John, 108

Hacker, Andrew, 92–93
Hackney, Sheldon, 11
Haitian immigrants, 206, 207, 210
Hall, Prescott, 29–30
Hamilton, Alexander, 110
Hamilton, Edward, 136–37
Handlin, Oscar, 104–5, 127
Hang 'Em High (movie), 114
Harrington, Michael, 134
Harte, Bret, 103–4, 112
Harvard Encyclopedia of American Ethnic Groups, 55, 61
Hawthorne, Nathaniel, 115
Heaven, Patrick, 134
Heritage Foundation, 222

Hispanic immigrants: and acculturation, 56; and antiassimilationism, 187–97, 208; authentic cultures of, 97–99; and bilingual education, 74–75, 163; and cultural pluralism, 96–97; diversity of, 187–88; intermarriage by, 160; and multicultural curricula, 12, 16, 77, 79, 175; naturalization rates, 215. *See also specific Hispanic groups*

Historical revisionism: and black Americans, 181–82; impact of, 8, 9–11, 80–83; and multicultural curricula, 73, 80–83; in popular culture, 114–16, 118–19

Holiday (movie), 117

Holmes, Steven, 170–71

Homestead Act of 1862, 33

Houston, Texas, 150

Howells, William Dean, 119–20

Huddle, Donald, 201

Hughes, Robert, 78

Human rights, 10, 21, 109

Hungarian immigrants, 209

Hunter College (New York City), 79

Identity, national. *See* National identity, American

Illinois, 24, 33, 150, 151, 203

Immigrants and the American City (Muller), 33

Immigration: and "alienness" of immigrants, 25–31, 145, 162; in American mythology, 105–8, 110, 116, 118; assimilationist policy for, 199–217; attitudes toward immigrants, 129, 138–39, 164; economic growth and, 22, 31–35, 124–25, 127–28, 130–31, 201–3; and expansionist drive, 20–24; fourth wave of, 135–42,

144–45; legislation restricting, 16–18, 23, 24, 29–31; nativist movements and, 25–31; political impact of, 24, 35–36, 51–52; population growth from, 22–23, 31–33; Protestant ethic and, 135–42; religious organizations, 36–37; second wave of, 144, 149, 150, 151; social organizations and, 36–37; third wave of, 144, 149, 151, 187

Immigration Act of 1917, 30

Immigration Act of 1924, 24, 30, 208

Immigration and Nationality Act amendments of 1965, 200

Immigration and Naturalization Service, U.S., 23, 32, 213

Immigration policy, 199–217; amnesty for illegal aliens, 204, 206, 207, 208, 212, 214; citizenship and, 210, 214–16; family-based preferences in, 203–6, 208, 212, 214, 216; geographic-diversity, 213–14; illegal immigration and, 16, 204, 206–8, 210–17; national-origins, 205, 208, 217; and nativist backlash, 16, 131, 200–201, 208, 217; occupational preferences in, 204, 208–9; reform proposals, 210–17; for refugees and asylees, 204, 209–10, 214, 217; restrictionist, 16–28, 23, 24, 29–31, 201

Immigration Reform and Control Act of 1986 (IRCA), 204, 206, 207, 210, 212

Immigration Restriction League, 24

India, 5

Indianapolis, 154

Indian immigrants, 152, 153, 205, 214

Industrialization: immigration and, 33–35; and Protestant ethic, 130, 131; unions and, 133

Inside American Education (Sowell), 82

Integration, 63–64, 169

Interethnic conflict, 16–17, 186

Intermarriage, 51, 53, 158–61, 173–74, 186

Iowa, 31

Irish immigrants: assimilation of, 144, 190, 215; ethnic enclaves of, 149, 150, 151, 153, 155; geographic concentration of, 72; occupational specialization by, 156; politics and, 35–36; and Protestant ethic, 123–24, 131–32; and public schools, 64, 68, 69–70; resistance to, 26–27, 29, 98, 131; as WASPs, 92–94

Italian immigrants: and acculturation, 56, 58; assimilation of, 144, 162, 187, 189, 190; and cultural pluralism, 96, 98; ethnic enclaves of, 72, 149, 150–51, 152, 153, 154; intermarriage by, 160; and multicultural curricula, 77, 79; occupational specialization by, 155, 156; and Protestant ethic, 124, 132; resistance to, 29–31; as small businessmen, 35; as WASPs, 93

Italy, 5

It Happened One Night (movie), 117

I've Seen the Best of It (Alsop), 93

Jackson, Andrew, 81

Jackson, Jesse, 46, 222

Jamaican immigrants, 145

James, Henry, 120

Japanese immigrants, 56, 69, 160

Jefferson, Thomas, 20, 110, 127, 169

Jeffries, Leonard, 97–98, 171

Jewish immigrants: and acculturation, 56, 58; and anti-Semitism, 35, 69, 117, 141, 181–82; assimilation of, 162, 187, 189, 190, 215; and cultural pluralism, 97, 98; ethnic enclaves of, 72, 149, 150–51, 153, 154; ethnic identity of, 13; intermarriage by, 159, 160; movies and, 116; and multicultural curricula, 77, 79; occupational specialization by, 35, 155, 156; and Protestant ethic, 124, 126, 132; and public schools, 68, 69; resistance to, 29–31, 175; and socialism, 134; as WASPs, 93

Jim Crow laws, 169

Jones, James, 167

Jones, Malcolm, Jr., 95, 96–97

Jones, Maldwyn, 28, 37, 54

Jordan, Barbara, 47

Kallen, Horace, 45, 47

Kansas City, 154

Karenga, M. Ron, 175

Keegan, John, 85–86

Kennedy, John F., 8, 160

Kennedy, Kerry, 160–61

Kennedy, Robert, 160–61

King, Martin Luther, Jr., 169, 182

King, Rodney, 172, 173

Kingston Technologies, 202

Know-Nothings (Native American Party), 19, 24, 26, 28, 131

Kohn, Hans, 95

Korean immigrants, 152–53, 155

Kotkin, Joel, 201–2

Kristol, Irving, 134

Ku Klux Klan, 24

Kwanzaa, 175

Labor-force participation rates, 137–38, 140, 188

La Raza, 189

Last of the Mohicans, The (Cooper), 115

Latinos. *See* Hispanic immigrants

Lau v. *Nichols*, 73

Leatherstocking Tales: The Deerslayer (Cooper), 115

Leaves of Grass (Whitman), 115

Lebanon, 101

Legitimacy, in assimilation, 49–51

Lerner, Max, 35, 38, 39, 54, 123, 124, 129

Letters from an American Farmer (Crevecoeur), 107

Lewis, Sinclair, 120

Libertarianism, 113

Lincoln, Abraham, 36, 64, 81, 104, 108–9, 110–11, 175

Lipset, Seymour Martin, 104, 130–31

Little Big Man (movie), 114

Lodge, John Davis, 160

London, Meyer, 110

Longfellow, Henry Wadsworth, 103–4

Los Angeles, 148, 150, 152, 203, 216

Louisiana Purchase (1803), 22

Luck of Roaring Camp, The (Harte), 112

McCabe and Mrs. Miller (movie), 114

McCann, Dennis, 135

McCarran-Walter Act of 1952, 208

McDougal, John, 28

McVeigh, Timothy J., 58

Madison, James, 110

Manifest destiny, 21–22

Mann, Horace, 7, 63, 64

Marriott, Michel, 173–74

Marshall, Thurgood, 169

Marty (movie), 118

Massachusetts, 7, 24, 33, 63, 150

Mayo-Smith, Richard, 52

Mazzoli, Romano, 206

Melting Pot, The (play; Zangwill), 10, 44–45, 47

Melting-pot metaphor, 44–49, 224; alternatives to, 46–49; assimilation and, 144–45; criticism of, 45–46; as "cultural genocide," 13; origins of, 10, 44–45; popularity of, 46

Melville, Herman, 115

Mexican American Legal Defense and Education Fund, 189

Mexican immigrants: assimilation of, 145, 187, 188, 190; illegal, amnesty for, 206–7, 208; percentage of, 205

Miami, 150, 203

Michigan, 33, 203

Middle Americans, 96

Midnight Cowboy (movie), 118

Military-industrial complex, 193

Miller, John, 17, 185–86

Milwaukee, 24, 33, 154

Minnesota, 24, 31

Monoculturalism, 77

Moynihan, Daniel Patrick, 10, 45, 144, 162

Mr. Smith Goes to Washington (movie), 111

Muller, Thomas, 27–28, 31, 33, 135

Multiculturalism. *See* Cultural pluralism; Ethnic federalism

Multilingualism, 157

My Fair Lady (musical), 65

Myrdal, Gunnar, 174

NAACP, 170–71

Nast, Thomas, 36

National identity, American, 224–26; language in. *See* English

National identity (*cont.*)
language; myth of influence of
WASPs in, 87, 92–94, 97;
mythology in, 101–21; and public school education, 61–71; values in. *See* American Idea. *See also*
Assimilation, American style
National Opinion Research Center,
144
National-origins immigration policy,
205, 208, 217
National unity, 9
Native American Party (Know-
Nothings), 19, 24, 26, 28, 131
Native Americans: authentic cultures
of, 97; impact on European cultures, 90; and multicultural curricula, 77, 78, 79; in the Western
genre, 113–15
"Native" language, right to use, 11
Nativism, 7, 25–31, 40; anti-immi-
grationism and, 144; Chinese
and, 28–30; and ethnic communities, 146; Germans and,
27–28; Irish and, 26–27;
Know-Nothing Party and, 19,
24, 26, 28, 131; Latinos and,
16; and nonassimilationist
assumptions, 146; and public
schools, 68; recent resurgence
of, 16, 131, 200–201, 206–7,
212–13, 216, 217; recurrences
of, 16, 55, 98–99, 131
Naturalization. *See* Citizenship
Neonativism, 16–17, 131, 200–201,
206–7, 212–13, 216, 217
Neuhaus, Richard John, 220
New American Poverty, The
(Harrington), 134
New Deal, 132
New historians. *See* Historical revisionism
New Jersey, 148, 150

New York (city): and the American
Dream, 118; bilingual education
in, 74–75; economic growth of,
33; ethnic enclaves in, 10, 58,
150–55; fourth wave of immi-
grants in, 137; as immigrant gate-
way, 10, 24, 58, 148, 149–56,
202–3; public school system, 63;
suburban diffusion in, 154; wel-
fare in, 132
New York (state), 63; Educational
Department, 74; immigrant pop-
ulation in, 148, 150; Social
Studies Review and Development
Committee, 14, 76, 77
New Zealand, 51
Nigerian immigrants, 145
Nixon, Richard M., 8
Norris, Frank, 119–20
North American Review, 29–30
Northern Ireland, 5, 57
Novak, Michael, 10, 88, 96

Occupation-based immigration pref-
erences, 204, 208–9
Of Thee I Sing (musical), 111
Oklahoma City federal office build-
ing bombing, 58
One Flew Over the Cuckoo's Nest
(movie), 118
On the Waterfront (movie), 118
O Pioneers! (Cather), 112
Ordinary People (movie), 118
Organizational life, 36–37, 53–54,
146–47
O'Sullivan, John L., 17, 21, 98
Outcasts of Poker Flat, The (Harte),
112
Out of the Barrio (Chavez), 74, 193

Paine, Tom, 20
Pakistani immigrants, 152
Park, Edward J. W., 201

Park, Robert, 49
Pathfinder, The (Cooper), 115
Pennsylvania, 24, 33, 63, 148, 150
Philadelphia, 24, 33, 150
Philadelphia Story, The (movie), 117
Piazza, Thomas, 170
Pittsburgh, 33
Plessy v. *Ferguson*, 63
Podhoretz, Norman, 87
Polish immigrants, 29, 153, 160, 189, 205
Political correctness, 192–93, 196
Politics of History, The (Zinn), 9–10
Polyculturalism, 95–96
Porter, Rosalie Pedalino, 74
Portes, Alejandro, 187–88
Portuguese immigrants, 153, 156
Poverty: and the Protestant ethic, 134–35, 137, 141–42. *See also* Welfare state
Prairie, The (Cooper), 112
Preferences, race-conscious, 14, 15, 189. *See also* Affirmative action
Presidency, citizenship requirement for, 6
Primary labor market, 138–39
Progress, and assimilation, 54–55
Proportional representation, 11, 189, 195
Proposition 187 (California), 16, 206–7, 213
Protectionism, 34
Protestant ethic, 123–42; and attitudes toward immigrants, 129, 138–39; as basis of assimilation, 6, 18, 38, 39–40, 124–26, 135–42, 176; and blaming the victim, 14; and children of immigrants, 15; described, 6; downside of, 129–31, 134–35, 141–42; economic growth and, 124–25, 127–28, 130–31; under ethnic federalism, 14, 15; and faith in money, 128–29; and immigrant versus native workers, 135–42; importance of, 39–40; origins of concept, 126–27; poverty and, 134–35, 137, 141–42; socialism and, 132–34; welfare state and, 8, 14, 132, 134, 136, 138, 141–42

Public schools, 61–83; in Americanization movement, 68–70; antiassimilationism and, 72–82, 191–92; as basis of assimilation, 7, 18, 40, 61, 64–65, 67–69; bilingual education in, 73–76, 163, 182, 189–91, 193, 195, 196; Catholic schools versus, 70; common schools, 63–65; district schools, 62–63; egalitarian approach in, 65–68; and German immigrants, 27–28, 38, 157; and historical revisionism, 73, 80–83; language curriculum in, 65–66, 67; multicultural curricula and, 14, 73, 76–83, 175–76, 191–92; private schools versus, 66, 70; teachers in, 67, 71
Public School Society of the City of New York, New York, 64–65
Puddington, Arch, 172, 177, 178–79, 196–97
Puerto Rican immigrants, 150, 151–52, 187, 190
Pulp Fiction (movie), 119
Pygmalion (Shaw), 65

Quotas, ethnic, 14, 16, 31. *See also* Affirmative action; Immigration policy

Racial Attitudes in America (Schuman, Steeh, and Bobo), 174
Racism, 10, 172–76, 178, 180–82
Railroads, 28–29
Rao, Neomi, 192

Ravitch, Diane, 86
Refugees, 204, 209–10, 214, 217
Religious conversion, 48–49, 159
Religious organizations, 36–37, 53–54, 91–92
Reservation wages, 138
Revolution of the 1960s, 8–12
Riders of the Purple Sage (Grey), 112
Riis, Jacob, 34
Rise of the Unmeltable Ethnics, The (Novak), 10, 88
Robertson, James Oliver, 101, 105, 107
Rochester, New York, 63
Rockwell, Norman, 104
Rodgers, Daniel, 126
Rodriguez, Richard, 76
Roosevelt, Theodore, 10
Root, Oren, 160
Roth, Henry, 120
Rumbaut, Ruben, 187–88
Russian immigrants, 209
Rwanda, 5

Sacco, Nicola, 132
St. Louis, 24, 33, 203
Saltonstall, Leverett, 160
Salvadoran immigrants, 205, 206, 207
Samuels, David, 194–95
San Diego, 202
Sands of Iwo Jima (movie), 111
San Francisco, 148, 150, 203
Saturday Evening Post, 104
Scandinavian immigrants, 124, 151, 154, 155, 157
Schaff, Philip, 3, 11
Schlesinger, Arthur M. Jr., 11, 76, 77, 82, 90, 91, 97–98, 185, 193, 196–97
Schuman, Howard, 174
Schurz, Carl, 35, 38
Schwartz, Benjamin, 87–88

Secondary labor market, 138–40
Sennett, Richard, 11
Sergeant York (movie), 111
Seven Days in May (movie), 111
1776 (movie), 111
Shalala, Donna, 193
Sharpton, Al, 171
Shaw, George Bernard, 65, 91
Shelley, Percy Bysshe, 105
Simon, Julian, 31
Simpson, Alan, 206
Simpson, O. J., 172
Skouras, Spyros, 160
Slavery, 21–22, 36, 78, 90, 168, 169, 224
Sniderman, Paul, 170
Sobol, Thomas, 79
Social class: black American underclass, 177–78; marriage and, 160; and public schools, 65–67, 70; in the Western genre, 113
Social Darwinism, 135
Socialism, 132, 133–34
Socialization, public schools and, 7
Social organizations, 36–37, 53–54
Solomon, Haym, 160
Somalia, 5
South Carolina, 169
Soviet Union (former), 5, 149, 205, 209
Sowell, Thomas, 52, 82, 83, 161
Spokane, Washington, 154
Sri Lanka, 5
State of the Union (movie), 111
Steeh, Charlotte, 174
Steinbeck, John, 43
Stewart, James, 111
Sturges, Preston, 117
Swedish immigrants, 154
Sykes, Charles, 82

Terrorism, 57–58
Texas, 150, 190

Thernstrom, Abigail, 193, 196–97
Thernstrom, Stephen, 59, 193, 196–97
Thomas, Norman, 133
Thoreau, Henry David, 115
Tocqueville, Alexis de, 53, 62, 64, 89, 105, 128, 147
Truman, Harry S, 169
Trust (Fukuyama), 53
Twain, Mark, 103–4
Tweed, Boss, 36

Ukrainian immigrants, 29
Unforgiven (movie), 114, 118–19
Ungar, Sanford J., 143, 145
Union Pacific Railroad, 28
Unions, 34, 131–32, 133–34, 138, 139
Urbanization: ethnic communities in, 147–55; immigration and, 24, 31–35
Urban League, 170, 171

Vanzetti, Bartolomeo, 132
Vietnamese immigrants, 145, 205, 209
Vietnam War, 10, 15, 118
View from the Bridge, A (movie), 118
Virginian, The (Wister), 112
Voltaire, 92
Voting rights, 21, 24, 169

Warhol, Andy, 116
Washington, Booker T., 169

Washington, D.C., 150
Washington, George, 81, 104, 110, 162
WASPs (White Anglo-Saxon Protestants): ethnic identity of, 13, 26; marriage and, 160; myth of influence of, 87, 92–94, 97, 102, 224. *See also* Protestant ethic
Weber, Max, 126
Webster, Noah, 65
Welfare state: and legal immigration, 216; and Protestant ethic, 8, 14, 132, 134, 136, 138, 141–42; reduction of benefits of, 16–17
West, Cornel, 172–73
West Indian immigrants, 149, 156
Wharton, Edith, 120
Whitman, Walt, 103–4, 115
Whitney, Craig, 6
Wilson, Woodrow, 105
Wisconsin, 24
Wister, Owen, 112
World Trade Center bombing, 57–58
World War I, 132
World War II, 23, 44, 117, 132

You Can't Take It With You (movie), 117
Yugoslavia, 101

Zangwill, Israel, 10, 44–45, 46, 47, 56
Zinn, Howard, 9–10